*Apostate Englishman*

# Apostate Englishman

## Grey Owl the Writer
## and the Myths

### ALBERT BRAZ

University of Manitoba Press

University of Manitoba Press
Winnipeg, Manitoba
Canada R3T 2M5
uofmpress.ca

Printed in Canada
Text printed on chlorine-free, 100% post-consumer recycled paper

19  18  17  16  15       1  2  3  4  5

Cover image: *Portrait of Grey Owl* by John Lavery, 1935
(*Illustrated London News*, 28 November 1936)
Cover design: David Drummond
Interior design: Karen Armstrong Graphic Design

**Library and Archives Canada Cataloguing in Publication**

Braz, Albert, 1957–, author
Apostate Englishman : Grey Owl the writer and the myths / Albert
Braz.

Includes bibliographical references and index.
Issued in print and electronic formats.
ISBN 978-0-88755-778-1 (pbk.)
ISBN 978-0-88755-504-6 (pdf)
ISBN 978-0-88755-502-2 (epub)

1. Grey Owl, 1888-1938.  2. Conservationists—Canada—Biography.
3. Nature writers—Canada—Biography.  4. Natural history literature—
Canada—History—20th century.  5. Passing (Identity) in literature.
6. Indians in literature.  7. Culture in literature.  8. Politics in literature.
I. Title.

E90.G75B73 2015          639.9092          C2015-903494-9
                                           C2015-903495-7

The University of Manitoba Press gratefully acknowledges the financial  support
for its publication program provided by the Government of Canada through the Canada
Book Fund, the Canada Council for the Arts,  the Manitoba Department
of Culture, Heritage, Tourism, the Manitoba Arts Council,
and the Manitoba Book Publishing Tax Credit.

*To Ali and Jon,*
*with love and gratitude*

# CONTENTS

*Photographs follow page 80*

# List of Illustrations

Scale

0          500          1000 km

Base map: © Her Majesty the Queen in right of Canada, 2015

NEWFOUNDLAND
& LABRADOR

QUEBEC

ONTARIO

Métis-sur-Mer

P.E.I.

Témiscouata

N.B.

NOVA
SCOTIA

Halifax

Biscotasing

Temagami

Mattawa

Montreal

Ottawa

Toronto

# Preface

A project like a book cannot be written without the assistance of many people, assistance that sometimes is provided inadvertently. This is certainly what happened with *Apostate Englishman: Grey Owl the Writer and the Myths*. Early in 2000 I happened to be meeting with John Wadland, then the director of the Frost Centre for Canadian Studies and Native Studies at Trent University. When he learned that I was preparing an essay on Armand Ruffo's poetic biography of Grey Owl, later published as "The White Indian: Armand Garnet Ruffo's *Grey Owl* and the Spectre of Authenticity," he invited me to present it at Trent's annual Temagami reunion, at Camp Wanapitei, Ontario, in the heart of Grey Owl country. Wadland then informed me that Gary Potts, the former leader of the Temagami First Nation and the Teme-Augama Anishnabai, was doing graduate studies at the Frost Centre and might attend my talk. This was a prospect that both excited me and triggered considerable anxiety, since at that early stage of my research I had no idea whatsoever how Indigenous people in the area felt about their long dead but still controversial English-born visitor.

The Temagami reunions are designed to help participants understand the land in light of Indigenous and ecological issues, and one of their aims is to introduce international students and scholars to Canadian culture. So, during the day there are guided hiking and canoe trips and in the evening there are lectures and other cultural activities. My talk was held at the historic Temagami Lodge. As I discussed Ruffo's long poem, I underscored that it provides a surprisingly sympathetic portrayal of the subject, which is significant considering that Ruffo is not only Anishinaabe but actually comes from a family—the Espaniels of Biscotasing—that welcomed the man then known as Archie Belaney into their midst during his early days in Canada. I also kept glancing around the room for signs of Potts but, perhaps because the lighting was somewhat limited, I could not spot him. However, once the presentation ended, there was a question from the back of the room. The speaker identified himself as Gary Potts and, after thanking me for my talk, proceeded to state that the critical response to Grey Owl is extremely hypocritical. He claimed that when Indigenous people are assimilated into the white world, white people show no concern. But whenever a white person chooses to identify with Indigenous culture over his or her own culture, it troubles them to no end. In other words, suggested Potts, what disturbs many white critics about Grey Owl is not voice appropriation but cultural apostasy.

Potts's intervention at Camp Wanapitei was clearly a fateful moment in my research on Grey Owl, leading me to explore the possibility that the at-times vitriolic response to the beaver champion's ethnocultural transformation may not just be about him. Of course, the fact that I was already presenting a paper called "The White Indian" indicates that I was receptive to that interpretation. Indeed, in many ways, the catalyst for my investigation of Grey Owl's writings and the evolution of his cultural image was the poetic biography by Ruffo. After all, it was my reading of *Grey Owl: The Mystery of Archie Belaney* that compelled me to start exploring what the conservationist had actually written and the relation between those writings and the ever-increasing representations of him.

While this study examines both the writings and the image of Grey Owl, it is very much centred on Grey Owl the writer. As I will show, Grey Owl owes much of his popularity with readers to his writing style. He possesses a rich vocabulary and can write eloquently. But his spelling is somewhat idiosyncratic, notably his predilection for capitalizing words such as Nature and Wilderness. However, with the exception of the occasional misspelling or grammatical error, I reproduce his texts as he published them. Also, as befits a study of the representations of Grey Owl, I obviously refer to numerous texts about him. But I wish to highlight my extensive reliance on two particular books: *Wilderness Man: The Strange Story of Grey Owl* (1973), by his London-based publisher and promoter Lovat Dickson, and *From the Land of the Shadows: The Making of Grey Owl* (1990), by the (now retired) University of Calgary historian and biographer Donald B. Smith. These are the two main biographies of Grey Owl and my reconstruction of his life and times is inconceivable without them.

I would like to take advantage of this opportunity to express my gratitude to everyone who, directly or indirectly, has supported my project. In addition to John Wadland and Gary Potts, as well as Armand Ruffo, I wish to thank the editors of the publications where different versions of my work on Grey Owl have appeared over the years: Stephen Bocking, Julie Rak, Janice Fiamengo, Julie A. Smith, Robert W. Mitchell, and David Jarraway. Thanks are also in order to the colleagues who, in various ways, assisted me during my research: Devon Bryce, Misao Dean, Shalene Jobin, Carolyn Kapron, Martin Kuester, Linda Quirk, Jennie Rubio, Mary Henley Rubio, Asma Sayed, Carl Spadoni, Elspeth Tulloch, and Tracy Ware. No less important, I would like to thank the staffs at the Bruce Peel Library at the University of Alberta, the Glenbow Archives, and the William Ready Library at McMaster University; the staff at the University of Manitoba Press, especially Glenn Bergen, David Larsen, and David Carr, who encouraged me to write this study for years and who waited patiently for me to complete it; and, for her understanding, my former chair in the Department of English and Film Studies at the University of Alberta, Susan Hamilton.

Finally, I would like to express my immense gratitude to the dean of Grey Owl scholars, Don Smith. Some scholars are terrified that others might steal their ideas. Don, instead, not only enthusiastically shares his research with other people in the field but frequently urges them to pursue their own projects. Most importantly, I would like to say a special thank you to my children Ali and Jon, their mother, Carolyn Kapron, and the newest addition to our family, Penny, the quartet that makes everything both possible and worthwhile.

# Archie Belaney's Transformation into Grey Owl

*In a time when the cowboys always won,*
*Archie [Belaney] wanted to be an Indian.*

—Jane Billinghurst

Grey Owl's death in 1938 triggered an international scandal. The controversy surrounding the untimely demise of the celebrated trapper-turned-conservationist had many causes. Not the least of these was that he was not of Scottish-Apache ancestry, as he often claimed, but rather a white Englishman named Archie Belaney. By the time he died, in the year he would have turned fifty, Grey Owl was the best-known conservationist and nature writer in the world. More precisely, he was the author of four best-selling books about wildlife in Canada, books that he had supported with numerous illustrated lectures in North America and Great Britain. Grey Owl had become particularly identified with the animal that he was instrumental in saving from imminent extinction: Canada's own national emblem, the beaver. But for most of his admirers, his passionate advocacy for wildlife seemed inseparable from his purported Indigeneity. So when people learned that the champion of the beaver was not (partly) Indigenous but a white man, they felt defrauded, betrayed. The visceral denunciations of Grey Owl after his death are often interpreted as a rejection of his appropriation of another culture. But in this study of both his writings and his cultural image, I argue that what troubled many people was not so much that Grey Owl had fooled them about his identity and embraced the North American Indigenous way of life but the fact that he had forsaken European culture. That is, he had committed cultural apostasy.

Apostasy is usually associated with religion. It refers to the behaviour of those individuals who either claim to have, or are accused by others of having, "abandoned the main practices and/or beliefs of their religious community, in extreme cases even turning against it" (S. Wilson 2004, 22). Apostasy, though, transcends the spiritual realm. It may also designate the act of rejecting any collectivity, especially when the person in question "turns aggressively against the organization he or she has fled" (S. Wilson 2004, 3). Thus, "moral apostasy" occurs when people embrace "religious or social views [that] differ from those of their society" and elect to "stand apart from the group by their thoughts and actions" (Gutsche 1986, ix). Even more germane in terms of Grey Owl is "cultural apostasy," the stance of individuals "whose thought rather than personal social behaviour challenge[s] one or more widely held cultural or moral assumptions" in their societies (Turner 1993, 44). Some scholars restrict the concept of cultural apostasy to internal dissent, but there is no justifiable reason for not extending it to those individuals who spurn the cultures into which they were born, as Grey Owl did. This is particularly true of the Americas, where there is a long tradition of people of European ancestry abandoning their communities to join Indigenous ones. By their actions, these so-called White Indians are deemed to have "foiled their countrymen's civilized assumptions" (Axtell 1979, 8), something that can also be said about Grey Owl's embrace of Indigenous culture.

Grey Owl is often accused of being not merely "one of the greatest impersonators, or wannabe icons" in history but "a wanton cultural appropriator" (D.H. Taylor 1999, 120). However, following the lead of Gary Potts, I interpret Grey Owl's behaviour less as an example of cultural appropriation than of cultural apostasy. Potts, who is a former leader of Ontario's Bear Island Anishinaabe, the community where Grey Owl was introduced to both Indigenous culture and woodcraft, contends that the sometimes vitriolic criticism of the conservationist has "less to do with his relations with Native culture than [his relations] with his own." As mentioned in the preface, Potts alleges that "white people do not seem very concerned when Aboriginal people are assimilated into white society." Yet they are profoundly troubled by "the idea that one of their own would willingly choose to join another group" (Braz 2001–02, 182; Potts 2001), since they are unable to conceive that any "civilized person in possession of his faculties or free from undue restraint would choose to become an Indian" (Axtell 1979, 6). In short, for Potts, Grey Owl's real sin was not ethnoracial impersonation but his forsaking one of the pre-eminent cultures of his time for an ostensibly less "advanced" one.

◻   ◻   ◻

Archibald (Archie) Stansfeld Belaney was born on 18 September 1888, in Hastings, England, a seaside resort town less than 100 kilometres southeast of London. He came from a family with "a strong literary bent" (Dickson 1973, 8), as both his paternal grandfather and two of his brothers were published authors. His grandfather Archibald Belaney, after whom Archie was named, was the author of a collection of poems entitled *The Hundred Days of Napoleon*; the volume was dedicated to Queen Victoria, whose letter of acknowledgement was "lovingly preserved thereafter by the family" (Dickson 1973, 15). Besides being a poet, the original Archibald Belaney had "quite a hard nose for business and became a prominent ship's broker." He had married an heiress named Julia Jackson and, even though he died when his children were all under the age of ten, the family was "able to continue living on a very comfortable scale" (Dickson 1973, 15)—Dickson identifies the Belaney matriarch as Juliana, but I follow the more recent scholarship (Smith 1990, 9). Moreover, the Belaneys probably would have been able to maintain that lifestyle for decades had it not been for the actions of Archibald and Julia's only son, George, the father of the man the world would come to know as Grey Owl.

The destructive behaviour of George is often partly attributed to his mother. Following the death of her husband, Julia Belaney reportedly became determined "to have a male family head," lavishing "all her attention on her son." To the shock of her two daughters, Carrie and Ada, she "spoiled" George, both as a child and as an adult, supporting all his early financial and romantic adventures (Smith 1990, 10). George, who is generally described as "a spendthrift" and a "chronic" alcoholic (Smith 1990, 10, 12), wasted a considerable portion of the family's fortune in ill-advised business ventures. Then he began a practice that his son would emulate—marrying often and easily, and failing to provide for his offspring. While still in his early twenties, George had to wed an innkeeper's "fifteen-year-old daughter," who was "already pregnant with his child" (Smith 1990, 10). Even before the baby's birth, he became romantically involved with another young woman, Elizabeth Cox. He and Elizabeth then moved to Florida, where he bought an orange grove and pursued game shooting and taxidermy. Elizabeth was later joined by her thirteen-year-old sister, Kittie (Katherine). Elizabeth would die in Florida and, by the time George returned to England, he was not only penniless and a drunkard but also accompanied by a new "child-bride," Kittie Cox, who was pregnant with Archie (Smith 1990, 11).

When Julia realized what had happened to her son, she was forced to accept that he was not going to change his ways. Within two years, George and Kittie had another son, Hugh. Yet it was evident that George was not readjusting well to life in England, as he seemed unable to hold a job and support his growing family. So Julia and her daughters decided that it was in the Belaney family's best interest that George go into exile, and they gave him "a small income on the condition that he never set foot in England again" and have no contact with either his wife or his sons (Dickson 1973, 22). Thus, when Archie was only four years old, he saw his father for the last time. He would not have much contact with his mother either. Kittie had been given "a comfortable income for life" in order to provide for her two boys. But when Julia and her daughters discovered that Kittie "had sent money to George," they not only "cut off her income" but also took Archie from her so that they could raise him themselves (Dickson 1973, 22). Curiously, they showed no such interest in Hugh, whom Kittie took with her when she moved to London (Dickson 1973, 11).

Following the clash between the Belaney women and his mother, Archie was basically raised by his paternal grandmother and her two unmarried daughters, Carrie (Caroline) and Ada (Adelaide). Ada, the younger of the sisters, would emerge as the dominant figure in Archie's young life, if not his whole life. Lovat Dickson describes their relationship, "She became both mother and father to him, and he never knew whether he feared or loved her" (1973, 30). Ada was a strict disciplinarian. Unlike her mother and sister, who tended to pamper the family's heir, Ada demanded that Archie apply himself. She not only exposed him to all sorts of books but also taught him music, especially the piano, which became one of his great passions through-out his life. Not surprisingly, Archie's attitude toward Ada was always highly ambivalent. Dickson states that the young "Archie adored his grandmother" and was in "constant fear of her dying, for then he would be left alone with the terrible-tempered Ada" (1973, 31, 32). Years later, Archie confided to his (fourth) wife, Anahareo, that Ada had him "scared to death for a while" and that he "thought of suicide quite a few times." Yet he added that, while his aunt would have loved to have him as "putty in her hands—to break my spirit," he "put up a fight, and she succeeded only in making a devil out of me" (qtd. in Anahareo [1972] 2014, 30). He further told Anahareo that he even attempted to kill Ada by dropping "a bust of Bach or Brahms" from an alcove onto her head. But when he pushed the bust, it came off its pedestal and

" 'crashed down on my head and knocked me out cold' " (qtd. in Anahareo [1972] 2014, 30).

Ada was determined to shape her nephew into a gentleman, someone very much unlike his own father. In her effort to mould the future head of the Belaney clan into her desired image, she went so far as to try to ensure that he cease writing with his left hand. As he would complain to Anahareo:

> "She was obsessed with the idea of turning me into some kind of genius, and the things that woman did to me shouldn't happen to man or beast...I'm a southpaw, and the punishment I went through on that account you'd never believe. She'd whack my hand with that pointer of hers, and many were the times that, if by accident I happened to touch a pen or pencil with my left hand, she pulled me off the chair by the hair. Then there were the music lessons and the Bible study. You'd imagine that those subjects would touch the heart of almost anyone and bring out the best in them, but that was a laugh. She was every bit as much the brute in that as she was in everything else." (qtd. in Anahareo [1972] 2014, 28–29)

As Archie described her, Ada was "always primped and starched, a perfectionist" who had "studied German as well as the violin in Germany. All she lacked was a human heart" (qtd. in Anahareo [1972] 2014, 28).

Yet it is this same Aunt Ada to whom, in the dedication to his first book, *The Men of the Last Frontier*, he gives credit for "such education that enables me to interpret into words the spirit of the forest, beautiful for all its underlying wildness." Whatever else she may have done, Ada was largely responsible for teaching Archie to write, a skill that would serve him extremely well during his Canadian years, especially once the beaver had become almost extinct and he could no longer make a living as a trapper. Anahareo remarks that "when Archie was saying his worst about Miss Ada Belaney, he was at the same time unintentionally revealing a most remarkable woman." She tellingly adds that after Grey Owl "started writing, he never once said a disparaging word" about his aunt ([1972] 2014, 178, 182). Still, one thing that Ada could not do was mitigate the fact that her nephew was living in an all-female household. The novelist Howard O'Hagan goes as far as to suggest that Archie Belaney's transformation into Grey Owl may have been "a form of revenge for the matriarch-ruled days of his boyhood, a revolt against the aunts and grandmother who had scorned his Indian games and wanted him to grow up to be a good commuter like all boys of his 'class' " ([1978] 1993,

107). In particular, it seems to have been a rebellion against a household that deliberately or otherwise had deprived him of access to his father.

The general verdict among Grey Owl scholars is that George Belaney was "a vain, lazy, spoilt, impetuous failure" (Dickson 1973, 20). As noted above, he also vanished from the life of his son when the boy was only four years old; George is believed to have died in the United States in " 'a drunken brawl' " (Smith 1990, 13). The "ultra-respectable, [upper-]middle-class" Belaney women "were shamed by the failure of the man of the family, and determined that the little boy [in their care] should not go the same way" (Dickson 1973, 23). But likely because of this antagonism, in Archie's mind his absent and negligent father became transformed into an icon. Significantly, his progenitor was no longer a ne'er-do-well Englishman with a taste for game hunting and young brides. Instead, he was a Scot who became "an Indian scout in the wars against the Indians in the south-western United States in the 1870s" and who then married an Indigenous woman, "Katherine Cochise of the Jacarilla band of the Apache tribe" (Dickson 1973, 3). As perhaps befits someone conceived in the New World, Archie gave himself an authentically American pedigree.

Archie's construction of his family tree was not accidental. At least since the beginning of his school days, he had begun to imagine himself as a North American Indian. As Dickson relates, "He tracked animals, imagining himself an Indian in the forest, feeling his way forward, every sense alert to betraying noise, crack of stick, the hushed warning call of an animal, or the sudden cessation of birdsong as, heads to one side, disturbed birds listened for confirmation or denial of what had alarmed them" (1973, 29). Ada, who was otherwise rather austere, "allowed Archie to keep his own menagerie" of animals in his room, including "rabbits, snakes, and mice" (Smith 1990, 14). For a lonesome boy growing up without either parents or siblings, the animals provided him with "a secret refuge" from his stultifying environment (Smith 1990, 14). They also gave him the opportunity to imagine himself living in a world in which animals reportedly were treated as well as humans, that is, among the Indigenous peoples of Canada.

Ada likely assumed Archie would "grow out of his obsession with Indians" (Dickson 1973, 37), but that was not to be the case. If anything, as he grew older, Archie became even more fascinated with Canada's First Nations. He acquired considerable knowledge of "the major linguistic divisions" among Indigenous peoples and, while still in his mid-teens, expressed his desire "to go to Canada and join the Indians, study their ways, and maybe write a book about them" (Dickson 1973, 37, 38). His grandmother and aunts tried to dissuade him, but to no avail. Finally, they reached a compromise: Archie would work in Hastings for a year to save as much money as possible for his journey and then, "if he still wanted to go to Canada, the family would agree" (Dickson 1973, 39). So after saying farewell to Ada, Archie departed Liverpool on 29 March 1906, on the aptly named steamship *Canada* (Smith 1990, 24). He would arrive at the port of Halifax, Nova Scotia, a week later, on 6 April 1906. He was seventeen years old.

One of the conditions that his grandmother and aunts imposed on Archie before allowing him to migrate to Canada was that "he would become a farming pupil and learn to be a farmer while he was getting used to the country. If he would farm until he was twenty-one, only four years away, then he could do afterwards what he liked." The reason for the proviso was that they hoped that "if life with the Indians proved less attractive than he imagined," then Archie would always have farming to fall back on (Dickson 1973, 39). But Archie had no intention of ever becoming a farmer, on either side of the Atlantic. There is some uncertainty as to what he did immediately upon arriving in Canada, the most common theory being that "he worked as a clerk in a men's-wear shop" in Toronto (Anahareo [1972] 2014, 44). Later that summer he travelled by train to northeastern Ontario. Initially, he was headed for Cobalt, a mining town by the Quebec border where silver had been discovered a few years earlier and which was experiencing an economic boom. Many Canadians, such as the good denizens of Stephen Leacock's Mariposa, "went simply crazy" once they learned that "this great silver country spread out to the north of [them], where people had thought there was only a wilderness" (Leacock 1912, 29, 33). Archie, in contrast, was more interested in the wilderness than in the silver fields. During his trip, he is believed to have overheard other "passengers talking about the fabulously rich hunting country in the Temagami Reserve" south of Cobalt. "On a sudden impulse he got off the train at Temiskaming" (Dickson 1973, 46), and so began his experience as a woodsman in Canada. Given his aim to learn about the wilderness, Archie was fortunate to meet the well-known white guide Bill Guppy, who would become his first mentor. Archie agreed to "work just for his grub during the coming winter" (Dickson 1973, 51). In exchange, Guppy taught him how "to snowshoe, and how to restring snowshoes when they were worn by the sharp ice; how to make his own axe-handles, how to load canoes and run the rapids, how to 'carry' a portage" (Dickson 1973, 52). In short, Guppy initiated the new arrival into life in the wilderness.

While working in Temagami, Archie also got to know the Anishinaabe people of nearby Bear Island. He became particularly intimate with a young woman named Angele Egwuna. In fact, by the summer of 1908, he applied to the Justice of the Peace in Temagami for "a licence to marry Angele" (Dickson 1973, 74). But the marriage did not take place right away, for later on the people of Temagami watched the English newcomer "paddling fast in a canoe, with half a dozen Ojibway canoes in hot pursuit, in one of which sat Angele." Although Archie never explained why the Anishinaabe came after him, the speculation is that he "must have been attempting to anticipate pleasures that only marriage sanctified" (Dickson 1973, 74). Archie and Angele would marry two years later, in August of 1910, and there is little doubt that his encounter with Angele Egwuna was one of the great turning points in his life, for she not only introduced him to the Anishinaabe language and culture but also "taught him basic woodlore and how to survive in the bush" (Smith, 1990, 41). Angele herself came to love "her Englishman" deeply. Even after the controversy surrounding his death, "she recalled, with a smile on her face, how he would say to her, 'I'll make a white woman of you, my l'Angel.' And she would reply, 'Oh no, Archie, I make the Indian of you!' " (qtd. in Smith 1990, 43). Archie appeared to have become "committed to the Indian way of life," wearing "moccasins made by Angele from skins he had trapped and cured himself" (Dickson 1973, 78). Following the birth of their daughter Agnes in 1911, he even "tried the unprecedented course of going to work at a mine" in order to support his wife and child (Dickson 1973, 79), but his attempt at domesticity proved to be short-lived.

The next summer Archie received a letter from his aunt Ada informing him that Julia Belaney had died. Even more shocking than the news of his grandmother's demise was his discovery that Ada believed her mother must have been terribly disappointed by her children, each of whom "had somehow failed her when they grew up, the girls by not marrying, and the son by spending all her inheritance." This sense of disillusionment extended to Archie, for whom "Granny had hoped for so much" and from whom "no word had come to her during the last year of her illness" (Dickson 1973, 81). Archie did not say anything about the death of his grandmother to Angele. What he did tell her was that he was going to work as a fire ranger in Biscotasing, a village some 200 kilometres northwest of Temagami commonly known as Bisco. He also "promised that he would return in the fall, and that meanwhile he would send her money" (Dickson 1973, 82). But Angele would not see her husband again for the next six years, by which time he would have fathered a son by another woman and married yet another one.

Dickson attributes Archie's abandonment of Angele and baby Agnes not only to the shock of his beloved grandmother's death but also to what Dickson identifies as "a Belaney characteristic, a domestic claustrophobia, a feeling that he must break out or die"(1973, 84). Donald B. Smith agrees, writing that "Archie certainly should not have become a father.... Having no role model for a father, he had no idea even of what the part demanded. He did not know how a real family should act. The birth of their daughter, Agnes, terrified him, and within a few months he planned his escape" (1990, 44). There are two other possible explanations for Archie's behaviour. First, during his early years in Temagami, he "discovered alcohol" (42). No less important, Archie had become aware of "his fellow whites' censure of his marriage," which might have "led him to question it." Smith points out that there were white people in Temagami who refused to shake hands with Archie after he married an Indigenous woman (44), which suggests that it was not always advantageous for a white person to associate intimately with Indigenous people, much less to try to pass as one of them.

Whatever his reasons may have been for leaving Temagami for Bisco, Archie spent the summer working as a fire ranger for the Ontario Forestry Department and the winter trapping. Despite his distance from his family, he did not allow himself to become too lonesome. In his second winter in Bisco, 1913–14, he persuaded a young mixed-race woman named Marie Girard to join "him on his trapline" and, by the time they returned to the village in the spring, she was "pregnant," although he may not have been aware of it (Smith 1990, 50, 53). Archie seems not to have had any strong feelings toward Girard, beyond sexual desire, and was probably relieved when he learned that the First World War had broken out. Girard would give birth to a son that winter, develop consumption soon after, and die within months (Dickson 1973, 98). The baby's father, though, was nowhere in sight during those events.

Instead, Archie had enlisted in the Canadian Army, eventually joining "the 13th Montreal Battalion, now known as the Black Watch" (Dickson 1973, 101). While serving as a sniper in Belgium, "he was struck by a bullet which damaged the bones at the base of the toes of his right foot" (Dickson 1973, 102). Because of his injuries, he was sent to convalesce at a Canadian hospital in Bromley, England, not far from Hastings. Given his proximity to his birthplace, he was able to reacquaint himself with some old friends. Among these was Ivy Holmes—also identified as Connie—with whom he had had a teenage romance and who was now a professional dancer. The relationship was enthusiastically supported by both families, neither of which had any inkling of his marriage to Angele, and before long Archie and Ivy were married (Dickson 1973, 102). However, the union was "not a success," not the least because Ivy began to find her husband "strange, secretive—almost sinister" (Dickson 1973, 103). Ivy agreed to Archie's "plan of beginning a life together" in the Canadian wilderness (Smith 1990, 63). But when the Army's medical board concluded that his foot would be "permanently deformed" and that he should return to Canada for "further therapy" (Dickson 1973, 103), the newly (re)married Archie sailed across the Atlantic alone.

Archie's return to Canada after the First World War obviously was not a triumphant one. He was handicapped physically and wounded psychologically. As he was undergoing therapy for his foot in Toronto, he must have learned that "Marie [Girard] had died and that he had fathered a son, a baby named Johnny [Jero]," who was being raised by a local woman (Smith 1990, 64). Those developments meant that he could not take Ivy to Bisco. Interestingly, during a moment of such turmoil, he turned for advice to "the one person he felt he could confide in—Angele" (Smith 1990, 64). The two arranged to meet twice in the central Ontario town of Lindsay and, years later, Angele would recall that Archie was "anxious to go back to Bisco again" presumably because "he was afraid of another person," a woman he had married in England (qtd. in Smith 1990, 65). But Angele appears not to have elaborated on how she felt about the fact Archie had acquired a new wife overseas and was not planning to rejoin her and their daughter.

Still, while Archie may have managed to escape Ivy (and Angele) by moving to Bisco, he was not able to evade his own demons. Ontario had gone dry during the war years and, like other trappers and hunters in the area, Archie started to make moonshine. He also consumed the concoction liberally, something that would transform him from "a perfect gentleman and a wonderful conversationist" into an erratic and violent individual (Smith 1990, 69). Fortunately, some local people came to his rescue, notably the Espaniel family. Alex and Anny Espaniel, who were Anishinaabe, welcomed Archie into their house for "two or three years" and let him join them for "two winters at their winter trapping ground" (Smith 1990, 71). According to their son Jimmy, who became a close friend of the young Englishman, it was from the Espaniels that "Archie learned the 'Indian way of doing things—which...the white man calls conservation'" (qtd. in Smith 1990, 71). Smith maintains that "Alex was the only father Archie ever had" (1990, 71), a view that is supported by the inscription Archie wrote in one of his books that he gave to Alex: "To one whom I am proud to call 'Dad,' & who taught me much of whatever I may know—Alex L'Espagnol" (Smith 1990, 196; see also Ruffo 1996, 162). Yet even the unstinting support of the Españiels—who coincidentally descended from a Grey Owl–like Spaniard (L'Espagnol) who moved to the region toward the end of the eighteenth century, married an Anishinaabe woman, and "adopted an Indian lifestyle" (Smith 1990, 71)—would not be enough to keep Archie in the area. The main reason Bisco initially appealed to Archie was its rich hunting grounds. But conditions had changed drastically during the war. As Dickson captures the situation, "What had been a Garden of Eden when he first came to Bisco in 1912 looked, only six years later, as though a drunken party had taken place" (1973, 113). The expansion of the timber trade was the great culprit, but the result of the seemingly indiscriminate cutting of the forest was that the habitat of many animals also had been destroyed. By 1925, Archie was becoming ever more dependent on guiding during the summer. Since Temagami was considerably more attractive to tourists, he gradually drifted south to the place where he had first landed in northern Ontario, which was also the place where his first wife and their daughter lived.

Paradoxically, Archie's move to Temagami would not lead to a reconciliation with Angele but to his meeting the great love of his life, Anahareo. Born Gertrude Bernard, Anahareo was eighteen years younger than Archie. There are many fascinating aspects to their relationship, some of them quite ironic. For one, while Anahareo was a Mohawk, she was urban. She was raised with little exposure to the traditional elements of her culture, and one of the reasons she became captivated by the man she called her "Jesse James, that mad, dashing, and romantic Robin Hood of America" (Anahareo [1972] 2014, 2), was that she hoped he would enable her to rediscover her Indigenous roots. In addition, Anahareo was very much a female version of Archie, someone who seldom allowed her desires to be subordinated to the needs of those close to her. As Archie wrote to her toward the end of their relationship, after she left home to go on one of her lengthy prospecting trips, "No, I'm not mad at you Gurdy, I only envy you.... This is a case of the student overtaking the master" (qtd. in Anahareo [1972] 2014, 158). Most important, Anahareo reportedly became the catalyst for the two main conversions in Archie's life, being instrumental in transforming him from a trapper into a conservationist and, to a lesser degree, into a writer. These were, of course, the transformations that would enable Grey Owl to be hired by Canada's National Parks Branch as a conservationist at Ajawaan Lake, in Saskatchewan's Prince Albert National Park, and then to write full time and to lecture about wildlife preservation on both sides of the Atlantic.

Anahareo would not be Archie's last wife or common-law partner. That
role belonged to Yvonne Perrier, an Ottawa health worker who had been an
assistant to "Elizabeth Smith Shortt, one of Canada's first female medical
doctors" (Smith 1990, 170). But there is little question that Archie (and the
world) came to see Anahareo as his real intellectual and spiritual companion, his soulmate. Because of her wanderlust, reflected in her passion for
prospecting for precious metals like gold and silver, Anahareo would leave
Archie, as well as their daughter Dawn, for extended periods (Dickson 1973,
226–28). She particularly found it difficult to accept that Archie would have
to devote so much time to writing the books that were making him (and her)
famous around the world. Still, there is no avoiding the fact that she occupies
a central place not only in his most celebrated book, the memoir *Pilgrims of
the Wild*, but also in many of the short documentary films that he showed
while he lectured. Indeed, no less so than the beaver, it is hard to imagine
Grey Owl without Anahareo.

Anahareo is critically important for yet another reason: the supposed transparency of Archie Belaney's transformation into Grey Owl. It has become
common to argue that "Grey Owl had little difficulty in convincing his white
audience of his Indian identity" but that he "failed to fool aboriginal people"
(Relke 1999, 257, 263; see also Egan 2011, 73). But this thesis is seriously challenged by Anahareo herself. As noted above, Anahareo was a Mohawk and
she must have been reasonably intimate with Archie, since they lived together
for several years and even produced a daughter. Yet she always maintains that,
during their relationship, "Never once did I suspect that Archie was anything
but what he said he was, Scotch and Indian, born in Mexico" (Anahareo
[1972] 2014, 176). As she underscores, "He was an Indian. He lived like one,
he identified with Indians, he took up their cause and he never did this for
himself" (qtd. in Fraser 1975, 17). It was only after his death, and particularly
after Anahareo travelled to England to meet his aunts, that she became "convinced that Archie was English," a realization that she says gave her "the awful
feeling [that] for all those years I had been married to a ghost, that the man
who now lay buried at Ajawaan was someone I had never known, and that
Archie had never really existed" (Anahareo [1972] 2014, 184). Considering

Anahareo's reaction, Archie's assumed identity must not have been nearly as obvious as some critics like to believe. Or, to phrase it differently, at least some Indigenous people were not aware of his metamorphosis.

The claim that only white people were duped by Grey Owl is often accompanied by the insinuation that today we are too sophisticated to fall for such antics, an argument that is not overly persuasive. After all, we live in an age of literary hoaxes. From Helen Demidenko and Binjamin Wilkomirski, through James Frey and JT LeRoy, to Margaret B. Jones, we have been subjected to an endless parade of texts produced by authors using false identities. The Alan Sokal affair, in which a physicist wrote an essay full of fabricated footnotes contending that quantum mechanics vindicated postmodern relativism and had it accepted by a prestigious journal (Sokal [1996] 2000, 11–45), demonstrates that even established scholars cannot always distinguish between genuine scholarship and satire of academic work. Settler societies, such as Canada and Australia, seem to be especially prone to hoaxes in which non-Indigenous writers pretend to be Indigenous. So pervasive have literary impersonations become in Australia that some critics "identify 'the hoax' as a peculiarly Australian phenomenon" (Nolan and Dawson 2004, vi). In light of the proliferation of such cases, it is difficult to accept that we are more discerning judges of texts than were Grey Owl's readers in the 1930s.

The relationship between a text and its ostensible creator is necessarily complex. "In theory," states W.H. Auden, "the author of a good book should remain anonymous, for it is to his work, not to himself, that admiration is due. In practice, this seems to be impossible" (1962, 14). The most conspicuous way in which authors impinge upon their writings is through such paratexts as prefaces and epilogues, in which they often attempt to control how the works will be interpreted. But these paratexts have an even more complicated function in the writings of what one might call trickster writers, those authors who deliberately mislead the reader about their identity or who provide such meagre and ambiguous information about themselves that it is almost impossible to determine who they are. Needless to say, Grey Owl is one such figure. Given the extent to which he fashioned a new identity, it is not surprising that in his books he was not very forthcoming about his background. This reticence, though, created major obstacles for someone who was producing what are professedly autobiographical works, writings based on his life experiences. Moreover, the problem was further compounded by his fear of being unmasked, which had to be a dominant concern once he became well known. As Grey Owl writes in the preface to his last book, *Tales of an Empty Cabin*, a collection of essays published two years before his death, "Most aspiring authors get their punishment at the very outset; mine, no doubt, will come later when it will hit the hardest, and I am waiting for the crash any time now" ([1936] 1999, ix). He does not specify what kind of "punishment" he has in mind, but one suspects that it likely has something to do with his tendency to conflate the factual and the fictive in his accounts of his life.

There is no question that the man first known as Archie Belaney engaged in ethnocultural passing, by claiming to be part of a group to which he had no genetic links whatsoever (Compton 2010, 24). Yet Grey Owl's passing, or "reverse passing," as some postcolonial scholars prefer to label the phenomenon when undergone by members of dominant groups (Huggan 2007, 103), is not without its complexities. For example, did he damage anyone by discursively inserting himself into a culture into which he was not born? That is, what did he gain by pretending to be Indigenous when there seemed to be few tangible financial or cultural benefits to such an identification? As Janet Billinghurst observes in the passage that serves as the epigraph to this chapter, Archie Belaney chose "to be an Indian" at "a time when the cowboys always won" (1999, 2). Similarly, what is the significance of his desire to abandon or escape his culture? Does it mean that he deemed it inferior to the North American Indigenous way of life? One cannot help but wonder what might be the reasons that led a boy born into one of the leading cultures of the time to feel that he did not belong there and that his true home lay in a far less technologically advanced society. Finally, is there some merit to his journey, the quest of someone who adopts a new ethnocultural identity because he is not at home in his own? The novelist Francine Prose has made the provocative suggestion that "since there are, as we now know, transsexuals—men and women who grow up knowing instinctively and beyond persuasion that they have been doomed to inhabit a body with a different gender from their brain and heart—surely there must be transculturals—people who have been born in the wrong society and for whom going native represents the equivalent of a surgical correction" (2002, 45). Or as the non-fiction writer Kurt Caswell asks, "If a man can...change his sex to become a woman, why can't a man change his heritage to become an Indian?" (2013, para. 29). In other words, could Grey Owl have been one such transcultural? Is it possible that he underwent some kind of transculturation once he arrived in Canada and came to identify more with Indigenous culture than with European?

All of these issues will be explored in this book. The first three chapters focus primarily on Grey Owl's construction of himself in his writings. Chapter 1 deals with his early magazine articles and his first book, *The Men of the*

*Last Frontier*, a collection of essays that significantly he had entitled *The Vanishing Frontier*; Chapter 2 examines his most influential text, the memoir *Pilgrims of the Wild*; and Chapter 3 analyzes his two remaining books, the children's novel *Sajo and the Beaver People* and the collection of essays *Tales of an Empty Cabin*, as well as some fugitive writings. Chapter 4 focuses on Anahareo's two memoirs about her relationship with the nature writer and conservationist: *My Life with Grey Owl* and *Devil in Deerskins: My Life with Grey Owl*. Chapter 5, which is by far the longest, traces and analyzes the representations of Grey Owl chiefly since his death. It begins with the work of Lovat Dickson, Grey Owl's London-based publisher, biographer, and greatest promoter, and ends with *Grey Owl: The Mystery of Archie Belaney*, the poetic biography by Armand Garnet Ruffo, a great-grandson of Alex and Anny Espaniel who celebrates his own family through the conservationist; the feature film *Grey Owl* by Richard Attenborough; and *Grey Owl and Me*, the memoir by the Ontario wilderness guide and canoeist Hap Wilson, who sees himself as a new Grey Owl. Finally, the book concludes with an overview of the Grey Owl story and why it is likely to remain a living narrative in the twenty-first century.

# CHAPTER ONE

## *Grey Owl's Search for His "True" Self:*
## The Vanishing Frontier/The Men of the Last Frontier

> *How many of us get to choose who we will become?*
> *How many of us dare to follow our own dreams*
> *and visions?*
>
> —Gilbert Oskaboose

Grey Owl often credited his writing career, as well as his transformation from a trapper into a conservationist, to his Mohawk wife, Anahareo. But while Anahareo undoubtedly influenced his decision to become a writer, there is much evidence that he had been preparing for the role at least since his teen years. As mentioned in the introduction, one of the reasons the young Archie Belaney wanted to come to Canada was to join Indigenous people, learn about their cultures, and possibly write about them. In addition, many of the people he befriended in his early days in Canada remarked how he was always recording his observations about the new world he was discovering. For instance, years after Grey Owl's death, Jimmy Espaniel reminisced about how his friend "used to take notes whenever he thought of anything in the bush. We worked from 4:30 in the morning until nine at night in those days, and when Belaney was finished he would sometimes make notes in his note-book." Then, after they returned to the Espaniel home in Bisco, "Belaney wrote from those notes. He had nearly a packsack of material written on padsheets when he left here. He would write so much and then roll it up and file it in the packsack" (qtd. in Smith 1990, 72). Grey Owl's oldest daughter, Agnes, also recalled how, when he visited her mother, Angele Egwuna, and her family at Temagami, he would spend all his time with her people and "take notes of everything they were saying" (Smith 1990, 75). Finally, the English-born fire ranger Bill Draper stated that, while the two were working in northern

Ontario just before the outbreak of the First World War, "he told me he was writing a book" (Smith 1990, 52). Again, Grey Owl's wish to be a writer had manifested itself long before he met Anahareo in the summer of 1925.

An unexpected person who played a pivotal role in the launching of Grey Owl's writing career was his mother. Kittie Cox had remarkably little impact on her oldest son after she gave him up to be raised by his Belaney grandmother and aunts when he was still an infant. The nature of their relationship is illustrated by the fact that, even though she visited him when he was convalescing near London during the war, "he left England without giving her his address" in Canada (Smith 1990, 82). Yet Kittie, who had changed her surname to Scott-Brown after she remarried, managed to locate him and wrote him a letter asking that he help his half-brother, Leonard Scott-Brown, get a job with the Hudson's Bay Company. Mother and son eventually initiated a correspondence and Kittie found one of Archie's letters "so poetic" that she decided to send it to the English magazine *Country Life*, which responded by inviting him "to write an article" (Smith 1990, 83). Archie soon prepared a substantial essay entitled "The Passing of the Last Frontier," which his mother forwarded to *Country Life* and which would appear in the magazine's 2 March 1929 issue. Ironically, reflecting this familial trajectory, the author's first major publication would bear the name "H. Scott-Brown" (1929, 305). Kittie then had to write a letter to the magazine explaining that the essay was not by her but by "my son, Archibald Stansfeld Belaney" (Grey Owl 1929, 342; see also Dickson 1973, 155–56), who thus begins his writing career as A.S. Belaney. Nevertheless, Grey Owl continued to find it difficult to acknowledge his biological relation to Kittie, describing her to Lovat Dickson as "a step-mother whom I am not well-acquainted with" (qtd. in Dickson 1973, 201). Judging by his writings, the only maternal figure in his life—and not a warm one at that—would appear to have been his aunt Ada Belaney.

As Grey Owl relates in *Pilgrims of the Wild*, so impressed was the editor of *Country Life* by this new voice from the Canadian wilds that he requested to see something more substantial, "a book" ([1935] 1990, 184). More precisely, he wanted Grey Owl to write his life story. But the crafting of an autobiographical text created some unusual problems for the neophyte author. As he started publishing his work, he changed not only his byline from A.S. Belaney to Grey Owl but also his identity from a white man to someone of mixed Indigenous and European descent and, at times, even to someone of strictly Indigenous ancestry. Consequently, Grey Owl chose "to write, not a personal biography, as requested, but a series of essays on the North itself" ([1935] 1990, 185). His decision, though, was probably shaped less by his desire to focus on his treasured wilderness than to avoid a much more perplexing subject, his evolving self. As Dickson encapsulates the situation:

> Archie could not find a way of giving an account of events in which he had acted not only as an observer but a participant, without what he thought of as an offensive use of the first personal pronoun. It was not modesty which hamstrung him, but the difficulty of combining the marvellous truth of what he observed with the un-truth about himself which he had established: his Indian birth and upbringing. His problem was not the artistic one of finding the right opening, but the moral one of telling a life-story that began with a lie. (1973, 195)

That is, Grey Owl's unstable biography would not only precipitate the greatest controversy in his (after)life but also determine the form of most of his writings, compelling him to avoid writing about himself even when detailing his own activities.

⊡     ⊡     ⊡

The use of the word "I" would pose a major dilemma for Grey Owl throughout his writing career, starting with his very first book. Most of the essays that comprise *The Men of the Last Frontier* were first published in the *Illustrated Canadian Forest and Outdoors*, the magazine of the Canadian Forestry Association (CFA) popularly known as *Forest and Outdoors*. In June 1930, just over a year after "The Passing of the Last Frontier" appeared in *Country Life*, Grey Owl had his essay "The Vanishing Life of the Wild" published in *Forest and Outdoors*. This would mark the beginning of an extremely close relationship with both the magazine and the CFA. Over the next eight years, he would have nearly thirty contributions published in *Forest and Outdoors*, not only his essays but also invited responses to essays by other writers and advice columns. In January 1931 he even served as a keynote speaker at the CFA's annual convention in Montreal, where he clearly made an impression, both verbally and visually. According to the CFA's official report, "Dressed in becoming Indian costume, Mr. Grey Owl made a picturesque figure on the platform, and his address, couched in vigorous and expressive English, dealt with the topic of wildlife conservation, with a first-hand knowledge and freshness of treatment which the audience relished greatly" ("Annual Forest Convention" 1931, 95). The "Famous Indian Writer" (qtd. in Grey Owl 1933,

229), it would seem, became as valuable a resource for the CFA as the CFA and its magazine did for him.

The relationship between Grey Owl and *Forest and Outdoors* started tentatively. He wrote "The Vanishing Life of the Wild" in response to another contributor's plea that we "not forget the lesson of our vanished beaver" and "combat the wolf menace" before the deer go the way of the beaver (Bates 1930, 137). While Grey Owl agrees with the other writer about the wolf problem, he uses his experience as "a trapper of lifetime experience" (1930a, 321) to make the case that the beaver can yet be saved. He also states that he has rescued "several pairs of these animals," which after he finishes observing them, he plans "either to place at the disposal of the Government or to restock with them a chosen territory where they will have adequate protection for all time" (361). As he closes his essay, the situation of the beaver is so dire that, "regardless of party politics or provincial differences," Canadians must "give our national animal the Dominion-wide protection that he so justly deserves, before he becomes as a tale that is told, existing only as a memory to those who knew him—before he vanishes forever from off the face of the earth" (364). In short, what is needed to save the beaver is nothing less than a national campaign, or perhaps better a national mission.

Judging by the way they frame his essay, the magazine's editors clearly share Grey Owl's vision. On the first page of "The Vanishing Life of the Wild," they insert a box in which they quote several paragraphs from a letter that was included with the submission. In the letter, Grey Owl asserts: "*Remarks on beaver protection may seem a little premature. But should they, like the buffalo, be brought back, NOW is the time to talk of ways and means, and a course of action decided on*" (1930a, 321; italics in text). He further adds that he is "*a native*" of Ontario and that he "*would be glad to enter into correspondence, through the medium of your magazine, with any persons resident there, who are genuinely interested in the preservation of our national animal, provided the interest is not pecuniary*" (321; italics in text). Perhaps more important, in the opening paragraph, he declares, "*I am a man of Indian blood, and am what might be termed a 'converted' trapper. My few observations are the result of practical experience, and deep thinking, based on the habitual observation and the insight into the way of the wild for which our race is noted*" (321; italics in text). That is, from the outset, the editors of *Forest and Outdoors* are under the impression that their new author is both a trapper-turned-conservationist and Indigenous, assumptions that could not help but affect their response to him and his writings.

Interestingly, as had happened when "The Passing of the Last Frontier"

was published in *Country Life*, there is some confusion about the identity of
the author of "The Vanishing Life of the Wild," whose name appears between
quotation marks, as "Grey Owl." But in his next contribution to *Forest and
Outdoors*, "Little Brethren of the Wilderness: Part One," the editors clarify
that "*Grey Owl...is his real and complete name. He is of Indian blood, a true
lover and conservator of wildlife, and possesses an uncommon facility in literary expression*" (qtd. in Grey Owl 1930b, 499; italics in text). Moreover, it is
not only the magazine's editors who are struck by Grey Owl's style; so are its
readers. In his article "King of the Beaver People: Part One" in the December
1930 issue, Grey Owl includes a letter from L.R. Schlosser, of Chicago, who
applauds the magazine for its commendable articles on "wildlife reforestation
and all constructive subjects. We have no outdoor magazines in the States that
compare with yours. They publish articles that incite hunters to ruthless killing instead of conservation." Schlosser is especially impressed by Grey Owl's
writings, which "show a wonderful command of the English language as well
as unusual knowledge of wildlife" (qtd. in Grey Owl 1930e, 686).

Schlosser also expresses the desire "to correspond with Grey Owl personally" (qtd. in Grey Owl 1930e, 686), and he must not have been the only
reader to do so. By the April 1931 issue, Grey Owl has been commissioned
to respond to essays by other contributors to the magazine. Thus, when one
W.A. Parker charges that " 'The Indian' is a big problem" regarding Canadian
conservation, since the Indigenous people "I have met in the bush know no
closed season" (1931, 195), Grey Owl counters with "The Indian's Side of the
Question," which is placed right in the middle of the first page of Parker's text.
Similarly, when a few months later the novelist Philip H. Godsell writes that
while Indigenous people are "usually blamed" for the scarcity of fur-bearing
animals across Canada, the real culprits are "white trappers" (1931, 340),
Grey Owl is enlisted to reply, which he does in "Comments on Mr. Godsell's
Article," to what he terms Godsell's "illuminating article," whose conclusions
he generally shares (1931e, 343). Then by the October 1931 issue, he has been
promoted to nothing less than the head—and presumably the only member—of the Bureau of Information for the Young, in which the magazine, as
he describes it in "And a Little Child Shall Lead Them," "generously" provides
him "the space for a corner in which I may answer, insofar as I am able, the
various and sometimes penetrating questions on wild animals and their ways
that these young citizens may put to me" (1931g, 40). As he acknowledges,
"One of the greatest pleasures resultant on my attempts to arouse a public
sympathy and interest on behalf of the Kindred of the Wild is the immediate
and universal response that has been evidenced by the scores of letters I have

received from widely distributed spots in both the United States and Canada" (1931g, 40). Considering the prominence that *Forest and Outdoors* gives to his writings, and the frequency with which his name appears in its pages, it is fair to deduce that Grey Owl had found his home and the magazine its central spokesman on wildlife preservation.

The sixteen texts that Grey Owl publishes in *Forest and Outdoors* between June 1930 and December 1931, about the time that *The Men of the Last Frontier* appeared, cover the gamut of wildlife issues and conservation. Several essays of course deal with the nature of the beaver and the urgent need to prevent the extinction of the species. Others, such as "The Fine Art of the Still Hunt," contend that, "paradoxical, as it may sound, it is none the less an indisputable fact that there are no more ardent advocates today of game preservation than the devotees of that ancient and honorable pastime, the fall hunt" (1935d, 624). Still other texts speak of the author's evolving strategy for leading people to embrace conservation by giving them direct access to the beaver he is raising. As he writes in a letter to the magazine that is excerpted in the opening page of the second part of his essay "King of the Beaver People," "*One thing I must warn you, on no account have any perfume such as talcum powder or after-shaving lotion on your person, as they object to it and can become very troublesome and unmanageable*" (1931a, 13; italics in text). Invariably, Grey Owl claims to speak from experience. He is someone who is supposedly intimately familiar with the wild and its human and non-human denizens, which, in addition to his writing style, is the main source of both his appeal and his power.

The editors of *Forest and Outdoors*, however, seem to have perceived Grey Owl as more than just an expert. He is a sage of sorts, someone who has "A Philosophy of the Wild." That is the title of a piece that appears in the magazine's December 1931 issue, written by the well-known conservationist Tony Lascelles, the pseudonym of Hubert H. Green, in "*collaboration*" with Grey Owl (1931, 15; italics in text). The authors open their manifesto with the declaration that "[i]n this age of tolerant opinions one may say with the privilege of conviction that, of all creatures, civilized man is the most terrible, for he alone kills and destroys without necessity and in excess of his needs" (15). Lascelles and Grey Owl present themselves and the magazine's readers as people "who know the wilderness and love the wild things" and are able to "appreciate full well the abysmal gulf which exists between the animal world and the human race—a gulf of man's creation rather than Nature's avowed purpose" (15). But they stress that this chasm was not produced by man as such but only by modern man, who "persistently destroys and distorts the face of Nature" (17). The divide between humans and non-human animals is therefore neither natural nor inevitable. As the authors reflect, "It is not unstrange to a wilderness philosophy to realize that pagan people have yet to be discovered who hunt for the pleasure of killing and in excess of their immediate and pressing needs. Aboriginal races uncontaminated by the influence and excessive demands of the white man, or his civilized colored cousins, take wildlife as did their remote progenitors" (15). For Lascelles and Grey Owl, the only way that modern humans will be able to stop defiling nature is by returning to their primal roots and embracing the ways of their early ancestors, ways that they maintain are still the norm among Indigenous peoples.

Although this is not openly stated in "A Philosophy of the Wild," one presumes that the main reason Lascelles feels compelled to collaborate with Grey Owl has to do with the latter's ostensible insider knowledge of Indigenous cultural practices. In their preamble to "The Indian's Side of the Question," the editors explain their decision by asserting that, "in view of the somewhat pointed references" in Parker's essay "to the 'Indian problem,' it was deemed advisable, in order to present a complete picture of the subject, to secure a further opinion from the view-point of the Indian. Accordingly, with Mr. Parker's consent, our correspondent, Grey Owl, was invited to comment on that subject" (qtd. in Grey Owl 1931d, 195). Again, for the magazine's editors, their author is not merely an expert in wildlife conservation and "a well-known writer of nature stories" (qtd. in Grey Owl 1932b, 289) but an Indigenous one. This is something that they frequently advertise in editorial notes that accompany essays both by Grey Owl and about him, in which they describe him as the "Famous Indian Naturalist" (Grey Owl 1938e, 37) or "the noted Indian author" (Lascelles 1932, 51). In "The Indian's Side of the Question," Grey Owl (1931d, 195) certainly sounds like someone who has intimate knowledge of the Indigenous world. He contends that Parker "forgets that the Indian has the prior right. He must live." No less important, anticipating "A Philosophy of Life" and his later writings, Grey Owl claims that "the Indian has no sporting instinct and kills only from necessity, and then only what he needs." As he closes the essay, "If the Indian is such a devastating feature of the landscape, how is it that at the time these people were most numerous, i.e., on the arrival of the white man, the country swarmed with game?" (195). That is, unless the First Nations have undergone a radical metamorphosis regarding their attitudes toward wild animals, it is difficult to imagine that they are the main culprits when it comes to the scarcity of fur.

It is worth noting that in "The Indian's Side of the Question" Grey Owl has·

a tendency to refer to Indigenous people in a somewhat distant manner, not as "us Indians" but as "the Indian," which could be interpreted to mean that he is not one of them. But he shows no such reticence in several of his other contributions to *Forest and Outdoors*. As we saw in the letter attached to his first submission to the magazine, "The Vanishing Life of the Wild," he identifies himself as being of Indigenous ancestry (1930a, 321). Then following his triumphant address to the 1931 CFA convention, the magazine includes a full-page biographical profile of the author, accompanied by a large studio photograph. Entitled "The Adventurous Career of GREY OWL (wa-shee-quon-asier)," the note presents "biographical facts" about Grey Owl that he provided to the magazine during his visit to Montreal. The text, which will be supplemented a few years later with "A Little History of Grey Owl," states that he was born into the "Jicarilla Apache [band] to which his mother belonged" in some unspecified place in either the United States or Mexico. His father, a free trapper like his father before him, "served as a Government scout and guide to waggon trains at various military headquarters and frontier posts" in the western part of the United States. Revolted at the "injustice and unfairness of the wars against Indians," he joined Buffalo Bill's show and travelled with the troupe to England. Grey Owl himself subsequently too "hired with Buffalo Bill and spent nine months in England." But he tired of the show and, "influenced by his father's tales of a trapper's life," came to Canada in the first decade of the twentieth century. Some years later, after becoming a trapper, he was "formally and ceremonially adopted by the Ojibway Nation, learned their language and methods of travelling and hunting, being now more of a bush Indian than he ever was a plains Indian" (1931, 118). Disgusted by the havoc that amateur white trappers and forestry conglomerates were causing in the Canadian wilderness, he had an epiphany that led him to cease trapping beaver and to fight to preserve the species.

So, in his writings for *Forest and Outdoors*, Grey Owl leaves little doubt that, while he may or may not be an Ontario native, he is, as he describes it in "The Indian's Code of the Wild," at least "partly of Indian blood" (1935b, 883). In his written account of his address of the CFA convention, "Who Will Repay?" he maintains that the reason he is qualified to address such an august body on the conservation of wildlife in Canada is not only that he has "many of the inside facts on the game situation" (1931b, 119) but also because of the perspective he represents. "To us, who dwell in the wilderness," he writes, "the bush and its denizens, the waters, the northern lights and the sunset are living breathing realities. The Forest, to us, has a Personality—a Soul" (120).

He adds that he has spoken with "not one, but hundreds of Indians, and it was always the same tale—NO FUR" (120). The extent of the consultation he has conducted perhaps explains why he appears to forego his individual voice in favour of a collective one. He concludes the essay with a clarion call, written in block letters: "THIS IS NOT THE VOICE OF GREY OWL THAT SPEAKS, BUT THE VOICE OF A MIGHTY AND EVER-INCREASING ARMY OF DEFENDERS OF THE WILD, VOICES THAT WILL BE HEARD. LET YOUR EARS BE OPEN" (122; see also Grey Owl 1938d, 397). One cannot help but notice that Grey Owl implies that he is Indigenous, instead of identifying himself openly as such. That is not the case in "Indian Legends and Lore," his contribution to the October 1931 issue of *Forest and Outdoors*. His essay is meant to counter the numerous "superstitions [that] have grown up by the long association with Nature of my people—a thoughtful, simple people—imbued with the spirit of the Wild." The reason he has the authority to challenge these fallacies is that, he writes, "I speak as an Indian" (Grey Owl 1931f, 23). Again, Grey Owl makes it clear to the magazine's editors and readers to which particular ethnocultural community he belongs.

Curiously, this is not the strategy Grey Owl employs in his longer writings. The problem of his personal identity is especially pronounced in his first book, a text that is related by someone with a rather unstable sense of personal identity, someone who can go from being a white man to an Indigenous one and who is very reluctant to discuss his ethnocultural background. *The Men of the Last Frontier*, which has been called "a significant landmark in contemporary Canadian literature" (Gaskell 1936, 3), was first published in London by *Country Life* late in 1931 and deals with life in the wilderness of northern Ontario. With titles such as "The Land of Shadows," "The Trail," "On Being Lost," "The Still-Hunt," and "The Altar of Mammon," the ten essays detail the trials and tribulations faced by hunters and trappers in what the author terms "the No-Man's-Land beyond the Frontier" (Grey Owl [1931] 1973, 6). More specifically, the book explores how an ever-expanding civilization seems to be leading to the ineluctable disappearance of Canada's forests and their denizens, both human and non-human. From the beginning, Grey Owl establishes a direct opposition between two Canadas: the modern Canada of "farming, mining, manufacturing, and like industries" and the natural Canada of endless forests, lakes, and streams. He remarks, with a back-handed compliment, that southern Canada is a land of "unequalled opportunities" and that "there can be found in her cities and small towns a civilization as prosaic and matter-of-fact as exists in many older and longer-settled countries" (5; see also Braz 2007, 214–15). But unperceived even by most Canadians, there is another Canada, a "region of illimitable distance, unknown lakes, hidden rivers, and unrecorded happenings; and changed in no marked way since the white man discovered America" (Grey Owl [1931] 1973, 30). This is a land where nature rules, and where one's subsistence is utterly dependent on the local fauna and flora.

Grey Owl, of course, favours the second Canada, "a land of Romance, gripping the imagination with its intensity, its boundless possibilities and its magic of untried adventure" ([1931] 1973, 30). He even suggests that it is the wilderness that gives Canada its identity, setting it apart from an increasingly industrialized and homogenized world. Sadly, what his co-citizens do not appear to realize is the degree to which their forests and wildlife are threatened. Particularly in "The Tale of the Beaver People" and "The House of McGinnis," in which he chronicles the genesis of his transformation from a trapper into a conservationist, he tries to dramatize the crisis by arguing that, if "the depletion of our game animals goes on much longer at the present rate, specimens of wild life will soon be seen only in zoos and menageries" (152). As he underscores, Canadians may be witnessing the last generation of people who live off the forests and, when those people die, they "will turn the last page in the story of true adventure on this continent, closing forever the book of romance in Canadian History. The forest cannot much longer stand before the conquering march of modernity, and soon we shall witness the vanishing of a mighty wilderness" (26). *The Men of the Last Frontier* is thus not so much a collection of essays about the wild as it is an ecological manifesto, an urgent warning to Canadians that, unless they protect their forests, they will lose the very elements that make their country distinct among the nations of the world.

Despite his zeal to save the wilderness, though, Grey Owl is quite ambivalent about it. On the one hand, he celebrates Canada's natural beauty and natural resources, writing that the northland is "a rich treasure-house, open to all who dare the ordeal of entry, and transformed by the cosmic sorcery of the infinite into a land of magic glades and spirit-haunted lakes, of undiscovered fortunes, and sunset dreams come true" (Grey Owl [1931] 1973, 45). Yet, on the other hand, he frequently stresses the hardships faced by those who must struggle to wrestle "a living from an unyielding and ungenerous wilderness" (11). Grey Owl characterizes portaging the contents of a canoe through an overgrown trail as nothing less than "the curse of Adam...fulfilled to the letter; sweat commences to pour into the eyes, down the body, dripping off the forearms. Vicious insects light and bite on contact. One hand is engaged in pulling forward and down on the top load to support the head, the other contains an axe or a pail of lard; so the flies stay until surfeited, and blood runs down freely with the sweat" (66). In addition, he details the loneliness and the constant danger of getting lost, which can result not only in one losing one's provisions and gear but one's very life. Still, for Grey Owl, there is no escaping the allure of the wilderness. Northern Canada, he asserts, is "the world as it was after the age of ice, the scratches and gouges of its slow passage still visible on the now solid rocks" (33–34). It is a place where "the soul of a man is stripped bare and naked, exposed for all to see" and where "his true nature will come out" (49). Compared to southern Canada and the rest of the industrialized world, it is an Eden.

When Grey Owl says that the wilderness is the site where men are tested and transformed by the environment, he does not mean all men but just the pathfinders who live "on the far-flung borderland beyond the fringe of Civilization," notably trappers ([1931] 1973, 6). Given his subsequent reputation as a world-famous conservationist, one of the most surprising aspects of *The Men of the Last Frontier* is that it is a paean not only to the wilderness but also to its apparent nemesis, the trapper. "Trapping," writes Grey Owl, is "a gamble on a large scale, the trapper's life and outfit against the strength of the wilderness and its presiding genii, to win a living" (20). He justifies the trapper's lifestyle in a statement that seriously undercuts his image as a sentimental lover of all things natural:

> Nature is cruel, and the flesh-eating animals and birds kill their prey in the most bloodthirsty manner, tearing off and eating portions of meat before the unfortunate animal is dead. The thought of this considerably lessens the compunction one might feel in trapping carnivorous animals, as they are only getting a dose of their own medicine and do not undergo a tithe of the sufferings they inflict on their victims, often hastening their own end by paroxysms of fury. (Grey Owl [1931] 1973, 41)

Grey Owl underlines that there is no reason for trappers to feel defensive about their means of earning a living, for nature itself countenances their profession. "Man is not the only trapper in the wilderness," he contends; there are many other species, from spiders to wolves, that prey on other members of the animal kingdom ([1931] 1973. 40). For Grey Owl, the trapper clearly belongs in "the enchanted world of which he is as much part as the ancient trees, the eternal snows, and the dancing Northern

Lights" (25). Or, to phrase it differently, the trapper is an essential part of the wilderness. Like the animals he hunts, he is a natural part of his environment.

It is true that, before the end of the book, Grey Owl comes to perceive the landscape around him as a "place of peace and clean content," where he is "the only profane thing, an ogre lurking to destroy" ([1931] 1973, 142). Part of his identification with wildlife has to do with the utter isolation of his occupation. "A man so much alone," he writes, "looks kindly on the numerous small birds and animals that congregate around his cabin and camping places" (14). But especially in the second half of the text, as he questions his right to take the lives of other creatures, he comes to assert that non-human animals have a greater claim to the wilderness than do humans, stating that a creature such as the beaver is entitled to live in the wild since "he was there before me" (143). Wild animals supposedly also have more "common sense" than do the people who hunt them, for of all the denizens of the forests, they are the "most helpless in the face of the vigorous conditions" they encounter (51). Yet, even then, Grey Owl seldom engages in the idealization of nature, the romanticization of the wild that purportedly made his work so appealing to "Canadian ladies" (Ross 1979, 79, 82). In his rather problematic words, "Civilization will not let you starve; the wilderness will, and glad of the opportunity" (Grey Owl [1931] 1973, 83). No less significant, whatever his qualms about his profession, he never disowns the trapper.

Like his attitude toward nature, Grey Owl's view of the trapper is conflicted. For Grey Owl, the trapper is the quintessential pioneer, the nation builder. Modern Canadians may extol the surveyor and the engineer, who open up the country for settlement and industrialization, but he argues that the trapper is the true trailblazer, someone who carves the path that the engineer and surveyor are merely following. At the same time, this great hero is an anachronism, if not a downright atavism. Grey Owl claims that the trapper may simply not be able to control what he does, for "[t]here is some sorcery in a beaver hide akin to that which a nugget of gold is credited with possessing, and the atmosphere of the trade in these skins is permeated with all the romance and the evil, the rapacity and adventurous glamour, attendant on gold-rush" ([1931] 1973, 148). Still, the trapper is caught in "the last battle-ground in the long-drawn-out, bitter struggle between the primeval and civilization" (29), a struggle he will lose unless Canadians wake up to what is happening to their country. As he writes, the frontier is quickly receding and "we who stand regretfully and watch, must either adapt ourselves to the new conditions, or, preferably, follow the ever-thinning line of last defence into the shadows, where soon will vanish every last one of the Dwellers amongst the Leaves" (45). Once more, trappers are threatened with extinction as much as the animals on which they depend, which may explain the author's empathy with them.

Excluding the polarity between non-human animals and humans, the central opposition in *The Men of the Last Frontier* is not between Natives and non-Natives but between professional (full-time) trappers and amateur ones. Grey Owl maintains that the crucial difference between the two groups is that "real" trappers have a sense of ownership about the wilderness, which impels them to protect their territory, for "[n]o man will burn his own property" ([1931] 1973, 179). This is supposedly the case for both Natives and non-Natives. As depicted in the text, there is no discernible ethical difference between Indigenous and non-Indigenous trappers. So when Grey Owl concludes that the only way to prevent the extinction of the beaver is by severely reducing the number of trappers, he targets solely recent arrivals from the South. The solution to the problem, he pronounces, is "the removal from the woods of all white trappers except those who could prove that they had no alternative occupation, [and] had followed trapping for a livelihood previous to 1914." That is, he wants to banish just "the draft evaders and others who hid in the woods during the war" (151). However, Grey Owl's partiality toward "the resident white trappers" may not be due solely to his considering them "genuine woodsmen" (150), and as ecologically responsible as their Indigenous counterparts. It may also reflect the likelihood that he is one of them.

The fact that Grey Owl normally addressed his audiences wearing Indigenous regalia leaves little doubt as to the ethnocultural identity he intended to project. His desire to be perceived as Indigenous, or at least as someone of mixed race, is also reinforced in his private correspondence with his editors. As he had done with *Forest and Outdoors*, just before the publication of *The Men of the Last Frontier* he informed *Country Life* that his book was "written by an Indian.... Refer to me as an Indian writer" (qtd. in Dickson 1973, 225). Along the same lines, when the publisher sent him the galley proofs of his manuscript, Grey Owl protested vehemently that it was wrong for the editors to standardize his spelling, especially his overuse of capitals, since his "book is not to be a shining example of English literature— far from it." Then, he added that his text was "written by an Indian about his own country, and from his point of view" (qtd. in Dickson 1973, 218). It is as if Grey Owl has forgotten that the editors had first learned of his writing through his British white mother.

Grey Owl's discovery that *Country Life* had tinkered with his writing would mark the first of several bitter conflicts between the two parties. An even more ominous dispute occurred when the editors sent Grey Owl the first copies of his book and he noticed to his horror that they had arbitrarily changed the title from *The Vanishing Frontier* to *The Men of the Last Frontier*. As the outraged author fulminated in a letter he sent to London,

> I was a little surprised to find that you had changed the title without consulting me. As it stands I have written a book about myself, a thing I studiously avoided. Although the critics might say I have written more about the men than the Frontier itself, I care little for the opinion of critics; it is the public I want to please, an entirely different idea. The original title has a greater appeal, it has the lure of the vast, though disappearing frontier, which in the nature of such a work as I tried to produce, dwarfs and belittles that of mere, short-lived man. That you changed the title shows that you, at least, missed the entire point of the book. You still believe that man as such is preeminent, governs the powers of Nature. So he does, to a large extent, in civilization, but not on the Frontier, until that Frontier has been removed. He then moves forward, if you get me. I speak of Nature, not men; they are incidental, used to illustrate a point only. (qtd. in Dickson 1973, 218–19)

Whether the *Country Life* editors misread the manuscript as egregiously as Grey Owl charges is open to debate, but it is unlikely, given the centrality of the authorial figure in the text. That said, there is no question that Grey Owl is correct when he claims that the new title puts considerably more emphasis on the human figure at the heart of the narrative than did the initial one. This is a prominence that the author does not welcome, since even he himself is not quite certain about his own life story.

In *The Men of the Last Frontier* Grey Owl is not explicit about his ethnocultural background. Yet, since the publication of his first book, he has been seen by critics almost universally as someone of mixed Indigenous and European ancestry, underscoring the degree to which analyses of texts can be influenced by paratextual information, not the least the biographical profiles of authors provided by publishers. Writing for the *New York Times*, R.L. Duffus describes the author as "the son of a Scotch father and an Apache mother" who had come to Canada as a young man, was "adopted into the tribe of the Ojibways, and became a trapper" (1932, 4). Similarly, in his assessment of the book for the *Saturday Review*, Edwin Sabin states that the author is "sprung from a Scot father and a New Mexican Apache mother—with name Grey Owl, bestowed upon him by the people of his adoption, the Ojibway of Canada" (1935, 5). Even W.T. Allison, writing for the *Winnipeg Tribune*, asserts that "Grey Owl is a half-breed. His father was a Scot, his mother an Apache Indian of New Mexico" (1932, 2). Allison, who as we will see shortly was the only critic who raised doubts about the book's authorship, makes one additional point about Grey Owl's identity. He explains that, although the author "was born somewhere down along the Rio Grande," he "thinks of himself, and has good reason for doing so, as a Canadian" (2). That is, through his writings, Grey Owl has earned his citizenship in the Great White North.

The response by the contemporaneous critics of *The Men of the Last Frontier* is puzzling because it is not easily apparent how they can reconcile a Grey Owl of mixed Scottish and Apache ancestry with the figure at the centre of his book. In retrospect, at least, there are numerous indications in the text that the speaker, Grey Owl, is not likely to have any Indigenous ancestry, indeed, that he is white, and probably of British stock. For example, when praising trappers and other frontier pathfinders, Grey Owl writes that they possess "the spirit of the true Pioneer. This is the urge that drove Champlain, Raleigh, Livingstone, and Cook into the four corners of the earth; the unquenchable ambition to conquer new territory, to pass where never yet trod foot of man." He further notes that the trapper "antedates" all other pathfinders and that his prototypes are individuals such as "Boone, Crockett, Bridger, and Cody" (Grey Owl [1931] 1973, 7). Even more germane, his antagonism toward part-time white trappers derives not only from the fact that they are supposedly "get-rich-quick vandals" who do not care about the welfare of the forest (150), but also that they are overwhelmingly of Eastern European origin. As Grey Owl alleges, the reason Canada's "noble forests" have been "reduced in a few hours to arid deserts" is that the " 'Bohunk' or 'Bolshie' is seldom seen without a home-made cigarette, hanging from his lower lip" (174, 175). These "South-eastern European" interlopers are guilty of other sins, too. They supposedly "work for less wages than the 'white' races," like "the English-speaking and French-Canadian nationalities," and, as a result, have "to a very large extent supplanted the old-time, happy-go-lucky lumberjack of song and story" (175). Grey Owl maintains that there is space in "Canada for some of the surplus population of the British Isles, and employment for them" (175), but not for everyone. He is thus perplexed why the Canadian government is allowing this "alien race" of "unwanted foreign-born 'settlers' " (177), this "clamouring multitude of undesirables" (178), to drive off the woods' bona-fide Canadians: those of British and French ancestry.

The author's apparent Britishness is also suggested by his descriptions of the beaver. For Grey Owl, Canadians should make a concerted effort to preserve the once ubiquitous rodent because it is the most intelligent of all the wild denizens of the forest. Therefore, to "inflict such torture on this almost human animal is a revolting crime which few regular white hunters and no Indian will stoop to" ([1931] 1973, 148). But there is another fundamental reason why Canadians ought to ensure that the beaver does not go "the way of the buffalo" and become extinct (149). Besides its natural acumen, the beaver possesses both great national iconographic value and identifiably Victorian traits:

> This little worker of the wild has been much honoured. He ranks with the maple leaf as representative of the Dominion, and has won a place as one of Canada's national emblems, by the example he gives of industry, adaptability, and dogged perseverance; attributes well worthy of emulation by those who undertake to wrest a living from the untamed soil of a new country. He is the Imperialist of the animal world. He maintains a home and hearth, and from it he sends out every year a pair of emigrants who search far and wide for new fields to conquer; who explore, discover, occupy, and improve, to the benefit of all concerned. (154)

Elsewhere in the text, Grey Owl makes similar British imperialist pronouncements, praising professional white trappers and other wily pioneers as "the people who are actually laying the foundation of an Empire overseas," the pro-nature "Empire-building" of which he approves (85, 87). Combined with the fact he also asserts that the "passage of the paleface through his ancestral territories is, to the Indian, in effect, what the arrival of the German Army would have been to a conquered England" (214–15), those statements cannot help but call into question the probability that he is of Indigenous heritage.

The most compelling reason for suspecting that Grey Owl is not Indigenous, though, is the way he usually presents the First Nations. He writes that he was "accustomed to hunting on the plains" before he moved to northern Ontario ([1931] 1973, 101), where he cast his "lot" with the Anishinaabe, who eventually adopt him as "a blood-brother" (225, 244). Tellingly, he does not declare that he is Indigenous, only that he is embraced by the Anishinaabe. As well, throughout the book, he tends not to identify himself as Indigenous. Thus, he affirms that one of the consequences of the

deforestation of Canada is the disappearance of the professional white trapper, adding that "with him will go his friend the Indian to be a memory of
days and a life that are past beyond recall" (26). More surprisingly, he states
that one of the advantages of modern hunting is that the "trapper of to-day
has no longer the menace of the hostile savage to contend with" (7), such as
in the early days of the fur trade, when "[m]en fought, murdered, starved and
froze to death, took perilous trips into unknown wildernesses, and braved
the horrors of Indian warfare, lured on by the rich returns of the beaver
trade" (145–46). Finally, he explains that when a trapper is afflicted with "the
'madness of the woods' " and becomes bushed, he begins to experience all
sorts of macabre apparitions, including those by "Indians [who] appear, stare
momentarily beyond him as though he were invisible, [only] to disappear
again, eluding his frantic efforts to attract their attention" (111–12). Needless
to say, the trapper through whom Grey Owl shows life in the wilderness may
inhabit a world dominated by Indigenous people but is not likely one of them.

As one comes to expect of almost any social relation involving Grey Owl,
his relationship with the First Nations is complicated. One certainly cannot help but notice that he invariably presents the wilderness of northern
Ontario as "Indian country" ([1931] 1973, 69). As he often points out to the
reader, "the Canada that lies back of your civilization, the wild, fierce land
of desperate struggle and untold hardship," is "the last stronghold of the Red
gods, the heritage of the true adventurer" (44). For Grey Owl, Indigenous
people have a special affinity with the land. So while many of the techniques
that professional white trappers adopt when hunting are "borrowed from
the animals," they are already "common amongst Indians" (17). Even in the
twentieth century, "the arts of woodcraft are practised as originally acquired
from the Indian, whose highly specialized faculties his white contemporary
has more or less successfully emulated" (22). Indeed, Grey Owl contends that
"the Indians were always conservationists, the first there ever were in this
country" (217). This is the reason he feels that the First Nations are the best
wardens of the wilderness, and should be assigned that role by the Canadian
government.

That said, Grey Owl's attitude toward Indigenous people remains problematic. For one, he tends to refer to the First Nations not only as "they" but
also in the past tense, as if he accepts that they are destined to vanish from
the face of the earth. To be fair to Grey Owl, he envisages the same destiny
for everyone who derives a living from the wilderness, including himself and
(other) white trappers. Still, while one deduces that the white trappers will
be able to change professions without losing their culture, it is not clear he

believes Indigenous people will manage to do the same. This is the impression
he conveys when he says that the Anishinaabe are "a fading people. Not long
from now will come one sunset, their last; far from the graves of their fathers
they are awaiting with stolid calm what, to them, is the inevitable" (Grey Owl
[1931] 1973, 226–27). Grey Owl seems so convinced of the fate progress has
in store for the First Nations that he hints it is preferable for the "Indian" to
disappear with a flourish, before he is "thrown into the grinding wheels of the
mill of modernity, to be spewed out a nondescript, undistinguishable from
the mediocrity that surrounds him, a reproach to the memory of a noble race"
(220, 221). As he quotes his Anishinaabe mentor, "To-night the sun sets for
the White Man for a day. Soon another sun will set for the Indian; and it will
be forever" (246). Again, what becomes apparent is that the authorial figure
in Grey Owl's book does not usually portray himself as being biologically
part of the Indigenous people amongst whom he lives.

   There is yet another reason to question the identity of the "I" in *The Men
of the Last Frontier* and that has to do with the author's language. In the text,
he invariably presents himself as an insider, someone who lives in and off
the wilderness. In the opening essay, "The Vanguard," he writes that in "a
territory beyond the jurisdiction of the police" (Grey Owl [1931] 1973, 17),
life is ruled by a few "unwritten" laws, such as the edict against stealing other
people's food caches or trashing their cabins. He then relates the story of "a
white trapper," who "returned one night to his camp to find it destroyed in
such a way as to be no longer habitable" (18), a cruel act of vandalism that
almost resulted in the trapper's death. He closes the episode by stating that
he "talked with the man in question," from whom he presumably gathered
the information (19). Similarly, in "The Still-Hunt," Grey Owl explains that
the practice of stalking an animal is extremely difficult to master. It is "an
art learned from the Indian, an accomplishment in which few white men
excel, save only those who have spent many days in the lodges of those silent,
thoughtful people, or consorted much with those who have" (87–88). But he
then goes on to add that he knows of "no greater thrill than that, after two
or three hours of careful stalking with all the chances against me, of sighting
my game, alert, poised for that one move than means disappearance" (91).
Once more, he implies he knows intimately the environment he depicts. His
authority derives precisely from his reputed first-hand knowledge of life in
the wilderness.

   However, if Grey Owl has spent most of his life in the wild, one cannot
help but wonder where he acquired both his fluid writing style and his considerable knowledge of Western culture in general and literature in particular.

His familiarity with a wide body of literature is especially evident in the epigraphs to his essays, which come from writers as diverse as Lord Byron, Robert Service, Robert Louis Stevenson, and Henry Wadsworth Longfellow, who is obviously his favourite. Grey Owl not only borrows four of the ten epigraphs from Longfellow, but even appends a note to the last one, affirming that "*Longfellow surely grasped the true spirit of the wilderness when he wrote* Hiawatha, *and shows a knowledge of Indian life and customs that is uncommon*" ([1931] 1973, 204; italics in text).

Perhaps even more striking than Grey Owl's erudition is his writing style. It is hard not to be affected by lines such as these:

> In the fastnesses of this rapidly fading frontier, the last one on this continent, reigns the Spirit of the North Land. Enthroned behind the distant mountains with the cohorts and legions of his last grand army massed about him, he sallies forth, brooding over the length and breadth of the land, seeking whom he may destroy, ever devising new means for the elimination of the invaders of his chosen realm. ([1931] 1973, 35)

> The real trapper (by which I mean the man who spends his days up beyond the Strong Woods, not the part-time hunter, or "railroad" trapper out for a quick fortune) is as much an integral part of the woods as are the animals themselves. In tune with his surroundings, wise in the lore of the Indian, he reads and correctly interprets the cryptograms in the book that lies open before him, scanning the face of Nature and forestalling her moods to his advantage. ([1931] 1973, 8)

The book's tone is set in the very opening paragraphs of the prologue, when the author informs us that the world he is about to depict is the "face of Nature as it was since the Beginning; all creation down the eons of unmeasured time, brooding in ineffable calm, infinite majesty, and a breathless and unutterable silence" (1). Needless to say, such writing is not likely to have been produced by someone with little or no formal education.

Ever since the publication of *The Men of the Last Frontier*, critics have found it difficult to accept that the author's style could belong to a trapper, particularly an Indigenous one. R.L. Duffus contends that "Grey Owl is no stuffed Indian. He is real and honest and he lets his readers behind the scenes." Yet for Duffus, "one's chief criticism is that Grey Owl is too literary.... He gives us, on the whole, not the vernacular of the trail but a translation of that vernacular into a language city people can grasp. Perhaps he has had to explain things to too many tenderfeet" (1932, 4). W.T. Allison, if anything, is even more perplexed by Grey Owl's language. The University of Manitoba English professor states that, as he read the text, he kept asking himself "how in the world could a half-breed trapper pick up such an elegant style. Even Longlance [Buffalo Child Long Lance], who was a college student, and had long years of experience as a newspaper and magazine writer, would not have produced anything so stylistic as the earlier chapters of this book" (1932, 2). His conclusion is that Grey Owl could not have written the book on his own and that his seamless style and rich vocabulary betray "the hand of the editor" (2), implying that Grey Owl had a "ghost" who helped him produce his book.

Anyone familiar with Grey Owl's writings, especially his letters and journals, is not likely to seriously entertain the idea that *The Men of the Last Frontier* is the work of anyone other than its ostensible author. For example, Prime Minister John Diefenbaker, who acted as a lawyer for Yvonne Perrier in a case involving the settlement of the Grey Owl estate following the conservationist's death, describes a trip he made to Ajawaan Lake with the Superintendent of Prince Albert National Park, James Wood. At the end, Grey Owl handed a manuscript to Wood to mail to his publisher. Diefenbaker read the text on his way back to town and was impressed both by the fact it was "filled with an imagery that only a lover of nature could possibly possess" and that it was "clothed in masterly English" (1975, 118). Still, Allison's response is legitimate, indeed, perceptive. The fact is that Grey Owl's language does at times sound incongruous for the figure at the centre of the collection. To be more precise, not only is the "I" in the text indeterminate, it does not always seem to refer to the same person.

As I have noted throughout this chapter, in his first book Grey Owl tends not to specify his collective roots. From his praise of the British Empire and his identification with European and Euro-American explorers, one cannot help but deduce that he might be of European extraction and likely British. Also, for most of the text, he does not define unambiguously who he is. But there are some exceptions, when he does provide concrete evidence about himself. About halfway through the book, Grey Owl writes that the reason he initially found the still-hunt as practised by the Anishinaabe so unusual is that he was used to hunting on the Prairies, "where the game is in pockets, in gulleys, river bottoms, or in bluffs of poplar or willows" ([1931] 1973, 101). Grey Owl further adds that an "old-time buffalo hunt was an inspiring sight. The strings of light-riding savages on their painted ponies, probably the best irregular light mounted infantry the world has ever seen" (86). But his purported Western roots may not be as deep as he insinuates. Considering that the last wide-scale bison hunts took place in the 1870s and that he is writing around 1930, one wonders what sort of hunts he could have been part of, or even witnessed. As well, this "indifferent plainsman" turned into "some kind of a woodsman" (118) eventually joins the Anishinaabe, who rename him in an "ancient ritual...before a gaily decorated and attentive concourse" (225). In particular, he is supposed to have been embraced by an elder named Neganikabo (also Ne-ganik-abo), someone he says "has pulled back little by little, the magic invisible veil of mystery from across the face of the forest, that I might learn its uttermost secrets, and has laid open before me the book of Nature for me to read" (227). Grey Owl must have been more successful in this endeavour than he implies, since Neganikabo ultimately tells him that, even though he is still young, "of all my people, you are the only one who remembers the way of our race" (243). That is, in the course of the book, Grey Owl undergoes a physical metamorphosis from being an unabashedly pro–British Empire white trapper to becoming the depository of the collective memory of the Anishinaabe. Or, possibly, he has always been more than one person.

Perhaps the clue to the identity of Grey Owl lies in the paratexts with which he frames his book, which testify to "the double image that he [has] created of himself" (Heidenreich 2000, 222). Grey Owl opens *The Men of the Last Frontier* with a prologue in which he describes a natural landscape that turns out to be that of northern Ontario. In the middle of this landscape appears "a bark canoe, yellow as an autumn leaf," in which "stands a white man, bedizened with the remnants of the lace and ruffles of the courts of Europe" ([1931] 1973, 1). Presumably, this white man is the figure that dominates the collection of essays we are about to read, or at least the early sections. For by the time Grey Owl closes his book, with an epilogue, the white man has been joined by another man, one with "the vigorous features and calm bearing of an Indian" (252). There are many resemblances between the two companions. The white man's "cheeks are hollow and his frame gaunt" (1) and his face, which has been "tanned to the colour of leather," is "ascetic almost" (252). The Indigenous man, "his long black hair confined at the temples by a buckskin band," has "the air of one who waits" (252). It is possible that Grey Owl comes to believe that he is both men, and that he cannot really distinguish between the two.

Grey Owl's attempt to pass as Indigenous, or partly Indigenous, would of course become the most controversial aspect of his legacy. We live at a time when identity is often perceived as contingent, when self-made consensual theories of group identity purportedly have displaced ancestral or hereditary ones. Grey Owl's "fancy for aboriginal ways" would thus appear to be "mere fashion in these days of cultural free-borrowing" (Casey 2009, 42). One might think that at least some people would admire his determination to be his true self. As the Anishinaabe critic Gilbert Oskaboose writes in the passage that serves as the epigraph to this chapter, "How many of us get to choose who we will become?" (2000, para 2). Yet discussions of Grey Owl and his writings still tend to be accompanied by a profound sense of outrage at his deception, indicating the general discomfort with the idea of a white man pretending to be an Indigenous North American. Perhaps one should not be surprised that Grey Owl's admirers were shocked when they learned that their hero was not partly Indigenous but a white man. Yet one cannot help but be somewhat perplexed by the level of vitriol that Grey Owl's "masquerade" continues to attract.

For some critics, Grey Owl is not just a "fake Indian" (Chapin 2000, 98) but "a pervert," who became famous because "he wore a disguise and grew his hair long" (Ross 1979, 79). This unequivocal, and highly self-righteous, condemnation of Grey Owl's actions is dubious because it seems willfully naïve. The notion of imposture is conceivable only in relation to some fully transparent subject, a transparency that has become increasingly untenable, particularly for scholars working in areas like life writing. Paul John Eakin, for instance, is convinced that fictions play such a central role in the construction of any life story that he considers it wise to speak, not of the individual self, but of "*selves*" (1999, x; italics in original). More important, so persistent has been the focus on Grey Owl's imposture that it has overshadowed every other aspect of his life, including the audacity of his disguise. One of the principal tenets of social identity is that, whatever else one may do, one cannot change one's biological ancestors. As the philosopher Horace Kallen writes in a celebrated (if androcentric) phrase, "Men may change their clothes, their politics, their wives, their religions, their philosophies, to a greater or less extent: they cannot change their grandfathers" ([1915] 1924, 122). This assumption has recently been questioned by advocates of theories of consensual affiliation or post-ethnicity, who challenge "the right of one's grandfather or grandmother to determine [one's] primary identity." Yet even those scholars note that an individual does not usually choose to be, say, "a Japanese American in the absence of an element of Japanese ancestry to begin with" (Hollinger 1995,

116, 117). But this is exactly what Grey Owl does. In his attempt to construct his ideal self-identity, he jettisons his whole biological family and embraces a new one to which he has no genetic connection whatsoever.

The relentless focus on Grey Owl's impersonation raises a series of questions. First, as Grey Owl's critics concentrate on his identity, they tend to simplify what may not be simple at all. That is, they create the impression that fictionality is not present in the construction of the self. But as we have discovered in the last few decades, one of the challenges in the study of life writing is that "we cannot say for sure where the 'I' begins and ends" (Eakin 1999, 181). Grey Owl's detractors also seem too certain about the author's psychological motivation, usually depicting him as a member of the "Wannabee" tribe, one of those "Indian poseurs" whose role playing is supposedly a form of cultural "genocide" (Green 1988, 44, 31). As well, they often claim that his "masquerade…was only successful with tourists and newcomers" (Chapin 2000, 95), conveniently ignoring that even after Anahareo becomes aware of Grey Owl's English past, after his death, she continues to insist that "[t]o me he was an Indian, as I was" (1940, 7). Besides, even if one were to accept that Grey Owl was guilty of Indigenous impersonation, his transgression may not be that uncommon. "Playing Indian," writes the historian Philip Deloria, "is a persistent tradition in American culture, stretching from the very instant of the national big bang into an ever-expanding present and future" (1998, 7). Since non-Natives had no "natural affinity with the continent," they reasoned that they could only acquire it by mimicking Indigenous people, which they supposedly have been doing almost since the first very first contact between the two cultures (5). If the phenomenon is as widespread as Deloria implies, then perhaps the hostility toward Grey Owl by some critics may simply reveal their fear of their own complicity in the process, the suspicion that they themselves may be playing Indian.

Another troubling aspect of the emphasis on Grey Owl's imposture is that it discounts the possibility of acculturation. This is particularly curious given the work of such Indigenous writers as Armand Ruffo and N. Scott Momaday. In his seminal essay "The Man Made of Words," the award-winning Kiowa author writes not only that "[w]e are what we imagine" but also that "an Indian is an idea which a given man has of himself" (2001, 87, 82). Momaday thus appears to sanction the notion of self-construction, something that becomes even more evident when he asserts that "fiction is a superior kind of reality. What we imagine…that's the best of us" (qtd. in Schubnell 1985, 47). A similar position is embraced by Ruffo, who in his poetic biography of Grey Owl seems determined to prove that his subject undergoes an ethnocultural transformation upon arriving in the New World. Throughout the text, Ruffo shows the Anishinaabe teaching the newcomer both their language and how to canoe and trap. As he writes, "Indian, can't say he is/can't say he isn't. Speaks the language though" (1996, 66). If Grey Owl has become proficient in Anishinaabe, then he must have experienced a significant linguistic and cultural transformation.

There is yet one other reason why one should not be too hasty to judge Grey Owl's adoption of an Indigenous identity, and that has to do with his motivation. The question we may wish to ask is, what did he gain from his disguise? After all, in the first half of the twentieth century, it was not the wisest of strategies to claim to be Indigenous. That was even truer of people of mixed descent. Throughout the 1930s, writes Donald Smith, "Canadians with Indian ancestry…simply had no incentive to declare it" (1990, 185). So the fact that Grey Owl invented an Indigenous past at a time when many people of mixed race camouflaged theirs suggests that his reasons for choosing his identity may have been more complex than some people would like to believe.

Furthermore, we should not forget that, while the First Nations are now often perceived as living in harmony with the environment, this has not always been the case. On the contrary, as far back as the 1770s, in his account of one of his journeys from Hudson Bay to the Arctic, the English explorer and fur-trader Samuel Hearne writes that it was "common among all Indian tribes" to kill not only as many deer "as were sufficient for our large number, but often several merely for the skins, marrow, &c." and to leave "the carcasses to rot, or to be devoured by the wolves, foxes, and other beasts of prey" ([1795] 1958, 25, 26). This is a tradition that lasted well into the twentieth century, as the debate between Grey Owl and W.A. Parker illustrates. No less a figure than the conservationist and nature writer Ernest Thompson Seton could present Indigenous people as savages with an uncontrollable "mania for killing" ([1911] 1981, 20). According to him, so bloodthirsty were the Indigenous members of his crew during an expedition to collect animal specimens in the Arctic that his guide had "to use all his influence to keep the Indians from slaughtering wholesale" (89; see also Dean 2007). For Seton, the only ethical killing of animals is for scientific collecting or sports hunting. That is radically different from Grey Owl, for whom conservation cannot come before sustenance, both of oneself and of one's dependents. As Grey Owl defends his position in *The Men of the Last Frontier*, "hunting to fill the pots of those families, who, as representatives of an entire people, are bravely struggling against adverse conditions and leading a life of deprivation and heavy labour, in their endeavour to bring some semblance of prosperity

to a bleak and savage wilderness, is nothing to be held up to public scorn"
([1931] 1973, 85). Also, in contrast to someone like Seton, Grey Owl strives
to see the environment he describes from the perspective of the people who
live in it, be they white or Indigenous. Notwithstanding the author's upper-
middle-class origins, and his ideological shortcomings, *The Men of the Last
Frontier* provides a working-class perspective of a field dominated by sports
hunters, scientists, and collectors. Of course, in order to become aware of
those nuances, one would have to be familiar with Grey Owl's writings. But
this very basic step is one that the controversy over his identity demonstrates
has not yet been taken.

CHAPTER TWO

# The Dual Conversion of Grey Owl:
## Pilgrims of the Wild

*Never have the animals been in*
*greater need of human compassion.*

—Chief Dan George

In 1935, four years after the appearance of *The Men of the Last Frontier*, Grey Owl published his most celebrated book, the work that would make him famous around the world. *Pilgrims of the Wild* ([1935] 1990) is, in many ways, the book that the editors of *Country Life* had wanted him to write, the story of his life. Although, in a letter to Lovat Dickson, Grey Owl called it "an epic poem" ([1934–35] 1938a, 56), it is really his memoir about his relationship with Anahareo, and about his conversion from a trapper into a conservationist, an odyssey that takes the couple from northern Ontario, through eastern Quebec, and finally to western Canada, when he is hired as a conservationist by the National Parks Branch, the precursor of Parks Canada. No less important, *Pilgrims* is the account of his transformation into a writer, for once Grey Owl decided to stop trapping animals, he had to find another means of supporting himself and Anahareo.

Considering that Grey Owl had such an unstable life story, it is not surprising that he hesitated to write his memoir. What is also not unexpected is that he would encounter numerous obstacles along the way. The first challenge faced by Grey Owl was finding a new publisher. His conflict with the editors of *Country Life* was real. He felt that by changing the title of his first book from *The Vanishing Frontier* to *The Men of the Last Frontier* without consulting him, to say nothing of getting his approval, *Country Life* had turned his collection of essays into "an extravaganza of adventurous men" instead of an "urgent and passionate account of the extreme pressure being exerted against the old Frontier and its inhabitants" (Dickson 1973, 219). Consequently, he severed his relationship with *Country Life* and started searching for someone else to publish him in Great Britain. At the instigation of his English-born Canadian publisher, Hugh Eayrs, someone who had become a close friend and in whom he had "complete trust" (Panofsky 2012, 99), Grey Owl contacted Lovat Dickson. This was a decision that would prove to be inspired for both parties. The Alberta-raised Dickson, who had abandoned a promising academic career at the University of Alberta and opened his own publishing house in London, promptly welcomed the author into his "little fold" (Dickson [1963] 1976, 163). Grey Owl had approached Dickson because he had been assured by Eayrs that Dickson was "a good Canadian" and "an honest man" (qtd. in Dickson [1963] 1976, 161). Still, he did not agree to sign a contract with Dickson and Eayrs until he was granted a "verbatim clause" that forbade the publishers to alter his prose (Grey Owl [1934–35] 1938a, 73), a right that he would soon exercise.

In a letter to Dickson, Eayrs advised his London counterpart that it was "imperative" for him to consult Grey Owl "on every possible point of every sort or kind up to getting his final O.K. ready for printing." In addition, Eayrs stressed that Dickson should consult his new author on "format, illustrations and everything else and make him feel that in no way whatever are you out to hurt him, but on the contrary your great desire is not merely to be a publisher to him, but also a friend" (qtd. in Panofsky 2012, 99). Above all, Eayrs wished to convey to Dickson how essential it was that Grey Owl's authorial rights be respected, something of which the reading public should also be aware. The extent to which he was determined to ensure that Grey Owl would be perceived as the sole author of the texts bearing his name is evident in the extraordinary foreword that Eayrs wrote for *Pilgrims of the Wild*, which reads in part:

> This is Grey Owl's book. It appears between these covers precisely as he wrote it. His publishers in Toronto, London and New York have suffered no hand to touch it. Written in the Wilderness (a capital W for you, Grey Owl!) he loves so well, in the time he could spare from his Little People and their care, it came, copied into typescript, to me. Grey Owl's eye was on it, page by page, to watch that from pen and ink to typewritten copy no word, no phrase, even no slightest punctuation mark should have been introduced into what was, in every particular, his own story. "It may be doctored by nobody," said Grey Owl. "It is to be published,

if it is worth it, just as I wrote it. It is my work, good or bad, and
nobody else's. Nobody else is going to tamper with it." He was, of
course, quite right. To attempt to shape, to edit, to dress such a
story as this in any way whatever, would result in robbing it of its
simplicity and its beauty. Grey Owl wrote his own story. Nobody
else could write it. Nobody else has written it. Nobody else may,
in any way, seek to varnish it. (1935, n.p.)

Eayrs adds that the reason his unusual preamble is required is that "all sorts
of wild legends" have surfaced not only about Grey Owl and his first book
but also his second, the manuscript he is introducing. However, he assures
the reader that, like the "delightful sketches" that appear in the book, the
writing is "Grey Owl's own work" (n.p.). In short, testifies Eayrs, *Pilgrims of
the Wild* is authentic.

The anxieties about Grey Owl's authorship of *The Men of the Last Frontier*,
and by extension of his subsequent books, were evidently triggered by W.T.
Allison's critical review, which was discussed in the previous chapter. Grey
Owl was extremely grateful to Eayrs for his foreword, claiming that it served
as a corrective to "all this misquoting, misunderstanding and misconceptions
that have arisen" (qtd. in Dickson 1973, 227). Yet Eayrs's intervention clearly
did not erase all the questions that had been raised about his authorship. In
*Pilgrims*, Grey Owl calls the allegation that *The Men of the Last Frontier* was
produced by a ghostwriter the "unkindest cut of all," suggesting that it is the
result of cultural chauvinism and class bias on the part of a snob who was
"mildly scandalized...that an uncultured bushwhacker of acknowledged
native blood should so step out of character and become articulate" ([1935]
1990, 255). But Allison's review had other ramifications beyond hinting at
the possibility of ghostwriting. As Donald Smith has perceptively noted, the
Winnipeg scholar also insinuated that Grey Owl "had carelessly prepared
and executed his masquerade as an Indian author" (1990, 106). Therefore,
Grey Owl's authorial transgression was not just that he had someone else
write his book, but that he was not able to fashion a consistent style, thus
conveying the impression that the figure at the centre of the narrative is not
always the same person. Or, to phrase it differently, the text appears to have
more than one author.

In his foreword, Eayrs also affirms that he "can think of few books more
revealing of their writer than this. The very essence of our Canadian hinterland is in these pages because Grey Owl is so completely of it, and one with
it" ( 1935, n.p.). The second sentence may be true, but the first seems unlikely,

even if another critic has described *Pilgrims* as "a classic of self-revelation" (Gaskell 1936, 4). If Grey Owl does reveal himself in his memoir, he often does so in spite of his concerted efforts to the contrary. Because of the inconstant nature of his life story, he is surely compelled to employ a curious discursive strategy. Although he is writing an ostensibly autobiographical text, he focuses less explicitly on his genealogy than on that of his (fourth) wife, the more incontestably Indigenous Anahareo.

⬚        ⬚        ⬚

Excluding its five-page preface, *Pilgrims of the Wild* is divided into two parts, or books. The somewhat longer Book I is called "Touladi" and traces Grey Owl's gradual realization that the beaver are being hunted to extinction and that, if the animal is to be saved, he must stop trapping and start a beaver colony. This is a development that will lead him and Anahareo to uproot themselves and move from Temagami to Lac Touladi, in the Témiscouata region of southeastern Quebec, by the New Brunswick and Maine borders. Book II, which is entitled "Queen of the Beaver People," relates his first attempts at rehabilitating the beaver. It focuses particularly on his trials raising first McGinnis and McGinty and then Rawhide and Jelly Roll, the last of whom becomes a "screen star, public pet Number One," "The Queen" of the beaver ([1935] 1990, 169, 197; see also Cory 1935, 25). The section also deals with Grey Owl's initial efforts at writing, an endeavour one of whose fruits is to bring his ideas to the attention of the National Parks Branch and to a new job as a conservationist initially at Riding Mountain National Park in Manitoba and then, permanently, at Ajawaan Lake, in Prince Albert National Park in Saskatchewan, where he would work until his death and where he would do most of his writing.

Dickson has stated that all of Grey Owl's books are elegiac, being "laments for the old days, thirty years before, when he had been young" (1973, 241; see also Mitcham 1980, 8). Paradoxically, one of the things that Grey Owl mourns in his memoir is the death of trapping. As mentioned above, *Pilgrims* is devoted mainly to the author's transformation from a trapper into a conservationist. This is a critical turning point in his life, one which Grey Owl later compares to the archetypal conversion in the Western tradition. His experience in the wilderness, he writes in *Tales of an Empty Cabin*, "finally aroused in me a distaste for killing, and brought a growing feeling of kinship with those inoffensive and interesting beasts that were co-dwellers with me in this Land of Shadows and of Silence. So that ultimately I laid aside my rifle and my traps and[,] like Paul, worked for the betterment of those whom I so assiduously persecuted" ([1936] 1999, viii). While *Pilgrims* is not a religious text, it is very much about a transformation. Indeed, one critic calls Grey Owl's memoir "a funny, new New Testament" about nature and its denizens (Kirk 1991, 45). As its title implies, *Pilgrims* depicts a pilgrimage undertaken by two individuals who, by the end of their journey, appear to have found their place in the world. This is certainly true of the author.

Grey Owl's "natural" epiphany does not occur in a void, but is shaped by his material circumstances. Even if it was not fated that Grey Owl would become a conservationist in general and the champion of the beaver in particular, it seems inevitable that he had to cease killing wild animals for a living, since trapping had reached a major crisis. He highlights the precarious state of the trapping industry in the opening paragraph of his preface. *Pilgrims of the Wild*, explains Grey Owl, has a dual focus. It is "primarily an animal story; it is also the story of two people, and their struggle to emerge from the chaos into which the failure of the fur trade…plunged the Indian people, and not a few whites, during the last two decades." Characteristically, in addition to fires and other natural disasters, he blames the loss of his livelihood on an "invasion by hordes of transient trappers and cheap fur buyers" ([1935] 1990, n.p.). As he depicts his former hunting grounds later in the text, a "railroad had been built through part of it," and now there were "miles of staring desolation. Riff-raff bushmen, dirty, unkempt; stolid European peasantry tearing down the forest" (10). The consequence of the decimation of wildlife is that he is forced to leave Bisco and move back to Temagami to try to become a tourist guide. Yet, as he observes, not everything is negative about his journey south. He writes that he had been corresponding with a young woman he had met at "a summer resort where I had guided for a short time the year before" (14), and that woman has now entered his life. Actually, besides being an account of his transformation into both a conservationist and a writer, *Pilgrims* is a romance, his chronicle of his love affair with Anahareo.

There are definite links between *Pilgrims of the Wild* and *The Men of the Last Frontier*, notably the latter's essays "The Tale of the Beaver People" and "The House of McGinnis," in which Grey Owl first documents his transition to conservationism. But there is also a crucial difference between the two books; in *Pilgrims of the Wild*, Grey Owl is no longer alone. Instead, he is in the company of Anahareo. As he portrays their courtship, with some humour, "The course of true love ran exasperatingly smooth; I sent the lady a railroad ticket, she came up on a pullman and we were married, precisely according to plan. The complications started afterwards" ([1935] 1990, 14). Anahareo's presence is simply essential to his memoir.

That said, while there are two human figures at the centre of *Pilgrims of the Wild*, it is worth noting that Grey Owl frames them in a strikingly distinct manner. For instance, he always presents Anahareo as a member of a specific ethnocultural group. When he introduces her, he explains that she is "a cultured, talented and personable young woman of the Iroquois, a cut or two above me" ([1935] 1990, 14). He then describes her as his "wife Gertrude, who will be referred to from now on by her tribal name of Anahareo" (15), although he notes that she is "called Pony by those that know her" (73). Grey Owl further adds that Anahareo is not only a "full-blood" (89) but also "a direct descendant of hereditary Iroquois chiefs," her father being "one of the original Mohawk river-men who had helped to make history along the Ottawa in the days of the great square-timber rafts; she came of a proud race" (16). That is, Anahareo may be "strictly modern" and "no butterfly" (16, 17), but she has a tangible collective identity. She, and the reader, knows exactly where she comes from.

This is not quite how Grey Owl portrays himself, however. When he relates his departure from Bisco, he says that it "had been my home town for the fifteen years since I had drifted down from the North" ([1935] 1990, 9). Thus, one is led to infer that he probably belongs to some First Nation from northwestern Ontario, but one cannot be certain which one. During his Quebec sojourn, he becomes nostalgic for the landscape of northern Ontario and, at one point, states that he "must speak again the language of the Ojibways, my adopted people" (280). Yet, again, he does not identify his own ancestral group. Grey Owl is equally ambiguous when he writes that he "had been a most appreciative husband, not at all indifferent or unattentive as the real Indians often were" (20), which suggests that he may not be an Indian, or at least not a "real" one. Similarly, he sometimes refers to Indigenous people as "they," such as when he writes that an "Indian" comes to see his beaver (39), or that the fate of the beaver has always been ignored, even by "the apathetic Indians" (51). But other times he declares that he and Anahareo are "representatives of two tribes" (38) and that "we are Indian" (163). Still, he does not specify the particular First Nation to which he belongs. Also, Grey Owl appears to make a Freudian slip when he attributes his "sense of justice" to his "imaginative ancestry" (25). In any case, in contrast to his propensity to link Anahareo to "her people, the Iroquois" (176), he is rather reticent about his own collective identity, making it extremely difficult to establish with any certainty to which ethnocultural group he belongs (see also Dawson 2007, 119, 125).

There are reasons for being wary of Grey Owl's motivation for emphasizing Anahareo's collective identity and lineage, a subject to which I will return before the end of this chapter. Grey Owl maintains that Anahareo's impact on him was immense. He invariably credits her with being the main catalyst for his change in attitude toward animals. Soon after they get married, he writes in *Pilgrims*, Anahareo joins him on the trapline. Part of the explanation may have had something to do with the tremendous loneliness she must have felt spending her days alone in their cabin, which reportedly makes her become "jealous of the bush" ([1935] 1990, 19). So she decides to become a trapper herself, to work alongside her new partner. Anahareo was supposedly a natural and, despite it being her first winter on the land, she became "so adept that she was able to take her turn breaking trail, took care of side lines herself, and was altogether a good deal more of an assistance than some men partners I have had" (23). But her fascination with bush life would turn out to be short-lived.

Almost as soon as she joins Grey Owl in the wilderness, Anahareo starts to make him aware of "the cruelties" of their "bloody occupation" ([1935] 1990, 23, 24). He slowly realizes that she is disturbed not only by the wholesale slaughter of fur-bearing animals, particularly the beaver, but also by "the great numbers of harmless birds and squirrels caught accidentally" in the traps, "often still alive, some screaming, others wailing feebly in their torment" (23). Equally important, Anahareo and the animals seem to respond to each other on an emotional level. Grey Owl notes how, on numerous occasions, "a doomed animal would look not towards me, to the death that was so near, but at her, staring as though in dumb hopeless appeal to her for the mercy it must have known that I would never give" (23). He writes that the most significant aspect of Anahareo's presence on the trapline is that "all at once I saw myself as I was, saw clearly the selfishness that had been bred in me during a life of solitary wandering, and realized how narrow was the rut that I had got into" (21). Or, more likely, Anahareo leads him to see himself as he imagines she sees him.

The pivotal incident in the transformation of Grey Owl's attitude toward wild animals involves a family of beaver. It is late in the season, and the only reason he is still trapping is that, because of a combination of missing game and low fur prices, his financial situation is so dismal he feels he has no choice:

> The hunt should have been over by now, and I was a little disturbed over the hardship I could not now avoid inflicting, as the young beaver were most certainly born by now, and would

perish after the old ones were removed. This proved to be the case. Whilst making a set at an old, renovated beaver house where I knew the female to be, I heard faintly the thin piping voices of kitten beavers. In apparent clumsiness, I allowed my paddle to drop with a rattle on the canoe gunnell [*sic*] with the intention of hiding the sound, but Anahareo had heard it and begged me to lift the trap, and allow the baby beaver to have their mother and live. I felt a momentary pang myself, as I had never before killed a beaver at this time on that account, but continued with my work. We needed the money. ([1935] 1990, 27–28)

However, the next morning, he changes his mind. After discerning that the mother is missing, he decides to look for the young beaver. When he finds the kittens, instead of killing them, he agrees with Anahareo's suggestion that he "save them," as some kind of "atonement" (29). Mainly because of this episode, Grey Owl comes to believe that it is "monstrous" to hunt such creatures and determines to "study them" rather than "persecuting them further" (53). This is a fateful turn of events that leads him to conclude that it might be viable for them to start their own colony.

Grey Owl's decision to build a sanctuary for the beaver is a moral one, being nothing less than some kind of penance for his life as a trapper, but it also reflects his profound identification with the beaver, with which he sides over amateur trappers. For him, the beaver cease to be prey to be hunted and become his "co-dwellers in this wilderness" ([1935] 1990, 49). Like Anahareo, Grey Owl is especially affected by the "queer language" of the beaver (93), which he considers the greatest evidence of their intelligence (Braz 2012, 54). "Their voices," he explains in *Pilgrims*, are "really the most remarkable thing about them, much resembling the cries of a human infant, without the volume but with a greater variety of expression" ([1935] 1990, 33). Grey Owl actually comes to see the beaver as his "comrades-in-arms" as well as his "unarmed fellow-country men," who need his assistance in their struggle against unethical part-time hunters, those "alien interlopers who [have] nothing in common with any of us" (50). In the process, he also envisages the wilderness as a homeland, adopting an idea of citizenship that includes all of its legitimate inhabitants, both human and non-human. Thus, for some denizens of the forest to prey on others, or to witness the latter being hunted by other parties, becomes a "form of treason" (50). This is something that he no longer can countenance and so he stops trapping beaver and starts to explore avenues to save the species from extinction.

Grey Owl testifies that his metamorphosis is gradual, "a slow, hard process fraught with many mental upheavals and self-examinations, and numerous back-slidings and reversals to type" ([1935] 1990, 22). Besides Anahareo's influence, he usually attributes his "newly awakened consideration" of wild animals to his purported Indigenous ancestry (24). It is because of his un-conscious adherence to some Indigenous values, Grey Owl maintains, that he starts to feel guilty about his role in the near extinction of the beaver. It is also because of his knowledge of Indigenous history that he resolves to ensure the beaver will not suffer the same fate as the buffalo. The beaver, he writes, is "an animal on which I had depended almost entirely for my living" and one who has become "so identified with my own destiny as to be something in the light of a patron beast" (47). Consequently, while he has "ably assisted at the destruction of this beast, now that he was in danger of extinction in the North," he has "a sudden feeling of regret, something of that vacant feeling of bereavement that comes upon us on the disappearance of a familiar land mark, or on the decease of some spirited, well-respected enemy" (47). He compares his response to what "the hide hunters [in the second half of the nineteenth century] must have felt as the last buffalo dropped, so that some of them abjured forever the rifle and the knife, and strained every nerve to bring them back again" (47). Grey Owl even adds that his idea of starting a beaver "colony of my own" is modelled on Michel Pablo's work with the buffalo in the 1880s (53). He simply does not want what happened to the buffalo to befall the beaver.

The mental transformation undergone by Grey Owl as a protector of the beaver is fraught with ambiguities, if not outright contradictions. Like the Tsleil-Waututh leader, actor, and poet Dan George, who provides the epi-graph to this chapter, he comes to realize that wild animals have never been in "greater need of human compassion" (George 2004, 68). Although Grey Owl fears that he may be seen as a monster for trapping fellow denizens of the wild like the beaver, he knows that he could be simultaneously perceived as "a renegade" by his fellow trappers for ceasing to hunt ([1935] 1990, 54). As well, his mission to build a sanctuary for the beaver requires many personal and material sacrifices. To begin with, since there are so few beaver left in northern Ontario, he and Anahareo must leave their "own wild friendly Northland" (67) and attempt to build their colony elsewhere, which is what they proceed to do. When told by a Mi'kmaq acquaintance that beaver are so numerous in Quebec's Lower Saint Lawrence that they are "over-crowded in some of the smaller streams" (60), they decide to relocate to Témiscouata.

Along with their canoe, guns, snowshoes, and cooking utensils, they take their two adopted beaver.

Grey Owl and Anahareo are not completely shocked when they arrive in Quebec and discover that there are no more beaver there than there were in Ontario. Still, it is in this distant land that the two begin their experiment, what he terms their "pilgrimage—or was it a crusade?" ([1935] 1990, 73). It is also in Quebec that they name their beaver kittens. Grey Owl writes that he "had long ago invested the creatures of the forest with a personality" (24). But it is only after he starts to interact with the two rodents on a daily basis that he feels the need to give them their own monikers. During the trip, the beaver had lost most of their hair, except for "a narrow mane that extended out of reach down the centre of their backs." Grey Owl says that their near baldness gave the animals "the appearance of the shaven-headed Indians we see depicted in the history books," so he and Anahareo decide to name them "Little Iroquois" (77), which would be only the first of their many appellations. Later, they rename the beaver "Immigrants," on account of their "queer language" (93). Finally, inspired by a book they were reading about the Irish workers who built the Union Pacific Railroad in the United States, Grey Owl and Anahareo settle on McGinnis and McGinty (119). Presumably, the reason they do so is that they feel the beaver are industrious like the Irish.

Not surprisingly, given the uncharted nature of their enterprise, Grey Owl and Anahareo suffer numerous setbacks as they attempt to build a sanctuary for the beaver. The first of these is unintentional. After they have been in Quebec for some time, Grey Owl and Anahareo at last manage to locate a family of beaver around which they can build their colony. Toward the end of winter they go to town to get their mail and to pick up provisions. As they head back to their camp, they notice "strange snowshoe tracks" along the trail, the tracks of someone who "did not straddle on his webs as does a white man but walked closed-footed, like an Indian" ([1935] 1990, 151). They are elated when they reach their cabin and find an old Algonquin friend named David White Stone waiting for them. But their excitement does not last long. As befits a professional trapper, White Stone has not been idle since his arrival and presents his hosts with a "gift" for their hospitality, "two full grown beaver, still wet—and dead" (152). Like Anahareo, Grey Owl struggles valiantly not to betray how devastated he is by White Stone's actions. Their friend is "an old beaver-man, one of the best," and he behaved exactly the way they would expect his kind to do. In Grey Owl's words, at this point there is "nothing to be done. The ancient law of claw and fang had after all prevailed" (153). So the only option left is to start all over again.

If anything, the next reversal is even more demoralizing. Following the incident with White Stone, what Grey Owl terms the "sacrifice at Birch Lake" ([1935] 1990, 156), he and Anahareo decide to relocate to another lake, where McGinnis and McGinty would be safe. But one night the two beaver head to their lodge and vanish without a trace. Grey Owl and Anahareo search for them everywhere, and wait expectantly for their return, but they "never" see the beaver again (159). Interestingly, as he relates the disappearance of McGinnis and McGinty, whom he introduces in *The Men of the Last Frontier*, Grey Owl admits that they were gone by the time he wrote his first book. He rationalizes his decision not to acknowledge their apparent deaths, explaining that "I made out in my writing that our lost friends still were living, and hoped my readers would forgive me the deception, if it was one, which neither they nor I will ever know" [1935] 1990, 202). Whether McGinnis and McGinty were alive at time is open to question, but there is no doubt that they were no longer living with Grey Owl and Anahareo. The episode thus demonstrates that Grey Owl is not above inserting some fictions into his "true" account (137), even if they are compensatory fictions.

Grey Owl and Anahareo eventually succeed in building their colony, starting with two beaver they name Jelly Roll and Rawhide. Through his writings and lectures about the pair, Grey Owl is able to start disseminating his message about the need to rehabilitate the beaver around the world. Not the least important of the people who become aware of his ideas are the administrators of the National Parks Branch, notably Commissioner J.B. Harkin and Publicity Director J.C. Campbell. Harkin decides to hire Grey Owl as a conservationist to raise beaver in a national park, since he is convinced that "Grey Owl would not only provide an attraction for tourists but could also illustrate branch efforts concerning wildlife preservation" (Hart 2010, 451–52). Both aims seem to be soon realized. According to the National Parks report for the fiscal year of 1934, "Grey Owl as a writer on Nature subjects has a wide following throughout Canada, the United States, and Great Britain" and his activities "have done much to impress people with the significance of the conservation of Canada's valuable wild animal life, and also given prominence to the National Parks of Canada as game sanctuaries" (*Annual Report* 1935, 16). Whatever the Canadian government's motivation for hiring Grey Owl, his new position working within the sheltered confines of a national park means that he is now able, as he writes in *Pilgrims*, to carry out his conservation aims "under the auspices of the Dominion Government, and at a regular salary. The safety of the beaver would be guaranteed as long as they should live, and they would never be taken from me" (Grey Owl [1935] 1990, 241).

To add to this sense of achievement, and jubilation, Anahareo gives birth to their daughter, Dawn (276–77), also known as Shirley Dawn. An elated Grey Owl notes near the end of his memoir that all his wishes have been "fulfilled, and more. Gone is the haunting fear of a vandal hand. Wild life in all its rich variety, creatures deemed furtive and elusive, now pass almost within our reach, and sometimes stand beside the camp and watch" (281). Or, as he closes his book, "The Pilgrimage is over" (282).

⊡        ⊡        ⊡

The conclusion of *Pilgrims of the Wild* can only be described as positively utopian. Besides the symbolism inherent in the birth of Dawn, it suggests that Grey Owl's transformation from a trapper into a conservationist is total. Yet there are indications in the text that his conversion may only be partial. Even after his epiphany, Grey Owl never fully condemns trapping, either by Indigenous hunters or full-time white ones. "A dead animal, decently killed," he declares, "was no great matter, but a crippled beast was a crime and the woods were full of them" ([1935] 1990, 49). His aversion is not to trapping as such, just to certain kinds of trapping, especially by what he terms the hordes of "get-rich-quick transient [white] hunters" who have been drifting north and who have "depleted the fur-bearing animals almost to the point of extinction" (8). His juxtaposition between good (full-time) trappers and bad (part-time) ones suggests why he remains so popular with large segments of the Indigenous community among whom he lived (Ruffo 1996, 145–46; see also Braz 2001–02, 179). It also underscores his pragmatism, the pragmatism that colours his very attitude toward wild animals.

I have no desire to minimize the impact of Grey Owl's conversion to conservationism, or to question its genuineness. It seems patently unfair to dismiss as insincere his statements, such as the one in which he declares that, once he embraces his new conservation ethic, he feels the need to perform a "gesture of atonement" for his earlier role in the decimation of the beaver ([1935] 1990, 45). Concerning his influence, no less a figure than the celebrated economist Harold Innis contends that "Grey Owl's experience reflects a change of the first magnitude in the fur-trade" (1935, 199). What it signifies, in fact, is an individual's transformation from someone who makes a living by killing animals into someone who makes a living by *not* killing them. While I once again do not wish to denigrate Grey Owl's achievement, it is apparent that his conversion is not unrelated to material forces, notably the depletion of the beaver.

As one reads *Pilgrims*, it is difficult not to notice the author's growing awareness that he must choose another profession. Time and again, he hints that something ominous is happening to the wilderness and the human and non-human animals that live in it. "At the termination of the Winter trapping season," he writes early in the book, "we went out to sell our fur. Prices had fallen, and were going down every week or so. Although we did not realize it, the day of the trapper was almost done. The handwriting was on the wall, but although it had been painstakingly inscribed there by ourselves, none of us were able to read it" ([1935] 1990, 26). Even prior to that, Grey Owl notes how people like him are being affected by the economic and environmental changes: "I encountered Indians, white woodsmen, real prospectors, each meeting an experience. But when their conversation turned to future plans there were evidences of a vague foreboding in their speech. No man felt secure. Fire, railroads, power projects, the aeroplane, they were tearing the old life apart. The Frontier was rolling back like a receding tide. I must hurry" (12). In short, "The Frontier was on its way. So was I" (13). Or, to phrase it differently, whether he likes it or not, he must find a new occupation.

What also becomes apparent about Grey Owl's transformation is that it is inextricably linked to his writing. In fact, it would not be an exaggeration to posit that it is his writing that makes his metamorphosis possible. Following the incident with the orphaned beaver kittens that he and Anahareo later name McGinnis and McGinty, Grey Owl makes a vow "to kill no more beaver" and then builds a lodge for the two kittens, which he sees as "the foundation of my colony,—the substantiation of a dream, the fulfillment of a big idea" ([1935] 1990, 110). But he soon discerns that his edifice sits on rather shaky ground, for it is basically a one-person operation. As he jokes with Anahareo, "I am now the President, Treasurer, and sole member of the Society of the Beaver People. How about a donation?" (54). The inescapable reality is that, having abandoned trapping, he must find another source of income to support not only himself and Anahareo but also their beaver colony, a dilemma that eventually leads him to contemplate the possibility of becoming a writer. More specifically, he ponders if, instead of killing wildlife, "a man might live by writing about it; I had the practical experience but could I use it in this way?" (139). Grey Owl at times appears shocked by what is happening to him, unable to grasp how fundamentally his circumstances have changed. Yet while he claims that the "thought of the possible unsaleability of my product never entered my head," it is evident that his transformation into a conservationist and nature writer is motivated by a considerable degree of expediency (140–41). As he says of the beaver, "They were more fun alive than dead, and perhaps if I could write about them they would provide many times over the value of their miserable little hides, beaver included, and still be there as good friends as ever" (141). Like those early twentieth-century naturalists who campaigned passionately "to substitute animal photography for hunting" (Altmeyer 1976, 108), Grey Owl concludes that he may not have to kill wild-life in order to make a living from it.

The centrality that writing acquires in his life and thought becomes most apparent when Grey Owl receives a copy of his first article, published in *Country Life*. Like most neophyte authors, he is thrilled just to hold his work in his hands. He confides in *Pilgrims* that it is astonishing to see in "actual print in that royal-looking magazine, the words and phrases that had been produced under such difficulties and in such humble surroundings," not the least the illustrations of their "cabin, the beaver dam, and McGinnis and McGinty themselves" ([1935] 1990, 148). But what drives Grey Owl to the throes of ecstasy is the sight of the accompanying cheque, and the economic and intellectual liberation it represents. "As I considered this pink slip of paper," he relates, "I was conscious of an indescribable feeling of freedom, of having stepped through some dark and long closed door into a new, unmapped territory that lay waiting with all its unknown and untried possibilities" (149). Writing attains such prominence in Grey Owl's thinking that sometimes even conservation seems to be subservient to it. That is definitely the impression he conveys upon receiving his first payment. When he and Anahareo walk back to their cabin, they are so buoyed by "the good fortune" that has visited them that they do not travel "in single file as usually, but side by side," in order that they may talk about their future. It is then that they decide "to build a kind of beaver house for our two Irishmen, to give them a start." The beaver house, though, will function as more than merely a home for McGinnis and McGinty. As he elaborates, he "would write about them, while Anahareo would supply the illustrations with her new camera" (150). At such points, it could be argued Grey Owl becomes a conservationist so that he may write about his experiences.

Writing, for Grey Owl, actually is not completely unrelated to trapping. In *Pilgrims* he states that the reason he rejoices at becoming an author is that "the bloodless happy hunting ground of my imagination was now within the bounds of possibility" ([1935] 1990, 150). To write about wild animals is to capture them in their habitat, but to do so without having to kill them. Once a story is written down, he emphasizes, it becomes "a palace of dreams" (138). Writing enables those animals to touch people who have never seen them and to continue to live even after their death, something that he appears to have achieved in *Pilgrims*, a book in which the reviewer for the *New York Times* contends "the wilderness, with its values, is made articulate" (Moffett 1935, 19). Writing can also be beneficial to the author. This is especially true when, as in his case after Grey Owl moves to Prince Albert National Park, he happens to find himself in what he considers exile, away from the northern Ontario landscape that inspires him. By producing his first article, he asserts, he is able to get "some stuff off my chest where it had been fermenting for a long time, and somehow the writing of that manuscript...partially appeased the feeling of home-sickness that had overcome me whenever I saw, smelled or heard anything that brought quick stabbing memories of the trails of yesterday" ([1935] 1990, 139). Through writing, one has the capability to create an ideal home for not only one's subjects but also oneself.

Needless to say, not every aspect of writing is positive, particularly for someone who has spent most of his adult life engaged in such a red-blooded occupation as trapping. In terms of his sexual identity, conservation itself can be problematic for Grey Owl. Among other things, it calls into question his masculinity, making him wonder "at times if it was quite manly to feel as I did toward these small beasts" ([1935] 1990, 36). This anxiety about his manliness is further compounded when he starts to write. The eco-critic Cheryll Glotfelty has observed that when a "natural" man like a cowboy becomes a writer, he often feels a sense of self-emasculation. "The cowboy," she asserts, "is America's symbol of rugged masculinity, while the artist is often regarded as effeminate." So when such an individual elects to "lay down his rope and pick up a pen" or trade his horse for a desk, his decision is bound to affect both his "relationship to nature" and his "sense" of himself as a man (2004, 128). The same would seem to be true of the trapper, who is one of the quintessential symbols of Canadian masculinity. As Grey Owl remarks in *Pilgrims* about the old-time trappers who are forced to become river guides for tourists, "fur was gone and this now emasculated occupation was their only means of subsistence" ([1935] 1990, 13). Regarding his own situation, as he devotes more and more time to his writing, he admits that he sometimes wonders if he is not just "another good bushwhacker gone wrong" (278). In a letter dated 4 January 1936, J.C. Campbell alleges that Grey Owl has become "obsessed with one idea and that is that he [is] a great backwoodsman. He tells me in his letters that he does not want to be known as an author as he thinks that is synonymous with being a crooner or gigolo par-fumier" (1936a, 1). That is, he fears that his writing will turn him into a pseudo-woodsman, one who attempts to hunt beaver with his pen rather than with his traps.

Another negative aspect of writing is that, especially if one is successful and reaches a broad audience, one cannot help but expose oneself to the world. This is evidently what the international popularity of *Pilgrims* did to Grey Owl, as his exchange of letters in 1935 with the influential Canadian literary critic William Arthur Deacon reveals. Deacon sent Grey Owl a note informing him that "an acquaintance of yours from the woods" has charged that "you are all Scotch without a drop of Indian blood in you" and that "you assume the Red Brother for artistic effect" (1988, 162). An outraged Grey Owl at first tries to discredit his alleged friend, declaring that "[n]o one living in this country knows anything of my antecedents except what I have chosen to tell them" (Deacon 1988, 162). Yet, after stating that "I have not analysed my blood mixture quite as minutely as some would wish," he proceeds to describe its "component parts" (162–63) in considerable detail:

> Mother–½ Scotch (American)
> ½ Indian
> Father–Full White, American
> reputed Scotch descent. (Deacon 1988, 163)

Grey Owl underlines that he is "a quarter Indian, a quarter Scotch & the rest reputed Scotch, tho unproven," and avers that, while he is technically someone of mixed ancestry, "my whole life-training, my mentality, methods, & whole attitude is undeniably Indian." He also insists that the only reason he told his editor he was "a bushwhacker, a man of Indian blood," was that "I was tarred with the brush, & felt I was admitting something" (Deacon 1988, 163). Again, the publicity generated by his writings has the power to call into question the self-identity Grey Owl has so meticulously constructed in those writings.

Still another problematic aspect of writing is that it can lead one to disclose facets of one's life that one had no intention of revealing. Grey Owl's account of his relationship with Anahareo is a case in point. *Pilgrims* could be seen as a paean to Anahareo, who has been rightly identified as the memoir's "heroine" (Gleeson 2012, 153). As noted earlier, Grey Owl often credits his Mohawk wife with being the catalyst for his transformation into a conservationist and seems to revel in describing her ethnocultural background in a way that he does not describe his own. In addition, he maintains that she is instrumental in his becoming a writer and a lecturer. He relates that when they married, Anahareo brought as part of her dowry "an ominous-looking volume en-titled 'The Power of Will,' five small tattered booklets comprising 'The Irving Writing System' " (Grey Owl [1935] 1990, 18). The booklets reportedly had been included by mistake. He explains that they belonged to Anahareo's sister and that he and Anahareo intended to return them but never did (19), and the booklets became extremely useful once Grey Owl determined to become a writer (199–200). Finally, it is Anahareo who encourages him to become a lecturer, always giving him "moral support" (175). In sundry ways, he supposedly owes his new career to her.

☒        ☒        ☒

In *Pilgrims,* Grey Owl also tends to portray his Mohawk partner as ever loyal, describing her as "Anahareo, my brave and faithful Anahareo, who [has] been through so much with me" ([1935] 1990), 181). She is his soulmate for, "before the coming of Anahareo," he had enjoyed human companionship "only intermittently" (197). Yet his text suggests that there is much discordance in their relationship; that their marriage is not always a meeting of minds. The conflict between Grey Owl and Anahareo could simply reflect the considerable difference in their ages, his being eighteen years her senior. It could also be the result of his commitment to his writing, which by necessity is a solitary activity. In her second memoir, Anahareo observes that, after she returns to Ajawaan Lake from one of her prospecting trips, "I'd been home five months…and I was happy to be there, but living with a person who is writing is worse than being alone" ([1972] 2014, 131). Or, as she would complain years later to their daughter Dawn, Grey Owl was "nocturnal and he would sit up and write…scratch…scratch…scratch all night long. Then he would lay on the bunk of the cabin and sleep most of the day." Consequently, Anahareo "became increasingly isolated from him, and missed their outings. This incompatibility grew between them" (qtd. in Richardson 83; ellipses in text). There is yet another possible reason why they drifted apart: the apparent lack of affinities between the two, reflected in the fact that Anahareo is not as concerned about the fate of the beaver as she is about searching for precious metals.

Particularly in light of the prominence that Grey Owl gives to Anahareo in both his life and his career, one striking aspect of *Pilgrims*—as of her two memoirs, which will be discussed in Chapter 4—is her prolonged absences from their home in her quest to make her fortune by locating a rich vein of gold or silver. Grey Owl informs us that Anahareo comes from not only an illustrious line of Mohawk leaders but also "a family of prospectors" ([1935] 1990, 56). Such is her passion for precious metals that she frequently leaves on trips to the northern bush, sometimes with other prospectors, usually strangers and all of them male, sometimes alone. Grey Owl often has little information regarding her whereabouts, much less her circumstances. As he describes one particularly harrowing period during the disappearance of McGinnis and McGinty when he is not even able to write her, "It was a long time since I had heard from Anahareo; not only was she far removed from any means of communication, but she herself would not return for months. The mine on which we had so depended had failed us, and unable to get out of the country she might become destitute among strangers" (231). Another time he relates how he returns "from patrol," his search for the lost beaver, "to find sitting in the cabin waiting for me, Anahareo! She had come out to civilization by plane." Since he proceeds to inform her of "the history of the past year and a half" (251), one deduces that this is how long she has been away not only from Grey Owl but also from McGinnis and McGinty, who are still missing.

There is a fascinating passage in *Pilgrims* that reveals much about both the relationship between Grey Owl and Anahareo and their dissimilar priorities. Early in the text Grey Owl remarks that it is David White Stone's passionate talk about having "found a [gold] mine, at present unstaked and unrecorded," that fires up Anahareo's "imagination" about prospecting (56). So when their old Algonquin friend visits them in eastern Quebec, his imaginary gold mine becomes central to the trio's contrasting projects. As Grey Owl outlines the situation, "This mine was apparently the only hope there was for any of us to carry out our ambitions—Dave's to retire, Anahareo's to prospect, and mine to create a beaver sanctuary" ([1935] 1990, 172–73; see also Ruffo 1996, 68). It is significant that, at this point, he does not link Anahareo to the rehabilitation of the beaver. It is equally noteworthy that when Grey Owl is offered a position as a conservationist at Prince Albert National Park, there is discussion of a house for Anahareo, yet she appears to be nowhere in sight during the discussion.

Anahareo's long absences raise a series of questions not only about her relationship with Grey Owl but also with the beaver, that is, about her conservationism. They also cannot help but make one wonder what his motivation is for giving Anahareo such a centrality in his life, a centrality that results in her overshadowing all his other wives or companions and, to a certain degree, even himself. Dickson's response when Grey Owl informs him that he and Anahareo may be breaking up, which the publisher confesses sounds to him "like a note of doom across our enterprise," is telling:

> I thought he could not be serious. It was as though Abelard had
> spoken coldly of Heloise. Anahareo had been the heroine of

> *Pilgrims of the Wild*: she was certainly the leading lady of those
> films the government had made. The photographs of her in her
> breeches and shirt and leather boots, a madonna-like smile on
> her beautiful face as she watched Jelly Roll falling asleep on her
> knee, or held out a finger for a whisky-jack to alight on, or bent
> forward to put something in a fox's mouth, had implanted on the
> consciousness of the English public an unforgettable image. Grey
> Owl had created her in this image. She must remain the heroine
> of this story to the end. (1973, 238)

For the public, Grey Owl has become inseparable from Anahareo. This is
due both to his books, notably *Pilgrims*, and the films that the National Parks
Branch commissioned about his activities with the beaver and which he used
as a backdrop to his lectures (see Arnold 1935, 4). Largely the work of the
brilliant Calgary freelance photographer and filmmaker W.J. "Bill" Oliver,
who is considered "unquestionably one of the best film makers of the [in-
terwar] period" (Morris 1992, 169) and whose name became "synonymous
with national parks publicity" (Hart 2010, 451), the films turned the beaver
and Anahareo into stars. At times, audiences actually seem more interested
in her than in him. As Dickson apprises Eayrs from London, "what people
love here is the Beavers and Anahareo, and they like to hear Grey Owl talk
about them or read what he has written about them." Following his lectures,
"all their questions…were about her" (qtd. in Smith 1990, 153; ellipsis in text).
In short, like England's Prince Charles with Lady Di, he has been eclipsed
by his consort.

The fact that Anahareo appears to have become more popular than
Grey Owl is profoundly ironic, since, as Dickson incisively points out, she
is to a considerable degree his creation. Grey Owl's portrait of Anahareo in
*Pilgrims* is clearly problematic. He may wish that his readers consider their
relationship a love story for the ages. As Grey Owl describes her role in his
transition from a trapper to a conservationist, Anahareo is the "woman who
had followed me through this grim ordeal with such uncomplaining courage
and fidelity." Out of this most trying of experiences, he underlines, "there had
been born a bond between us, deeper and more binding than any marriage
tie or duty could impose, the steel-tempered, unbreakable bond between
comrades who, side by side, have fought a hard won victory over nameless
tribulations" ([1935] 1990, 103). Yet throughout his memoir, he often calls
into question the idea that they are driven by the same goals. Anahareo's
passion for prospecting, in particular, suggests that conservationism is not

nearly as important to her as it is to him. While Grey Owl presents her as a great defender of the beaver, it is evident that she cannot be tending to them when she is searching for gold.

Grey Owl's celebration of Anahareo is also questionable because it is achieved at the cost of effacing all his other wives or common-law-partners, especially Angele Egwuna, the woman Diefenbaker describes as his "true wife," the one "whom he met when he first came" to Canada (1975, 119). Given his desire to escape his English (and European) past, one can easily understand why Grey Owl does not wish to draw attention to his marriage to Ivy Holmes. Similarly, considering the brevity of their relationship, even if it did produce a son, one can reckon why he does not dwell on Marie Girard. But it is extremely difficult to fathom why he utterly expunges Angele from his life. After all, Angele is essential to his self-Indigenization, since she is the one who provides him access to a living Indigenous culture. Their daughter Agnes asserts that it was her "mother's uncle John" who gave the young Englishman "the name 'Grey Owl'" (qtd. in Mitcham 1981, 55). More significant, she claims that her mother taught her father "much of what he knew about trapping, about the habits of the animals, about the ways of the camp" (qtd. in Mitcham 1981, 57). Indeed, for Agnes, her mother plays at least as vital a role in her father's life as does Anahareo.

In order to understand why Grey Owl structures *Pilgrims* around Anahareo instead of Angele, one temptation might be to follow the lead of the literary critic A.W. Plumstead and interpret the ostensible memoir as a work of fiction. In a provocative essay entitled "What's the Matter with Grey Owl?" Plumstead contends that the reason the conservationist "has been ignored by the Canadian academic establishment" is that he has been erroneously read as a non-fiction writer, even though it is widely known that he was "a notorious liar about himself" (1997, 55, 56). The solution, for Plumstead, is to acknowledge that Grey Owl is essentially an author of fiction. Even *Pilgrims* is "a work of fiction," Plumstead asserts, being "more poetic and mythic than historical" (56). Plumstead, who like most other critics considers *Pilgrims* Grey Owl's "finest book," deems it "a spiritual autobiography, deliberately fictionalized, heightened for effect." He adds that its "closest analogues… are *Robinson Crusoe* and *Walden*" (58), echoing Dickson's judgment that "*Pilgrims of the Wild* is to life in the Canadian wilderness what *Robinson Crusoe* is to life on a desert island" (1973, 231). Plumstead goes further, however, and posits that Grey Owl's "text is not primarily about beavers, nor about saving the wilderness. It is about a human identity crisis, in which a hunter and trapper narrator, who drags his beloved princess into unknown territory to provide her with food, clothing, and adventure, discovers that he has been misled by inflated stories of an Edenic spot of abundant game" and undergoes a life-changing metamorphosis when "his princess persuades him to save two tiny beaver kits who will starve or drown without protection" (1997, 58–59). Thus, the value of *Pilgrims* is that it dramatizes how a "depressed trapper turns into a fascinated amateur biologist and anthropologist, then loving father-protector," and finally into "a reborn man," culminating in the author's transmutation from Archie Belaney to Grey Owl (Plumstead 1997, 59). In other words, the text is really about the possibility of human transformation, human growth.

　　While compelling, Plumstead's contention that *Pilgrims* should be perceived as a work of fiction is problematic. To begin with, much of the power of the book, and of Grey Owl's writing in general, derives from the assumption that it is based on reality, not imagined. Also, even if the text is a fiction, it is a fiction with a difference, for at least in the case of Anahareo, it is a fiction about real people. Most critical, Plumstead's thesis does not address why Grey Owl elects to celebrate Anahareo over Angele, which in fact may not be unrelated to our conception of princes and princesses. Grey Owl's daughter Agnes has an interesting theory as to why her father places Anahareo at the centre of his life narrative, instead of Angele. Anahareo, states Agnes, was "educated. She was also naturally smart and she understood my father's talents. She encouraged his speaking and writing. She could help him in the outside world whereas my mother could not" (qtd. in Mitcham 1981, 57–58). That is, Grey Owl favours Anahareo over Angele because of social or class factors. In Plumstead's terms, Anahareo fits the archetypal image of the princess, including being dependent on Prince Grey Owl in a way that Angele is not. But I believe that there is an even more fundamental reason why Grey Owl glorifies Anahareo. The fact is that, unlike Angele, who knew Archie Belaney when he first arrived from England and was fully aware of his origins, Anahareo took him to be who he said he was, proving that his ethnonational transformation was accepted not only by whites but also by some Indigenous people, a detail that helps to explain the curious shape of *Pilgrims of the Wild* and suggests that his metamorphosis was more effective than some critics like to believe.

# CHAPTER THREE

# *The Modern Hiawatha:* Sajo and the Beaver People, Tales of an Empty Cabin, *and Other Writings*

*I am an Indian and have spent all my adult life
in the woods,
yet never have I met one who so sincerely loved
and appreciated
the wilderness as [Grey Owl] did.*

—Anahareo

Grey Owl was extremely ambivalent about the writing profession. Even after the publication of two best-selling books, he could still write to Lovat Dickson that "I am not a real author, and don't want to be, don't ever intend to be" ([1934–35] 1938a, 75). Part of the reason for his attitude may have been his awareness that his becoming a writer was directly connected to his ceasing to be a trapper. His change of professions was positive in the sense that it enabled him to stop killing animals for a living. At the same time, it took him away from a dynamic life in his beloved wilderness to a rather sedentary one in a lone cabin. This meant that he could go for weeks without meeting another human soul, to say nothing of the fact that it evidently also undermined his masculinity. Grey Owl certainly came to feel that his change in lifestyle was too sudden, and that both "my health and peace of mind are suffering from the so-entire cessation of my former manner of living," something he tried to counter by hiking "20 miles a day" through the woods ([1934–35] 1938a, 54). Of course, his isolation as a writer may have been partly responsible for the rift between him and Anahareo, but there were other complications arising from his new career. In particular, when one writes professionally, one has to deal with a multitude of largely anonymous people in the industry, not the least copyeditors, many of whom are convinced they have a better command of the language than does anyone else, especially authors.

Notwithstanding all these irritants, there is no avoiding the fact that Grey Owl always aspired to be a writer. As discussed earlier, one of the reasons he wanted to come to Canada as a youngster and live with Indigenous people was so that he could write about them. Like most other writers, he also derived much pleasure from reading positive assessments of his work. Grey Owl notes in a letter that book reviews are "encouraging" and of "inestimable value to me, as they help me to line up my work to suit the public taste, in so far as I am able, and give me tips on writing technique that I would not otherwise get" ([1934–35] 1938a, 62-63). He even acknowledges that "I am human enough to want to show them to all my friends, but will refrain; though I must confess myself elated on reading them" (63). Ever since the publication of his first essay in *Country Life,* in 1929, he had also been writing prodigiously. As his correspondence with Dickson attests, he usually worked on several projects at once and would invariably contemplate future ones. For instance, only three months before he claimed that he did not consider himself an author, he informed Dickson that he was planning to write two novels. In the first one, he states, "I am going further back into the past, back into history this time, and am going to try and write a novel of the old Indian and French wars around 1750–60–70 in Canada." He provides two main reasons for this historical focus, starting with the assertion that it allows him to "get in lots of scouting and woodcraft and Indian lore and bush atmosphere," as it would be "written from the Indian angle" ([1934–35] 1938a, 60). His other explanation for striving to access his collective past through the imagination is political, saying that "we [Indigenous people] live in the past, because the future holds so little for us" (59). The second novel, which is "far off as yet," would be quite different, portraying "the adventures of an intemperate half-breed in a civilized atmosphere" (60). The text would thus focus on one group that Grey Owl frequently lambastes for not respecting the ancient ways of their Indigenous ancestors, a somewhat ironic reaction, given that he usually styles himself as being of mixed ancestry.

Apparently, Grey Owl had intended to produce yet another book, which would be his final work. Anahareo asserts that he had become aware that she deeply resented his devoting the overwhelming majority of his time to his writing, and little to her, noting that they "had grown pretty far apart" and "several times when I was planning on a trip, I remember Archie saying, 'The only way I can hold you...is by letting you go'" ([1972] 2014, 170; ellipsis in text). In one of those occasions, as they were discussing the First World War and his Aunt Ada's influence on him, Grey Owl reportedly promised Anahareo that "the next book, which I must write, will be my last, but I don't need to…because once they've read *The Devil in Deerskins*—that's what I'm going to call it—they'll never read another line from me…" (qtd. in Anahareo [1972] 2014, 171; ellipses in text). When she inquires why he would want to write a book that he is certain no one would read, he replies that the book will be "about me—things that even you don't know, and will never know; at least, not from me…," for the manuscript would not "be published until I'm dead" (qtd. in Anahareo [1972] 2014, 171; ellipsis in text). Although Grey Owl does not specify the exact nature of the book, one infers that this would have been his true autobiography, the text in which he would have revealed his ethnocultural background. Interestingly, Dickson maintains that Grey Owl's "last book" would have been a meditation on his relationship with nature. Based on a notebook written by their mutual friend Betty Somervell, which she kept during his return voyage after his second British tour, Dickson quotes Grey Owl in "The Passing of Grey Owl" as saying that he would write his final work "'in the mighty comprehension of the Wilderness'" (1938b, 10). In other words, it seems clear that he had no intention to stop writing. Grey Owl would die before he could produce either the historical novel or the mixed-race one. He also never managed to compose *The Devil in Deerskins*, the book in which Anahareo contends "he would have squared himself with the public" ([1972] 2014, 176)—and whose title she subsequently borrowed for her second memoir. But Grey Owl did complete one extended work of fiction, the 1935 children's novel *Sajo and the Beaver People*, which he illustrated with seventeen of his own sketches, and which Dickson considers "perhaps the greatest of his literary achievements" (1939, 303). Published in Great Britain as *The Adventures of Sajo and Her Beaver People*, the manuscript was first titled by the author *The Adventures of Chilawee and Chikanee*, the latter being the names of the two beaver kittens at the heart of the narrative. The title was later changed in order to draw more attention to Sajo, a pre-teen Anishinaabe girl who becomes very attached to the beaver. The alteration was made at the instigation of Dickson, who came to question whether "it was a very good suggestion" (qtd. in Grey Owl [1934–35] 1938a, 57). Admittedly, one of the things that the title change does is shift the focus from wild animals to humans, something against which Grey Owl had railed during the controversy over the naming of *The Men of the Last Frontier*.

In his preface to *Sajo*, Grey Owl asserts that his "intention was to write a child's story that could be read, without loss of dignity, by grown-ups" ([1935] 1977, xvi). This comment echoes what he had communicated privately to Dickson in a letter, in which he states that while the two beaver kittens appear throughout the novel, "the main interest centres round two Indian children, particularly the little girl, Sajo. It could be read by grown-ups without loss of dignity, and perhaps with some profit" ([1934–35] 1938a, 57). The book thus both is and is not a children's novel; or, more likely, Grey Owl was hoping to retain his adult readership with a novel that dealt mostly with young people. As with all his other books, he declares that *Sajo* is based on "actual fact," remarking that despite being a work of fiction, his "modest tale" derives from "personal experience and from first-hand narrations by the participants themselves" ([1935] 1977, xv; see also [1934–35] 1938a, 57). Besides, in the letter he sends to Dickson along with the manuscript, Grey Owl warns his publisher that, "in spots, you will catch glimpses of my insidious propaganda in favour of conservation and consideration for the weaker brethren" ([1934–35] 1938a, 58). Again, the function he envisages for his novel does not appear to differ radically from that of his non-fiction, be it his memoir or his collections of essays.

The rather dissimilar titles of Grey Owl's children's novel reflect the fact *Sajo* has a dual focus. It is about the adventures of two sibling beaver kittens named Chilawee and Chikanee, respectively "Big Small and Little Small" ([1934–35] 1938a, 50), as well as those of Sajo and her older brother, Shapian. Considering that the two sets of siblings, beaver and human, have such strong fraternal relationships, the initial title *The Adventures of Chilawee and Chikanee* seems more appropriate than *Sajo and the Beaver People*, since Sajo is always accompanied by her brother and their actions revolve around the two beaver. The plot is relatively simple in *Sajo*. A widowed Anishinaabe man from northern Ontario named Gitchie Meegwon, or Big Feather, saves two beaver kittens from certain death when their dam is broken by an intruding otter. He then gives one of the kittens to his fourteen-year-old son, Shapian, and the other to his daughter, Sajo, as a gift for her eleventh birthday. The children miss their mother, and Sajo becomes especially close to Chikanee, who is "not as strong as Chilawee," and who is also "quieter and more gentle" ([1935] 1977, 55). But because of the lack of game that year, Big Feather is forced to sell one of the beaver to the trader in the area's fur-trade post at Rabbit Portage. The trader, a "white man, a stranger" (63), who has only recently moved to the region, chooses Chikanee. Not knowing what to make of the situation, Chilawee becomes afraid and withdraws "into his little cabin, alone" (66). So, when their father has to join a canoe brigade carrying supplies on a month-long trip to a distant post in order to support his family, Sajo and Shapian take advantage of his absence and attempt to buy back Chikanee. This is an epic journey that takes them and Chilawee first to Rabbit Portage, a week away by canoe, and then to the southern city to whose zoo the trader sells Chikanee. Sajo and Shapian eventually succeed in their mission, and the novel concludes with the two children reunited with both their father and the beaver kittens back in their home village.

Grey Owl is often commended by other nature writers for the "studious detail" with which he portrays wild animals, a feat that amounts to "a revolutionary approach in this field of scientific observation" (Cantwell 1963, 114). Moreover, his meticulous rendering of natural life is not restricted to fauna; it also applies to flora. One of the most powerful episodes in the novel is actually his depiction of "The Red Enemy," which is the title of a chapter he devotes to a forest fire. With their father away with the canoe brigade, Sajo and Shapian decide to travel to Rabbit Portage to retrieve Chikanee. But no sooner have they and Chilawee begun their journey than they encounter an unexpected and implacable enemy, a forest fire. At first, the menace is almost imperceptible. As Sajo and Shapian wake up one morning by a lake, they detect "a faint smell of wood-smoke in the air, a smell of burning moss and scorching brush and leaves, and they knew that somewhere, seemingly far away, there was a forest fire" (Grey Owl [1935] 1977, 79). The blaze is much closer than they realize, though, as they soon discover.

After Sajo and Shapian paddle their canoe to the middle of the lake, with Chilawee in tow, the fire becomes more intense and more widespread. The smoke rising from it, we are told, is "no longer a pillar, but a white wall that seemed to reach the sky, and rolled outwards and down in all directions, becoming thicker and thicker until the sun was hidden, and the air became heavy and stifling, and very still" ([1935] 1977, 79). So extensive is the conflagration that it threatens not only the two children and Chilawee, but every creature in the forest, all of which attempt to save their lives by jumping into the water, forgetting their traditional enmities. The narrator describes the chaotic scene:

> Animals that seldom wetted their feet were swimming in the pool—squirrels, rabbits, woodchucks, and even porcupines. Deer leaped through or over the underbrush, their white tails flashing, eyes wide with terror. A bear lumbered by at a swift, clumsy gallop, and a pair of wolves ran, easily and gracefully, beside a deer—their natural prey; but they never even looked at him. For none were enemies now; no one was hungry, or fierce, or afraid of another. And all the people of the woods, those that went on two legs and others that had four, and those with wings and some that swam, animals and birds and creeping things, creatures, some

of them, that dared not meet at any other time, were now fleeing, side by side, from that most merciless of all their foes, dangerous and deadly alike to every one of them from the smallest to the greatest—the Red Enemy of the Wilderness, a forest fire. ([1935] 1977, 83–84)

In a moment of such horrific crisis, the fire leads all the animals to act as one. This solidarity, of course, is not likely to last long, certainly not beyond the mayhem produced by their incendiary foe.

The forest fire is merely the first of a seemingly endless multitude of obstacles that Sajo and Shapian encounter as they search for Chikanee. Once they reach Rabbit Portage and find the white trader, they discover that the kitten "had been sold again," this time to some people in an unidentified southern city who own "a park where wild beasts [are] kept in cages" ([1935] 1977, 100). They also learn that a live beaver is more valuable than a dead one and that it will cost them "fifty dollars" just to buy back Chikanee (101). Since Sajo and Shapian cannot imagine where they might be able to get such a sum, they become dispirited. Luckily for them, they soon learn that not all white people are "hard-hearted" like the trader; that some of them are "kind" (101, 102). Among these compassionate whites is a blond missionary called Yellow Hair, who not only speaks Anishinaabe but also knows their father. When Yellow Hair becomes aware of the situation facing the two siblings, he organizes an emergency meeting at the local Indian school to raise money to send Sajo, Shapian, and Chilanee to the city to get Chikanee. A group of American tourists is particularly touched by the children's attempt to recover their beaver kitten and, feeling they have "got to do something about it," they contribute generously to their trip (112). So effective is Yellow Hair with his appeal that even the white trader drops "a tightly folded little wad of bills" into the donations can (113), although he does so surreptitiously, unwilling to broadcast that he supports such a worthy cause.

In addition to delivering all the money collected to Sajo and Shapian, Yellow Hair writes one note to the railroad station agent to sell the children two return tickets and another introducing them to some people in the city. Thus, when the siblings, and "their small fellow-traveller Chilawee," arrive in the "world of noise" that is the city ([1935] 1977, 133), they do not feel completely lost. This is especially true once, thanks to Yellow Hair's letter, they meet an affable policeman named Patrick O'Reilly. Of Irish extraction, as his surname suggests, O'Reilly develops an instant liking for the northern visitors, even if this is partly due to a linguistic misunderstanding. When O'Reilly first sees the two children, he asks what they are carrying in their basket. Shapian, who like his sister has a limited command of English, says "A-mik," the Anishinaabe word for beaver. But O'Reilly assumes he has called him "a Mick," and is thrilled that the boy "knew I was Irish right away—sharp as a di'mond, the little haythen" (136). Since O'Reilly keeps referring to himself as "a Mick," Sajo in turn deduces that the policeman belongs "to some strange race of white men who called themselves 'Beavers,' a very honourable title indeed!" (136). Needless to say, the two Anishinaabe children and the Irish cop make an immediate connection.

The following morning, O'Reilly takes Sajo, Shapian, and Chilawee to the zoo where Chikanee has been kept in a "jail of iron and concrete" ([1935] 1977, 123). However, instead of being immediately reunited with Chikanee, they suffer yet another setback. The young clerk at the zoo agrees to sell the kitten back for the same price the zoo had bought it, fifty dollars. But when he counts the money that Shapian hands him, he finds only "fourteen dollars," and promptly returns it to the boy (148). O'Reilly is as devastated by this turn of events as the children, who momentarily seem to lose their power of speech. Sajo is the first to regain her composure and tries to comfort her brother. She asks Shapian to tell the clerk that, since they will not be able to take Chikanee home with them, "I—give him—Chilawee—too." With that, she sets "Chilawee's basket upon the desk and step[s] back, her face like a sheet of paper, her lips pale, and her eyes wide and dry, staring at the basket" (149). The clerk is caught off guard by Sajo's Solomonic gesture but, once he recovers, he shows his pleasure at the exchange. At that point, the hitherto silent O'Reilly howls out a thundering "NO!!" before proceeding to threaten to arrest the clerk for "conspiracy, an' fraud, an' misdemeanour, an' highway robbery, an' assault, an'—" (149, 150). The terrified clerk is about to flee when the zoo's owner suddenly materializes. He informs O'Reilly and the children that he had been following the discussion from an adjoining room, since he wanted to listen to Sajo and Shapian's "*whole* story" so that he could be sure "it was not a fraud" (151). Sajo's determination to keep the two beaver kittens together, even at the price of losing both of them, persuades the zoo's owner of their honesty. Consequently, he tells Sajo and Shapian to go "*get the other one.* He is yours; you most certainly have earned him" (153). To complete the story, as Sajo and Shapian pick up Chikanee, their father arrives. After he rushes home from his canoe trip, Big Feather is horrified to find the "cabin empty" and his children missing (116). Thanks to his chief, he learns that they had "escaped the Red Enemy" (118), and had gone to the zoo to try to

retrieve Chikanee. So he travels to the city just in time to be able to take both
his daughter and son and the beaver kittens back home.

◻ ◻ ◻

Like Grey Owl's other books, *Sajo and the Beaver People* was extremely well
received by critics at the time of publication, most of whom were struck
by both its simplicity and its (perceived) authenticity. In a profile of Grey
Owl as a "Pathfinder and Artist," the poet and critic Eric Gaskell lauds the
novel as a "delightful" and "enchanting" work. "The descriptions of wild
life," writes Gaskell, "are as authentic as a lifetime of association with such
things can make them" (1936, 4). Similarly, in her review for the *New York
Times*, the children's author Anne Eaton praises the text for possessing "the
friendly convincing quality of a tale told by word of mouth" (1936, BR 11).
Eaton further asserts that, even if one were not told in the preface that *Sajo*
is based on the author's life in the Canadian wilderness, one would still "feel
sure that this tale of two little beavers and an Indian boy and girl is a true one.
It has the genuine quality that comes only from knowledge and sympathetic
observation." As she concludes, it is because Grey Owl knows "the life of the
woods and the rivers as he does" that he "has a magic to make the reader feel
that he is actually observing at first hand" (BR 11). That is, the power of the
writing is supposed to be inextricably bound to the author's own experience,
and Grey Owl does not so much imagine his creative universe as reproduce
the real one.

    *Sajo*'s singular combination of simplicity and authenticity is also what
appeals to E.K. Broadus. In his review of Canadian fiction for 1935 for the
*University of Toronto Quarterly*, Broadus explains that he will not claim that
Grey Owl's book is "the best Canadian 'novel'" of the year, since it has become
impossible for anyone to define a novel. Yet he then adds that, "whatever
category *Sajo* belongs in, it is, as far as my reading goes, the best work of the
creative imagination, in the field of fiction, produced in Canada in 1935"
(1936, 368). Broadus may not have been totally disinterested in his assessment of *Sajo*, not because of his relation to the book's author but to its London
publisher, Lovat Dickson. An American who left a position as a professor of
English at Harvard for health reasons and moved to the University of Alberta,
Broadus became "a legendary figure in that small upland world" in Edmonton
(Dickson [1959] 1975, 219). He had legions of protégés among his students,
notably the young Dickson, who was effusive in his admiration of his mentor

(219–70). Still, whatever his motivation, Broadus is impressed with what he terms Grey Owl's "'simplified' style," whose "artlessness is indigenous, natural, primitive. It is not merely lucid. It becomes at times prose poetry" (1936, 368). Broadus states that, when it comes to "the quality" of their prose, Grey Owl is a superior stylist to Morley Callaghan, whose novel *They Shall Inherit the Earth* he is also reviewing (369). Grey Owl thus should be read not just because he is the voice of the wilderness, but because he is a fine writer.

Broadus also contends that one of the reasons Grey Owl is so masterful in his portrayal of the beaver is that, in his novel, "there is no artificial humanizing. He is content to tell you what he has seen beavers do" (1936, 368). The latter point is not quite true. Grey Owl does not merely show us what the beaver do; he also explains the reasons for their behaviour, sometimes by getting inside their heads, as if they were human characters. Indeed, he has been accused of engaging in the sort of "anthropomorphism" that professional scientists are "trained to shun" (Scheffer 1977, xiv). This is something he does throughout his work, starting with his essays for *Forest and Outdoors*, where he writes that "the fox" is "the evil genius of the north country" (1930c, 574) and that "the weasel's the gangster of the beaver country, a murderous, slinky no-account" (1936, 270, 282). Yet the reality is that, for Grey Owl, there is little difference between humans and non-human animals, especially the beaver. Also, *Sajo* is a didactic novel, even if its didacticism is gentle and fable-like. Despite its success with both readers and critics for over three-quarters of a century now, it never camouflages its preferences.

*Sajo* is particularly partial to two different groups, the beaver and the Anishinaabe. The text's identification with the beaver becomes apparent in the very episode that serves as the catalyst for the narrative: the destruction of the beaver dam that leaves Chilawee and Chikanee homeless and separated from their family. The dam is not simply broken. It is deliberately destroyed by "Negik, the otter, bitter and deadly enemy of all the Beaver People," who is "on the war-path" ([1935] 1977, 15). Moreover, Negik's behaviour is utterly predictable, since he is nothing less than the nemesis of the beaver. As the text describes the intruder, "Negik the Otter, the hungry, the cruel, and the sly, having broken the dam and so drained the pond, could now get what he had come for—kitten beaver meat! Now was his time. His snaky body blocked the plunge-hole; there seemed to be no escape. He gathered his legs beneath him, ready to spring" (25–26). Were it not for the heroic actions of their parents, who "would fight to the death in defence of their young ones" (27), and who valiantly battle Negik, Chilanee and Chikanee would have become part of the wicked otter's diet.

In addition to the courageous and selfless manner in which they defend their offspring, the beaver are unique among wild animals for two other reasons: their intelligence and their language. The beaver, the narrator informs us in the opening chapter of *Sajo*, are among the "very wisest" of wild animals. They "build themselves warm houses, store up water in which to swim, and put up large supplies of food for the winter months, working almost like men, often talking together when resting from their labours ([1935] 1977, 5). Although Indigenous people must kill beaver in order to feed their families, they admire the "cleverness and industry" of the beaver, looking on the rodents "almost as separate tribes of people, of a kind little different from themselves" (5). As the narrator elaborates, "Beavers are especially respected, and some Indians can understand to a certain extent what they are saying to one another, as their voices are not unlike those of human beings" (5–6). Actually, it is because of the affinities he recognizes between the beaver and humans as he watches Chilawee and Chikanee's parents defend their dam that Big Feather comes to the realization that he can no longer continue to trap. For him, beaver and humans ultimately belong to the same family, and it would be immoral to kill one's kind.

The other groups favoured in *Sajo* are Indigenous people in general and the Anishinaabe in particular. The Anishinaabe are the people who have made northern Ontario "their home, calling it the Land of the Keewaydin, the North-west wind" ([1935] 1977, 1). According to the text, "They are a race of people so ancient, and they have been there so long, that no one, not even they themselves, know where they came from or how they ever got here" (1–2). Because of their rootedness in the land, the Anishinaabe are at one with their environment, and with one another. After a successful hunt, they share their harvest with the whole community. No less important, they derive their education not from organized schools but from nature itself. "The forest is their school," writes Grey Owl, and "their studies are plant and tree life, the ways and habits of animals and how to track them; how to catch fish at all times of the year and, most important of all, how to make fire in any kind of weather, such as rain, wind or snow" (3). Given this kind of knowledge, especially the fact it must be transmitted orally from one generation to the next, tradition is fundamental to the survival of the Anishinaabe. This is something that people of mixed ancestry allegedly fail to realize, especially urban ones. The narrator claims that, unlike "real bush Indians," mixed-race people hunt out of season and fail to respect each other's hunting grounds (11). Because of their lack of appreciation for the age-old ways of their Indigenous ancestors, they thus endanger their culture.

While Grey Owl stresses the centrality of tradition among the Anishinaabe, he also hints that tradition can be flexible. Or perhaps rather, that there are culturally sanctioned ways of avoiding the weight of tradition in extreme circumstances. For instance, Shapian becomes persuaded to try to recover Chikanee only after Sajo has a vision by the waterfalls in their village. One day a despondent Sajo is sitting with Chilawee by the falls, significantly known as The Place of the Talking Waters, when she begins to hear murmurs emanating from the turbulent waters. She soon is able not only "to make out the words," which advise her to travel to the city, but also becomes certain that the aqueous sounds are really her "mother's voice" ([1935] 1977, 72). As she relates to Shapian, "we must go to the City for Chikanee. My mother has told me. I *know*" (73). The fact that Sajo and Shapian allow their course of action to be determined by what they believe a waterfall has communicated to one of them suggests that they are fully integrated into their own culture. But since their father is away with the canoe brigade, something of which the entire village is aware, they decide not to tell anyone else about their plans. The narrator explains that the reason Sajo and Shapian slip out of their village in the early hours of the morning is that they "fear the old people might try to stop them. The old Chief especially might forbid them" (77). That is, while Sajo and Shapian supposedly respect Anishinaabe traditions, they avoid being censured by the community simply by not apprising its leaders of their scheme.

One particular Anishinaabe individual who is celebrated in *Sajo* is Big Feather, someone who, one cannot help but notice, bears more than a few resemblances to the author. The first time we encounter Big Feather, he is described as "a lone Indian in a birch-bark canoe" ([1935] 1977, 8). The text then expands, "He was a tall, gracefully built man with keen dark eyes, and long black hair that fell in two braids over his shoulders. He was dressed in a suit of fringed buckskin that had been smoked to a rich brown, and altogether he looked a good deal like those Indians you see in pictures, or read about" (8). What is most striking about this sketch of Big Feather, beyond its remarkable likeness to the public image of Grey Owl, is the apparent link between the Anishinaabe hunter's ethnocultural authenticity and his similarity to popular culture's idea of the North American Indian. As we learn in the text, Big Feather constitutes the pinnacle of Indigenousness, especially manliness and fatherhood. Yet for an insider like the narrator, his genuineness seems to be connected to his proximity to the dominant idea of the Indian, which suggests that filmic and literary representations of Indigenous people are not external projections but rather capture the essence of the people being portrayed.

There is yet another strong parallel between Big Feather and Grey Owl. Like the author, Big Feather undergoes a life-changing metamorphosis from a trapper to a conservationist. When Big Feather witnesses Chilawee and Chikanee's parents fight the fiendish otter Negik in order to protect their young, he has an epiphany and determines that "[n]ever again would he make war on the Beaver People!" ([1935] 1977, 29). The narrator describes the hunter's reaction by saying that "as he watched, he could not help feeling, somehow, that it was a great shame ever to kill such creatures, that worked so hard to protect their babies and their humble home, and seemed to have such real affection for each other—almost like killing little people, he thought" (29–30). In fact, it is because of this incident that Big Feather reaches the conclusion that, since he has made his "living killing beavers for their fur," it is "only fair" that he now help to protect them (34). This is the reason that, when he realizes Chilawee and Chikanee have been separated from their family in the aftermath of the attack by Negik the otter, he decides to rescue them and take them home to his own children.

Notwithstanding these notable similarities between Big Feather and Grey Owl, there is at least one glaring divergence between the two men—their contrasting attitudes toward fatherhood. Big Feather, as noted, is a model parent. His wife dies when Shapian and Sajo are young and, from that moment on, he and his children become virtually inseparable. "The three of them," we are told, "were great friends and were seldom parted, and every place he went their father always took them" ([1935] 1977, 11). Two rare exceptions to this rule occur when Big Feather finds Chilanee and Chikanee, for "he expected to have trouble with some poachers" (11), and does not want to expose his offspring to unnecessary danger, and when he joins the canoe brigade, which he does in order to buy much needed provisions for his children. All evidence in the text points to theirs being a "happy circle" (67). This is clearly not the case with Grey Owl, who grew up without parental guidance or even company and was then an absent parent to his own children. So perhaps one fruitful way of interpreting his portrayal of Big Feather is as a fantasy, the trapper who undergoes a spiritual conversion that leads him to protect the beaver that he had been hunting for a living, and who manages to show as much love to his own children as he does to the Little People of the Wild.

⊡     ⊡     ⊡

My reasons for personalizing my reading of Grey Owl's characterization of
Big Feather, and his construction of *Sajo* as a whole, are strongly supported
by the text. Throughout the novel, the narrator intimates that he is an insider
to the culture he is depicting. At the very outset, as he explains how "chance
travellers" from distant regions may one day get to tell their own stories "to
these black-eyed, smiling Indian children," he asserts that "I…once was one
of them" ([1935] 1977, 4–5). Later, while describing the table spread at Big
Feather's cabin, he says that "Sajo made good bread," something to which he
can attest, since "I have eaten it many's the time" (40). He contends that he
not only has ocular proof that Sajo is a good baker but also that she is "quite
a little dancer, for I myself was there [in her village] and saw her, and saw
Shapian, too" (164). Further evidence of the narrator's cultural insiderism is
suggested by his use of Indigenous words at key moments in the narrative.
Thus, when Sajo hears her dead mother's voice by the waterfall, the words
appear first in "the Indian language" and then in English:

> Sájo, Sájo,
> Máh-jahn, máh-jahn.
> Sájo, Sájo,
> 'Den-na jah-dahn.

> Sajo, Sajo,
> You must go.
> To the city
> You must go. (72)

Finally, when the narrator closes the novel, he reiterates that the child protagonists "were real people," and real were also the "two little beavers that
loved them, and who really lived, and loved each other" (182–83). We also
should trust his tale because he is telling it from a "wigwam" (182). That is,
he is speaking from the heart of Anishinaabe culture. He is speaking about
beings that he knows intimately, his own kind.

Needless to say, a narrator's claims of cultural insiderism prove nothing.
Often, they are simply part of a rhetorical strategy to attempt to persuade
readers that a particular figure has the authority to speak about the world he
or she is describing. Yet it is hard not to be struck by how personally engaged
Grey Owl becomes with his writing, even something purportedly as light as
a children's novel. When he submitted the manuscript of *Sajo and the Beaver
People* to Dickson, Grey Owl wrote that he did "not expect to be given quite
the same latitude in my punctuation, construction, etc., that I was accorded

in the Pilgrim book, which was, in a way, my own story, as this work is supposed to be not only entertaining but a little educational in nature, as well." In the letter, he assured Dickson that if he were to accept the book, "I am prepared to make whatever alterations you deem necessary in the interests of sales value, etc." ([1934–35] 1938a, 58). But when Grey Owl received the copyedited version of his manuscript, he had a rather different reaction. As he complained to Dickson, "I am very disturbed by a number of alterations in the text of my book. There has been an attempt on the part of someone to Anglicize the book. This I cannot possibly permit. I have nothing against English phraseology, as such—perfectly all right in an English production, but not in one from Canada" ([1934–35] 1938a, 71–72). He added that it was as if someone were trying to force him "to express myself in the English way, which is not my way," someone with "a phobia against our North American style of speech." He then gave the example of how the word "haunting" had been turned into "hunting," since the copyeditor must have felt that children "can 'hunt around' but not 'haunt around' " (72). So disgusted was Grey Owl by this attempt to modify his prose that he categorically demanded that no changes be made to his text without his prior approval:

> I can allow no reader's or printer's private opinion to over-ride my intentions. I did not expect to invoke that "verbatim clause", but it looks like I must, as whoever monkeyed with my prose may make further adjustments to suit his ideas of how I ought to write, and as this is my last opportunity to see the text before it goes into the final process, I'll take no further chances. It must go *verbatim*. Then I know it's all right. I mean *verbatim* as revised in the proofs *by me*. ([1934–35] 1938a, 73)

It is noteworthy that Grey Owl never insinuates Dickson may be responsible for these editorial changes; it is always some anonymous copyeditor or reader. He also attempts to demonstrate that his refusal to have his style corrected is not whimsical, observing that while "one critic referred a little scornfully to my style, every one of the others, where they mentioned it at all, said that the odd queer turns of phrase I used added to the 'charm' of the book." As he concludes: "My style, if I have any, is what is getting me by, and I cannot have it distorted that way" ([1934–35] 1938a, 74). In short, he is just not willing to have his rustic Canadian language translated into proper British English. Whatever the consequences, he is determined that his work reaches his readers exactly as he produces it.

Grey Owl's last book was the collection of essays *Tales of an Empty Cabin*, which was published in 1936 and was supposed to have appeared before *Sajo*. In a letter to Dickson on 29 October 1934, just as *Pilgrims of the Wild* was about to go to press, Grey Owl informs his publisher that if his memoir should "pay its way, with sufficient profit to cause you, as a firm, to consider any further work of mine, the next book, which I intend to complete this Winter, will be *Tales of an Empty Cabin*" ([1934–35] 1938a, 53). He stresses that he "cannot concentrate" on his children's novel "while I have this other on my mind" and then adds that the new manuscript is "already half-written, as I worked on it after the MS of *Pilgrims* was sent away, and it will not take so long" ([1934–35] 1938a, 54). Something must have interfered with his plans, for *Sajo* ended up being published one year before *Tales*.

In the same letter to Dickson, Grey Owl also writes that *Tales of an Empty Cabin* will consist of "about twenty or so tales of the many that were told before the open stove door, that lonely and long (but for the beaver) Winter on Birch Lake" in eastern Quebec ([1934–35] 1938a, 53–54). He further explains that, although "the Tales will be very varied, each [will be] complete in itself" (54). The text is indeed heterogeneous, being divided into three autonomous sections, or books. Book One, the longest, is entitled "Tales of the Canadian Northland" and comprises fourteen essays on life in the Canadian wilderness. Book Two, "Mississauga," includes four essays on Grey Owl's favourite river, the Mississagi of northern Ontario (which he consistently spells as Mississauga). Finally, Book Three, "Ajawaan," is composed of eight essays dealing primarily with his experiences with the beaver in Prince Albert National Park.

Since the three sections of *Tales* are so different, I will discuss them separately. However, the collection remains unified because of its focus on nature and on Grey Owl's steadfast campaign to preserve it. The author's passion for conservation becomes apparent from the beginning. The long preface with which Grey Owl introduces his collection could be seen as either a personal manifesto on the relations between humans and the natural environment or as an *apologia pro vita sua*. He maintains that the wilderness is being threatened chiefly because of the human conception of our place in the order of things. As he opens his preface, "Man, that is civilized man, has commonly considered himself the lord of creation, and has been prone to assume that everything existing on this planet was put there for his special convenience, and that all animals (to say nothing of the 'subject' races of his own kind) were placed on earth to be his servants" ([1936] 1999, vii). Such a notion supposedly has had disastrous consequences not only for the earth's so-called "lesser creatures," but for the earth itself. Grey Owl contends that the only way environmental catastrophe can be averted is if humans reverse their attitude toward nature, beginning with the wilderness. "Man should enter the woods," he writes, not with his too typical arrogance and sense of entitlement, "but rather with the awe, and not a little of the veneration, of one who steps within the portals of some vast and ancient edifice of wondrous architecture. For many a man who considers himself the master of all he surveys would do well, when setting foot in the forest, to take off not only his hat but his shoes too and, in not a few cases, be glad he is allowed to retain an erect position" (vii-viii). In other words, it is imperative that humans realize that they are not the owners of the earth but merely some of its myriad subjects and thus treat it with the reverence it deserves.

In order to illustrate how people have the power to change their attitudes toward the natural world, Grey Owl recounts his own story in *Tales*. He affirms that it is because of his "reflections" on his place in nature that he develops "a distaste for killing" and "a growing feeling of kinship with those inoffensive and interesting beasts that were co-dwellers with me in this Land of Shadows and of Silence" ([1936] 1999, viii). These affinities, in turn, inspire him to establish a beaver colony to help the rodents replenish their rapidly dwindling numbers. But his choice of the beaver, as opposed to some other animal, does not seem to be completely accidental. As noted earlier, Grey Owl often states how affected he is by the beaver's "remarkable mental attributes," particularly their highly advanced language. Yet he also confides that "I have found that in the beaver, with its almost human, very nearly child-like appeal, I had seized on a powerful weapon" (ix). Or, as he describes his initial aims in a letter to J.B. Harkin, he had hoped to use the beaver "to teach an object lesson, to preach a parable that would have resounded across the length and breadth of the continent to elevate them in the public mind to the position that rightly belongs to them, to the end that preservation of animal and other forms of wild life would be supported by widespread public opinion so that our national animal would become more than just a name; conservation would follow as a matter of course." He admits that he feels "a little queer at times putting the beaver through their paces before a crowd, but never lose sight of the ultimate object; seed may be sown in a number of instances where little suspected" (qtd. in Hart 2010, 453). Although Grey Owl is helping the beaver to repopulate, they are also assisting him in his campaign "to arouse public interest, to enlist public opinion on my side" ([1936] 1999, viii). Or, to put it differently, even his devotion to his favourite animal appears to be informed by a considerable degree of pragmatism.

In *Tales,* Grey Owl's ultimate goal of course is to save not just the beaver but wildlife in general. To this end, he will do anything, and he feels that, through "the medium of articles, books and moving pictures, and later, the lecture platform," he has already achieved "some small success" ([1936] 1999, ix). Still, Grey Owl emphasizes that "the half is not yet done, nor anywhere near it, and I fear my kinsfolk, human and animal, are leaning on a reed that if not quite broken, at least bends at times quite dangerously" (ix). Consequently, one is led to deduce that the main function of his book is to alert people to the urgency of saving the natural environment while there is time. As he closes his preface, through his pen, he is attempting to bring to his readers "something of the spirit of Romance, something of the grandeur and the beauty, a little of the Soul of this untamed and untameable Northland" (xii). In the process, he hopes that those readers will come to see the denizens of the wild differently, not as insentient creatures that one may exploit with impunity, but as fellow beings that deserve to live in peace as much as humans do.

Curiously, although *Tales of an Empty Cabin* is a collection of essays, it is not supposed to be written but told. The book is ostensibly related to us by a "Narrator," who "sits before a fire smoking, musing, lost in meditation, as the Past lives again in the changing embers" ([1936] 1999, 3). The narrator is in a small cabin by "a nameless lake" and most of the stories were originally "told to a woman by a man one lonely Winter long, long ago" (5, 8). Given the book's genre, and the fact that Grey Owl has already informed us in the preface that "once I told" most of these tales to Anahareo (xi-xii)—Anahareo herself claims that "the inspiration" for the manuscript was their "proud Birch Lake cabin" in Témiscouata ([1972] 2014, 94)—it is not clear why he feels the need to create a third-person narrator. The existence of this semi-fictional device becomes even more puzzling when, in order to counter any potential suspicions that "this spectral band of my familiars is but a figment of my dreams, conjured up by loneliness and long hours spent in visualizing old familiar landmarks," Grey Owl stresses in *Tales* that "I myself have been there many times" ([1936] 1999, 10, 9). Again, the text's veracity is determined by the author, not the narrator.

In fact, as one would expect in a collection of personal essays, it is impossible not to be aware of the author's presence throughout the book. Whether Grey Owl is describing an event he either participated in or witnessed, or whether he is reflecting on the socio-political ramifications of some development, he is always in the text. Thus, in both the opening and closing pieces of the first section, "Tales of the Canadian Northland," he explores the significance of Canada's seemingly endless northern wilderness, the sparsely populated area that lies north of the continental divide, which "separates those waters which run South from those that empty into the Arctic Ocean." In addition to its vastness, what Grey Owl finds most important about the Canadian "hinterland" is that it supposedly has not yet "been brought under the sway of modernity" ([1936] 1999, 11). He even suggests that Canada's southern and northern regions may not be part of the same polity, at least culturally and psychologically. As he states, "The settled country to the South is, to the dwellers in this Wilderness, a world apart, and those leaving for a rare visit to the railroad, are said to be going 'down into Canada,' as though they were making an expedition into a foreign country" (11). Paradoxically, the South's ignorance of northern realities augurs well for the future of the country. Since most Canadians know so little about the North, he writes, they are not likely to attempt to transform it into a copy of the region where they live and so to industrialize, or modernize, it.

Grey Owl's contention that the Canadian North has not been affected by modernity is clearly problematic, as he demonstrates. In the fifth essay, "A Day in a Hidden Town," he states that "[m]odern influences have taken away much of the romance, picturesque appearance and exotic atmosphere from Indian camps." Because of their contact with and "exploitation" by the outside world, many Indigenous people reportedly have lost their "racial pride" and no longer know how to live off the land ([1936] 1999, 33). If this is true, then modernity has already infiltrated some areas of the North. That said, this apparent contradiction does not detract from his main thesis that it is the wilderness that sets Canada apart from most other countries and gives it its national identity, a sentiment that is broadly shared in Canadian culture (Francis 1997, 129).

In the *Tales'* last essay in the section aptly titled "Canadiana," Grey Owl asserts that Canadians are extremely ambivalent about the North, if not outright embarrassed by it. They are predisposed "to hide that part of our light that emanates from the North, under a bushel, though it may yet prove to be the brightest ray of our national illumination" ([1936] 1999, 145). This collective discomfort about the North is evident in the practice of applying "foreign nomenclature" to the "prospects of sublime grandeur that typify so much of our Canadian scenery," as if Canadians wished to apologize for "its existence and sought to gain something for it by means of a borrowed appellation" (146). In other words, he charges, most Canadians are still not at home in their own land.

Grey Owl is quite aware of the commercial imperatives for exploiting the North's natural resources, but he warns Canadians about the dangers of becoming "a nation of hard, sharp-appearing bargain makers." After all, "Our souls need something too" ([1936] 1999, 147). Grey Owl links the preservation of Canada's wilderness and wildlife to spiritual and cultural concerns. He writes that every individual or people "needs an aesthetic release" and that, "aside from the arts," in Canada that aesthetic release will be found in "the lakes and streams and woodlands of our North as nowhere else" (148–49). Besides, conservationism supposedly can be financially profitable:

> It is not as though we would have to take a loss if we set aside, for the good of our souls, good-sized areas of the original Canadian scene with the intention of keeping them inviolate for all time.... And as I just said, we do not stand to lose, not in the long run. There's a pay streak in it, and a heavy one. Did you know that Canada's wild life, *alive*, and her natural scenery (and I mean *natural*, real forests of big trees, not burnt-over areas or lumberman's leavings) have made the tourist traffic one of Canada's foremost industries? But the wild life and scenery *must* be here for these guests of ours to see, or they won't stay long and won't come back, won't leave their dollars here any more. (149–50)

As he encapsulates his position, "Skyscrapers and [the price of] hogs may rise and fall, but that Northland of ours is one of our best possessions and should be heard from" (146). However, in order to be "heard from," the North must be preserved.

Grey Owl's privileging of the North reflects his view of Canada as nature, which is widely considered one of the three dominant images of the country—the other two being Canada as "a peaceable kingdom" and Canada as "a victim" (Rutherford 1993, 278–79). Needless to say, his focus on Canada's need to embrace its natural patrimony also reflects his own identification with nature, and with nature's champions. One of the most powerful, yet anomalous, pieces in *Tales* is "The Mission of Hiawatha," which is not a tale by any stretch of the imagination but a literary essay. It opens with the contention that it "has become a pose of modern ultra-sophistication to scoff at those works of Fennimore [*sic*] Cooper and Longfellow that portray the life of the North American Indian" ([136] 1999, 79), which is followed by a passionate defence of the two authors. Grey Owl questions the authority of his contemporaries to judge the two nineteenth-century writers, since most people at the time could not even make their way through the woods.

*Archibald Belaney at the age of fourteen. Hastings, England, c. 1901.*
*Photo by A.R. Perry. Library and Archives Canada, MIKAN no. 3191794.*

*Treaty payment day at Lake Temagami, Ontario, 1913. Chief and second chief in centre. Photo by Frank Gouldsmith Speck. Canadian Museum of History, 23991. Angele Egwuna is standing second from the left. The child immediately in front of Angele is her and Grey Owl's daughter, Agnes.*

*Anahareo (Gertrude Bernard), c. 1925. Glenbow Archives, PD-393-3-59.*

*Grey Owl standing beside canoe at a lake, c. 1930–1938. Glenbow Archives, PA-3947-83.*

*Grey Owl feeding a beaver, c. 1930–1938. Image courtesy of the Bruce Peel Special Collections Library, University of Alberta.*

*Grey Owl, with Lovat Dickson, standing beside a car, England, 1936. Glenbow Archives, PA-3947-101.*

*Grey Owl with a beaver on his shoulder, c. 1930–1938. Image courtesy of the Bruce Peel Special Collections Library, University of Alberta.*

*Photograph of Grey Owl, inscribed to Hugh Eayrs, 7 October 1935.*
*Macmillan Company of Canada Fonds, William Ready Division of Archives*
*and Research Collections, McMaster University Library, Hamilton, ON,*
*Canada.*

*Grey Owl, Ottawa, 7 February 1936. Photo by Yousuf Karsh. Library and Archives Canada, MIKAN no. 4103894.*

*Grey Owl at Beaver Lodge, Prince Albert National Park, Saskatchewan, c. 1930–1938. Glenbow Archives, PA-3947-76.*

He writes that Cooper and Longfellow "lived a great deal closer to the days and affairs that they described than we do, and it is reasonable to suppose that they had access to sources of information (much of it at first hand) that are closed to us" (80). While he appreciates the historical novelist Cooper, he is almost reverential toward the poet Longfellow, the creator of *The Song of Hiawatha*. Grey Owl concedes that much of the once-celebrated epic poem about the fabled Indigenous peacemaker and champion of the wild is "allegorical and much is legend"; still, he admires the fact that it focuses on "the abolition of all war and describes the warriors throwing away their weapons, washing off their war-paint, and the opposing tribes fraternizing together" (81). Also, he is impressed by Longfellow's purported knowledge of Anishinaabe language and culture. "So authentic is the treatment" of Anishinaabe society in the poem, writes Grey Owl, "that the whole thing could have been written by an Indian had there been one skilled enough to do it" (81). Thus, through his scholarship and empathy, Longfellow presumably has been able to capture the essence of a First Nation's way of life.

Grey Owl is full of praise for Longfellow's achievement in *The Song of Hiawatha*, but his appreciation of the New England poet transcends aesthetic matters. The fact is that Longfellow's hero is his ultimate model. As Grey Owl notes, he himself has done "a little propaganding on behalf of my own Little Brethren" ([1936] 1999, 86), and he owes most of his inspiration to "the Man the Beasts Loved," the "Messiah of the Wilderness" (89). Hiawatha may have "failed" in his attempts to unify the Indigenous peoples of North America, but "he seems to have succeeded with the animals, and he became the champion of these inarticulate and humble creatures, who appear to have been strangely attracted to him, and whom he called Little Brothers" (87–88; see also Longfellow [1855] 1983, 193). Not the least of his achievements is that he is credited with having "learned" the language of the beaver (88), something that Grey Owl says he believes and which would definitely appeal to him.

The degree to which Grey Owl models himself on Hiawatha becomes particularly evident in his private correspondence. In his letters to Dickson before his first lecture tour of Great Britain, he suggests to his publisher that "in your advertising you should stress the modern Hiawatha appeal; so far as animals go, that is what my work amounts to, or will do if I go at it right" ([1934–35] 1938a, 65). He elaborates that in his marketing of the lectures, Dickson should "lay little if any stress on my humanity, benevolence, etc.," for, "I am really considered rather a tough egg by those that know me" (68). Instead, the focus should be on his prowess as a woodsman, such as his canoeing ability, and his conservationism. "In fact," he underlines, "I think the truest definition of my status, (though I do not of course estimate myself his equal) is that of a modern Hiawatha and perhaps an interpreter of the spirit of the wild. Read Longfellow's *Hiawatha*. Use it in your publicity; not too much of the saintly St Francis of Assisi" (68–69). Grey Owl further reminds Dickson that not only is he "not gentle, nor religious," he is "not even a Christian." But then neither does he wish to be perceived as "a kind of a Gypsy Smith" (69). He is simply a modern version of Longfellow's Hiawatha, someone who has dedicated his life to the protection of his voiceless brethren, the creatures of the wild.

There is one other aspect of Grey Owl's conception of Hiawatha worth noting, and that is the legendary figure's ethnonational indeterminacy. In "Canadiana," Grey Owl remarks that the original Hiawatha became an Indigenous hero and conservationist despite the fact no one knows to which nation he belonged. Although Grey Owl is "certain" that there was a Hiawatha, he acknowledges that the latter's collective identity "has never been definitely established," and the "Iroquois claim him, and so do the Ojibways, the Malecites, the Micmacs and several other Indian nations" ([1936] 1999, 87). But as he points out in a rare footnote, the one group that has adopted Longfellow's epic and its protagonist as its own is the "Algonquin Indians of the Garden River Reserve," near Sault Ste. Marie, Ontario, who "claim that Longfellow lived among them for some time gathering the material for the poem." He writes that the people of Garden River had the poem translated and, for years, "commemorated his visit by an annual performance of the story of Hiawatha, staged on the waters of Lake Huron and in the neighbouring woods" (83; see also McNally 2006, 105). Ironically, considering that Longfellow gave the name of a Mohawk semi-mythical figure to an Anishinaabe cultural hero, it is not evident whether the people of Garden River are engaging in cultural appropriation or cultural redemption. In any case, their embrace of *The Song of Hiawatha* suggests that the instability, or at least fluidity, of cultural figures and events is not exactly a novel phenomenon.

The main reason Hiawatha's ethnonational indeterminacy is so crucial is that the author's own identity is ambiguous. Even in his last book, Grey Owl continues to construct his ethnocultural background in contradictory ways. It is telling that one of the most affecting pieces in the first section of *Tales* is "The Sage of Pelican Lake," which is about an old man who lives with two families just outside Prince Albert National Park. The man is so acculturated into Indigenous life that Grey Owl assumes he is Indigenous, "until he stated that he was a white man" ([1936] 1999, 56). More significant, in "A Day in a Hidden Town," Grey Owl writes that he had the unique privilege of visiting one of the few isolated villages where Indigenous people still live traditionally. This is a rare occurrence, since "[w]hite visitors, or intruders of any kind, are not welcomed at these villages" ([1936] 1999, 35), a curious sentence that suggests he may be white. Such an interpretation is further supported by the reaction of the village's residents upon seeing the visitors: "'who are all these people? Are they Kitche Mokoman? (The Long Knives, Americans)'" or, later, "'Shaganash! Kitche Mokoman!'—White people! Americans!" (37, 39). One would think that, if Grey Owl and his party were Indigenous, the local people would have recognized them.

Similarly, in his discussion of *The Song of Hiawatha*, Grey Owl states that he is qualified to judge the authenticity of Longfellow's portrayal of Indigenous culture by virtue of the knowledge he has "gathered from my own residence among semi-primitive tribal encampments in the North" ([1936] 1999, 82). Again, it is not clear whether he is a non-primitive Indigenous person or whether he is not Indigenous at all. This ambivalence is also evident in "The Tree," his famous tale about some 650 years in the life of a Rocky Mountains tree, from the moment "a squirrel picked up a jack-pine cone" and inadvertently "planted it" (117, 123), to the day a group of "practical" engineers unceremoniously felled it in order to build a "new highway through the mountains" (141, 142). "The Tree," which was later published in book form (Grey Owl, 1937) and which the self-described militant atheist Nigel Sinnott claims he cannot read without being "reduced...to tears" (2009, para. 15), has been described as "Grey Owl's own parable of his frontier mystique" (Rashley 1971, 64). It definitely reveals the author's vacillation about his collective identity through his discussion of the trapper. In *Tales*, Grey Owl writes that, during the life of the tree, "Civilization had come to the West, and *now* the West was wild—the great 'Wild West' of romance, and song, and story" ([1936] 1999, 134–35). The first figure to arrive in the region, he elaborates, was "the trapper, who nosed out all the secret places of the Wilderness and discovered or made routes to all kinds of supposedly inaccessible spots" (135). For him, trappers are the real trailblazers in the West and the North. In fact, "the reputed 'explorer,' who was seldom in the vanguard," usually followed "the trappers lead," but ended up "getting the credit and often inflicting his name on portions of the scenery" (135). Yet given that the trapper was succeeded not only by the explorer but also by "the missionary..., the prospector, the whisky peddler, the cow-boy, the surveyor and the land agent" (135–36), it is not easily evident if he should be perceived as a hero or as a scourge. More important, it is not clear whether the trapper is meant to be seen as non-Indigenous, like all the other emblematic figures discussed.

The puzzle of Grey Owl's identity is further complicated by what is undoubtedly the strangest piece in the collection, "A Letter." Addressed to a "DEAR MISS NURSE" and dated 3 February 1918, it opens with a prefatory note that is worth quoting in full:

> This epistle was written by a North American Indian, an ex-sniper in the Canadian Expeditionary Force in France during 1915–17. It was addressed to a nurse in an English hospital where the Indian had lain recovering from his wounds, previous to being sent back to Canada for discharge. It is interesting to note the contrast, amounting almost to a conflict, between his original style and spelling, and that resulting from his attempts at self-education. The newly acquired erudition stands out rather incongruously in spots and was, happily, beyond the power of the writer to maintain throughout. ([1936] 1999, 91)

Contrary to what Grey Owl implies, it is not only the style of "A Letter" that makes it intriguing; everything about it is peculiar. To begin with, the piece does not even pretend to be an oral work, a tale that someone would relate by a fire one long winter evening. As both the title and the note inform us, it is incontestably a written document, one reputedly produced by "an Indian" who fought for Canada in Europe. Also, while the letter appears in Grey Owl's book, he does not state that it is his own work, and its diction differs radically from the rest of his writing.

Grey Owl's writing style has always been somewhat conspicuous, especially considering that the author was supposed to have had little formal education. This is also the case in *Tales*, where he crafts phrases such as, "I was obliged to extemporize considerably" ([1936] 1999, 42); "[t]here is a story about this graceless prevaricator" (49); and "richly laden argosies came in from mysterious, unknown places" (171). That, though, is not how the author of "A Letter" writes. Whatever education he may have managed to acquire, it does not seem to have included either much grammar or spelling. As he informs the unidentified English nurse, "The little wee sorryful animals I tol you about sit around me tonight, and so they dont get tired and go away I write to you now" (91). Or, "Well Miss Nurse this is somewheres around the last of March. Half of the snow is went now" (94). Some scholars have concluded that the ex-sniper is Grey Owl himself and that the epistle was designed to illustrate the progress he had made as a writer between the First World War and the mid-1930s (Smith 1990, 65–66). But it is difficult to discern any direct link between the two writers, except as an exercise designed to deceive readers about its author's ethnocultural origins—to convey the impression that, like the soldier, Grey Owl is an Indigenous man with no formal education.

▣     ▣     ▣

The second section of *Tales of an Empty Cabin*, "Mississauga," is considerably more unified thematically than the first one, focusing mainly on Grey Owl's cherished northern Ontario. Along with the author's unswerving promotion of conservationism, one of the most striking elements that surfaces in the preface to the collection is a certain wistfulness, if not nostalgia. Grey Owl seems to regret some of the sacrifices he has to make in order to become a writer, not the least his own domestication through an occupation that keeps him largely indoors. As he laments, his "self-imposed task at times is onerous; nomadic instincts have to be suppressed" ([1936] 1999, x). In particular, he resents being uprooted from the landscape of his early days in Canada. So even though he is writing on the shores of Saskatchewan's Ajawaan Lake, in the middle of the Prairies, he often imaginatively drifts back to northern Ontario, his ideal and idealized Land of Shadows.

In the first essay of the section, "Requiem," Grey Owl writes that he has lived all across Canada, from "the impenetrable cedar jungles of far-off Temiscouata," through "the distant, unknown North," and finally to his current home in the "spruce-clad lowlands of the upper Saskatchewan" ([1936] 1999, 157). He asserts that every one of those regions has "its special claim on the imagination," being "imbued with the fantastic lure of the unknown that, like some all-powerful enchantment or magic spell, pervades the unpeopled places of the earth's surface." Yet, for him, all these places "lack the austere magnificence and the rugged grandeur of the highlands of North Ontario, with their bold, romantic scenery, uncounted and uncountable deep-water lakes and wild-rushing rivers" (157). Such is the charm of the northern Ontario landscape that, although Grey Owl is "happy" at Ajawaan, he cannot escape his memories of "the old, wild, carefree days when I roamed at will through the rock-bound Ontario wilderness," with all his "worldly goods loaded into one small, swift, well-beloved canoe" (157). That is, one of the sacrifices he must make in order to build his beaver colony in Saskatchewan is to exile himself from his favourite landscape.

For Grey Owl, his old days in Ontario were a period of both freedom and community. Most of the tales in the section focus on "the wild, romantic, spirit-haunted" Mississagi River, which he terms simply "the River" ([1936] 1999, 163), thus allowing him to revisit his "first love, the canoe" (159). As he writes nostalgically in "Rivermen," while describing the adventures of the fast-vanishing canoeists and their arduous journeys, "I too was once a Riverman, the canoe my trade, such men my boon companions" (172). Furthermore, it is not just the Mississagi River that he misses; he is also nostalgic for his hometown of Biscotasing, which sits at the head of the Mississagi. Grey Owl candidly admits that Bisco does not amount to much more than "a collection of small wooden houses gathered, or scattered rather, around the rocky hillsides that enclose a sheltered bay of Biscotasing lake" (169). Still, for him, it is "the town. My town. It doesn't belong to me, no; I belong to it" (168). Despite the fact he grew up not far from London and is believed to have lived in Toronto, Bisco is "apparently the only town in the world which Grey Owl viewed with affection" (Mitcham 1981, 31), underscoring its almost mythical significance for him.

It is not difficult to imagine why Grey Owl would come to idealize northern Ontario, both its rugged landscape and its "fraternity of freemen," where people presumably are judged not by the colour of their skin or by their speech, but by their versatility in the wilderness ([1936] 1999, 172). For someone now living in isolation from any sustained human contact, and burdened with massive commitments both to the beaver and to his publishers, those old days on the Mississagi must have seemed like a golden age of freedom. As one reviewer of *Tales* perceptively remarks, Grey Owl had not become merely a "friend" and "protector" of the beaver; he was also their "slave" (Maurice 1936, xx). The fact is that the beaver became all-consuming for Grey Owl. Whether he was tending to them or writing and lecturing about them, he had little time left to do anything else. He certainly did not have the liberty to simply disappear into the woods for any extended period. So onerous a commitment do the beaver become for Grey Owl that he comes to question his own reality. As he asks at one point, "Have I dreamed the last twenty years, or imagined them, and they never really happened? Maybe I was out with the boys last night; I don't seem to remember" ([1936] 1999, 168). Therefore, one of the compensations of his writing is that it enables him to escape, at least mentally, to what now seems a much freer time in his life.

The extent to which Grey Owl has become a prisoner of the beaver, both in real life and metaphorically, is evident in the reviews of *Tales*. In their assessment of the collection, several critics warn their readers that they "may feel a touch of impatience," since "it is not till we reach the third and last section of the book that we find ourselves again at Ajawaan, and are admitted again to the enthralling company of 'Beaver Lodge,' and to the wild life that surrounds it" (Maurice 1936, xx). Even those commentators who consider the book either "superb" (Cantwell 1963, 118) or his "most ambitious" (Maurice 1936, xx) seem disappointed that the author does not restrict his text to depicting the travails of the beaver. The response is particularly surprising, considering that the reviewers acknowledge that Grey Owl "looks back rather wistfully" to his old days as a canoeist and woodsman (*New York Times* 1936, 33). As the text frequently shows, Grey Owl appears to have considerable regrets about the life he was forced to abandon when he became a conservationist.

⊠     ⊠     ⊠

The final section of *Tales*, "Ajawaan," is indeed centred on Grey Owl and his life at Beaver Lodge, the log cabin that the Canadian government built for him in Prince Albert National Park so that he could establish his beaver colony. Beaver Lodge, he writes, is "more or less a replica of the House of McGinnis, that faraway Winter camp in Temiscouata which was the beginning of all things, the Empty Cabin of the Tales I lately told you." More significant, "Beaver Lodge is not only my home; it is the home, too, of my Beaver People and is the gathering place of many other creatures, denizens of the forest that encircles it on every side" ([1936] 1999, 281). "Ajawaan" is really a biographical-historical account of his experiences with the beaver following his transformation from a trapper into a conservationist, notably after he was recruited by the National Parks Branch. He details his first attempt, also described in "The Great Adventure" ([1931] 1995), to build a beaver colony at Riding Mountain National Park, in Manitoba, which he had to abandon when he discovered that the water supply was inadequate. That failure forced him and the National Parks functionaries to search farther west in Prince Albert National Park, which proved "more suitable to the requirements" of the colony ([1936] 1999, 241). So Grey Owl and his beaver charges made the journey to the neighbouring province of Saskatchewan, where they finally found a home.

Although Beaver Lodge was designed to accommodate not only Grey Owl but also Jelly Roll and Rawhide, this cohabitation created some unexpected problems, especially for a writer. As Grey Owl notes, his non-human brethren "engage themselves in projects that create a great deal of noise, quite oblivious of the fact that I am trying to write a book" ([1936] 1999, 251). In addition, Jelly Roll and Rawhide have a propensity for upsetting papers and destroying furniture. But there may be another reason why Grey Owl is not totally concentrated on his writing—he seems uncertain that writing is the most effective medium to disseminate his ideas about conservation. Even though he is constantly writing, in his account of his life with the beaver at Ajawaan there are numerous references to photography and film. For instance, early in the section, he states that, while his descriptions of the goings on at Beaver Lodge may seem implausible, "the camera has provided an incontestable record of its actuality" (225; see also Cory 1935, 106). That is, he appears to consider the camera to be a more reliable instrument than the pen. This may explain why the author and the National Parks Branch are willing to spend "[s]everal thousand feet of film" on Jelly Roll and Rawhide in order to make their "activities a matter of photographic record" ([1936] 1999, 241, 256). Film, they believe, has a reach that writing lacks.

By the end of the book, Grey Owl's relationship with the beaver has become extremely close. For better or worse, they are his only companions. Except for his "animal friends," he writes, "I live here quite alone," even if he stresses that, despite being "far from the haunts of my fellow-men, I am seldom lonely" ([1936] 1999, 274, 282). Still, he insists that there is much continuity between the rather contrasting phases of his life. He states that "I am still a hunter, in a little different way. The camera is my weapon today." Or, as he adds, "Some prefer to have a den full of trophies; others a hunting-lodge decorated with skins, maybe. Each to his own taste; I like mine alive" (332). Considering that Grey Owl professes that each and every "animal has his separate personality, easily distinguishable to one who knows him" (291), it is not surprising that he comes to contemplate how the creatures to whom he has dedicated much of his life may feel about him. As he says of Jelly Roll, when "he sits sometimes so motionless, regarding me so steadily with his cool and watchful eye, I often wonder what he thinks of me" (322). Perhaps, ultimately this is the only judgment that truly troubles Grey Owl, that of the beaver and other wild animals with whom he shares his life.

◻    ◻    ◻

Although *Tales of an Empty Cabin* was the last book Grey Owl published, it was not the last piece of writing he produced. Soon after his death, Dickson assembled a "tribute" to his best-selling author entitled *The Green Leaf.* Along with a deeply personal testimonial by Dickson and a series of letters from Grey Owl to his publishers, the volume includes his "Precepts" and

his "Farewell" to the children of Great Britain after his second tour. As
Dickson explains in "The Passing of Grey Owl," at the end of his visit, Grey
Owl met with the British royal family at Buckingham Palace, an event that
"gave him great personal satisfaction" and that attests to his phenomenal
popularity (1938b, 21; see also Massey 1963, 254–55). At the same time,
the British Broadcasting Corporation (BBC) refused "to allow him to make
his farewell broadcast unless an alteration, which he was adamant in his
refusal to make, was effected in the script of his talk" (Dickson 1938b, 21).
The talk in question was scheduled to be broadcast in a program called
*Children's Hour* on 20 December 1937, and the part of the text that the
BBC attempted to have altered concerned fox hunting. More specifically, in
"Farewell," Grey Owl was planning to tell British children that the "world
is not altogether ours" but "belongs to all who live upon it, both animals
and people" ([1937] 1938b, 104), a sentiment that encapsulates his whole
philosophy. As he addresses his young audience:

> Could you promise me never to take advantage of the weak-
> ness of another, human or animal—never to take the life of a
> poor defenceless animal just merely for amusement?
>
> I'll ask you, too, if you will never join in a chase where
> foxes, stags, or otters or hares, are driven to the last extremity of
> terror, and misery, until at last, with no chance of escape, they
> stand there looking for mercy, but finding none, surrounded
> by a horde of dogs, and men, and sometimes, I am ashamed
> to say, women and even children, and then, defenceless, terri-
> fied, helpless, and *alone*—no one near to help them—they are
> literally mobbed to death.
>
> Is that fair play? Is that sport? ([1937] 1938b, 105)

Grey Owl concludes with a calculated appeal to the local sensibilities,
stating that such one-sided contests cannot possibly constitute "good old
British fair play" (105). But, needless to say, the BBC felt otherwise.

Beyond its ability to generate controversy, Grey Owl's "Farewell" is im-
portant for what it reveals about the author's construction of his collective
identity. In his introduction to *The Green Leaf*, Dickson asserts that "Grey
Owl…never said he was an Indian" (1938a, 14). This is clearly incorrect, as
"Farewell" proves. Grey Owl opens his talk with the statement: "I am Wa-
Sha-Quon-Asin, Grey Owl, North American Indian, champion of the Little
People of the Forests" ([1937] 1938b, 103). Then, he closes it by saying that

"now, my wife, Silver Moon [Yvonne Perrier], and I, Grey Owl, two Indians, must leave you" (108). In other words, there are at least a few times when Grey Owl declares, quite unequivocally, that he is Indigenous. The most significant aspect of "Farewell," though, is the way it illustrates how threatening Grey Owl's ideas about animal rights can be. At the very moment that he is being feted by Great Britain's royal family, parts of his work are summarily rejected by the country's national broadcaster, which leads him to storm out of the "BBC's studios rather than submit to censorship of his remarks" ("Grey Owl Hushed" 1938, 17). As he states in "Grey Owl Pleads," he "deplore[s]" the British broadcaster's response, "but I simply could not cave in before going. I would be ashamed to face the wild animals and trees back home" (1938d, 397). Notwithstanding his frequent claims that he is not a real writer, it is evident that his writings have the power to affect people, for good or ill. This of course begs the question of what sort of place he occupies among nature writers, notably following the disclosure that he had no Indigenous ancestry.

In a letter informing Dickson of the circumstances of Grey Owl's death, which he delayed writing because of "the controversy which has raged not only in this country but also in England in regard to his nationality" (Wood 1938, 28), the Superintendent of Prince Albert National Park, James Wood, declares that "I care not whether he was an Englishman, Irishman, Scotsman or Negro. He was a great man with a great mind, and with great objectives which he ever kept before him" (30). In the passage that serves as the epigraph to this chapter, Anahareo similarly affirms that, even though she is "Indian" and Grey Owl is not, she has never met anyone "who so sincerely loved and appreciated the wilderness as he did" (1940, 23). However, the reality is that Grey Owl's biography has often impinged on the interpretation of his work, as reviews of a recent edition of his last book illustrate.

*Tales of an Empty Cabin* was reissued in 1998, an occasion that elicited several reviews by contemporary writers, including two strikingly dissimilar ones by the Canadian poet-scholars Adam Dickinson and Stephanie McKenzie. Dickinson is effusive in his review. He asserts that "Grey Owl sculpts his stories into finely crafted revelations" and that his writing is "robust and well-textured; the sentences sometimes continue for half a page unwinding their rhetorical complexities like a web of river systems" (2000, 108, 109). McKenzie, in contrast, has little to say about the writing style of the author she is reviewing—in truth, nothing at all. She implies that the new edition is linked to the appearance of Richard Attenbourgh's film *Grey Owl* (2003, 149)—which will be discussed in Chapter 5. She also praises the visual elements in the book, especially the photographs of Grey Owl and the beaver. Yet McKenzie bemoans the fact that the publisher provides no "indication why this text was reprinted at a time when contemporary Native literature is thriving and when debates about appropriation of voice have been challenging old publishing practices" (2003, 150). For McKenzie, Grey Owl apparently does not have the right to write even about his own experiences raising beaver or canoeing on the Mississagi, since by doing so he supposedly prevents Indigenous writers from being published. Thus, she devotes her whole review to the author's problematic biography and to voice appropriation, anything except his writing.

Ironically, in his last collection, Grey Owl anticipates exactly such a focus on biography and attempts to counter it. In his meditation on "The Mission of Hiawatha," he remarks: "It is notorious that a man's true worth is not usually recognized until he is dead, and the longer he remains dead the more famous he becomes" ([1936] 1999, 85). Perhaps even more significant, he adds that "examination into the private lives of mighty personages of history has been often disappointing." So he suggests that we "disabuse our minds of the fetish of super-men of days long past, and love our heroes, ancient and modern, for their very humanness" (85). In his own case, one deduces, he probably would prefer that future critics focus more on his books than on his private life. That is, that we read his texts, not the author, which admittedly is not always easy to do when dealing with someone who writes primarily first-person narratives. Yet what he feared is largely what has happened. Critics seem much more interested in the historical figure than in the writings he produced. Indeed, they frequently judge him as a person, and as a writer, without even deigning to read his work.

CHAPTER FOUR

## The Passionate Prospector: Anahareo, Grey Owl, and the Idea of Indigenous Transparency

*An Indian can tell who's Indian.*
*Grey Owl can't sing or dance.*

—Armand Garnet Ruffo

It could be argued that the three women who played the most important roles in Grey Owl's life were, chronologically, his aunt Ada Belaney and his wives Angele Egwuna and Anahareo. The impact of the first two women on Grey Owl is incontestable. Along with her sister, Carrie, and their mother, Julia, Ada Belaney raised the young Archie and, among other things, taught him to play the piano and to write. Angele Egwuna, in turn, introduced him to the Anishinaabe way of life and, inadvertently, made possible his subsequent transformation into Grey Owl. But considering the self-image that he projected in his writings as someone of mixed Indigenous and European ancestry, Grey Owl could not openly acknowledge the influence of either his white aunt or the Indigenous woman who met him soon after he arrived in Canada from England. Thus, for the overwhelming majority of his readers and the public at large, there is only one woman in the conservationist's life: Anahareo.

While Grey Owl's privileging of Anahareo over Angele Egwuna and Ada Belaney may be unfair, even cruel, it is not accidental. The fact is that, in order to create the impression that Anahareo had such prominence in his life, and to camouflage his European origins, Grey Owl had to minimize the roles played by the other women who shaped his destiny. His elision of Angele is particularly disconcerting, since he owed so much to her. The question that one will never be able to answer satisfactorily is whether Grey Owl would have had the same impact as a conservationist and nature writer had people been aware that he arrived in northern Ontario as a teenager fresh from Europe, and that he owed his knowledge of woodcraft to the people he met there, not the least Angele and her family. That is, was his effacement of Angele really necessary? Moreover, there are other troubling aspects to his treatment of her. To begin with, Angele was one of the few people, notably women, in whom Grey Owl was able to confide many of the existential problems that assailed him from an early age. No less disturbing, it is not easily apparent why he would risk romancing Anahareo right in Temagami, so close to the home of not only Angele but also their daughter, Agnes; in fact, Agnes was only five years younger than Anahareo and later claimed that she was "disappointed" when her "chum" started dating her father (qtd. in Mackey 2000; see also Mitcham 1981, 57). Given his dependence on Angele, Grey Owl appears to have been needlessly insensitive toward her when it came to his relationship with Anahareo.

There is no doubt that Grey Owl saw something in Anahareo that he did not glimpse in his other romantic partners. Indeed, she was a free spirit who achieved much at a time when women's freedom of movement was severely restricted, and she did so chiefly on her own terms, despite facing blatant sexism and racism at the time. Some explanations for his favouring the young Mohawk over his other wives, including Angele, are obvious, as they involve matters of class, education, and aesthetics. In addition to being young, urban, and formally educated, she was very photogenic. As the numerous photographs of her illustrate, Anahaero was a "timeless stylish" New Woman (McCall 2013, 28), quite a contrast to the dependable but rustic Angele. Most important for Grey Owl, she seems to have been the first Indigenous person he met who accepted that he was of mixed Indigenous and European ancestry, even trying to rediscover her Indigenous roots through him.

Anahareo occupies an extremely paradoxical place in the life, and my-thology, of Grey Owl. She is the most independent of his romantic partners, someone who supposedly "didn't give a damn about the status quo" (Swartile xii). Yet, to a considerable degree, she is also his creation. Whatever at-tracted the then trapper to Anahareo, it clearly was neither her domesticity nor her docility. As Allison Mitcham has noted, Anahareo was very much a female Grey Owl, the young Grey Owl. She treated him with the disdain that he showed to all his other wives and lovers and eventually abandoned him, "for essentially the same reasons which had motivated Grey Owl's for-mer flights. She simply could not stand being cooped up" (1981, 75). Grey Owl must have suspected that there were considerable risks involved in his

apotheosis of Anahareo, as he would eventually discover. People became so
enamoured with her that they insisted "she remain the heroine" of his story
even after the two of them had separated (Dickson 1973, 238; Smith, 1990,
153). Still, he had no choice but to foreground Anahareo, for, whatever else
she might be, she was a necessary fiction. Considering that Grey Owl had
such an unstable life story, he needed to draw attention to the "full-blooded"
Anahareo in order to be able to imply that he was Indigenous without actually saying so.

❖　　❖　　❖

At least in the terms of the public images they constructed, Grey Owl and
Anahareo were utterly dependent on each other. This is particularly true of
Anahareo, whose narrative appears unthinkable without reference to the
man first known as Archie Belaney. The centrality of Grey Owl in Anahareo's
life is conspicuously evident in her two memoirs, both of which refer to the
trapper-turned-conservationist in their titles. Anahareo's first book, published in 1940, is called *My Life with Grey Owl*; her second one, published in
1972 and reissued in a new edition in 2014, is entitled *Devil in Deerskins: My
Life with Grey Owl*. While the two works appeared thirty-two years apart, they
cover much of the same territory. Yet there is a discernible difference in tone
between them. In the first book, even though Anahareo seems determined
to defend the authenticity and legitimacy of Grey Owl, she presents herself
as an independent woman, quite autonomous from her partner. But in the
second book, which was written late in her life, she tends to portray herself
basically as the flag-bearer for Grey Owl, someone who derives much of her
identity from her connection to him.

*My Life with Grey Owl* was published only two years after the death
of Grey Owl and, not surprisingly, deals extensively with the ramifications of
his untimely demise. But there is one topic in which the memoir revels even
more than in Grey Owl's "astonishing life chapter" and that is his romance
with Anahareo, a singular liaison that purportedly makes them the Abélard
and Héloïse of the wilds (1940, vii). The book opens with a four-page preface titled "Introducing Anahareo," which states that the death of Grey Owl
marked the end not only of his seminal "experiment in animal conservation" but also of "a love-story...of unsurpassed beauty: the love story of Grey
Owl and Anahareo" (vii). The unidentified author, presumably representing
the publisher, asks readers to imagine the protagonists "as two young but

innocent lovers, making their solitary but happy way into the depths of the forest in mid-winter, with no fear or care but that which they had for each other" (ix–x). Needless to say, the writer completely glosses over the substantial age difference between Anahareo and Grey Owl and the revelations about the latter's polygamy and alcohol abuse, which suggest that by the time he met his Mohawk love he was neither innocent nor particularly young.

Still, judging by the description of Anahareo in *My Life with Grey Owl*, it is not hard to see why Grey Owl would fall madly in love with her. According to the text, "this strange, fascinating creature of the wilds" is "made up of contrasts," being simultaneously natural and sophisticated (1940, viii). Anahareo, we are told, "has the overpowering sense of humour of a high-spirited child, but she can lapse suddenly into stillness, and sit as unmoving as one of the little beavers whose habits and moods she and Grey Owl have done so much to make known, staring in sadness before her" (viii). She possesses a "slim, iron-muscular figure…and in the woods she can carry a load almost as heavy as that a man can bear. She can paddle a canoe as swiftly, can cook, make camp, find her way along any wilderness trail" (viii–ix). Above all,

> she is beautiful. The [eleven] photographs [of her] included in this book, with one or two exceptions, were taken in the open air with uncomplicated, old-fashioned cameras, and by very amateur hands. They show something of her slender, attractive strength, but nothing of the light and play of her features, her golden skin, her straight, deep-set brown eyes; the little tricks of gestures, the one dark eyebrow that lifts itself quizzically over a laughing eye when she is at her ease and indulging the slow, lazy, humorous sense of the backwoods. Nor the even white teeth, or the slim column of her neck rising from an open shirt that holds her small well-shaped head so proudly back. (ix)

In short, Anahareo was the ideal partner for the champion of the beaver, the beautiful and loyal mate who made his career possible.

Kristin Gleeson, who has written extensively on Anahareo, asserts that she was "not happy" with her first book, since "Lovat Dickson instructed her to refrain from mentioning Grey Owl's background." Anahareo was particularly displeased with the early part of the text and for several years afterwards, she "took to checking the book out of libraries and removing the first chapter," realizing that "she had, in some degree, surrendered control over Grey Owl's image and her own by giving in to the publisher's concerns" (2011, 307; see also Gleeson 2012, 178–79). That said, the memoir remains fascinating for what it reveals about Anahareo's image of both Grey Owl and herself. Even if a portion of the opening chapter of *My Life with Grey Owl* bears the imprint of the publisher, it still conveys the two most conspicuous elements about Anahareo: her sense of being unconventional, "a rebel" (McCall 2013, 28), and her romantic nature. In the first pages, Anahareo writes that she was "one of many children in an Indian home that a few generations back would have been a lodge in an Indian village" (1940, 1–2). She adds that, at the time of publication, "my Father and my brothers are employed by the White Man, for all my people—perhaps it was in our Fate—have come down in the world, as you would say" (2). One of the reasons for the decline of her family's fortunes was that her mother died when Anahareo was four years old, which resulted in her being raised by her paternal grandmother and her siblings by other relatives (3). In addition, Anahareo notes that her "family, like most other Indian families [in the region], was Catholic. We took our religion very seriously, and never failed to do our duty at the appropriate seasons" (2). But her Catholicism, along with her Indigeneity, turns out to pose somewhat of a challenge since, she confesses, "I wasn't cut out to follow a conventional life" (2). From the outset, she underlines that she feels alienated from a culture in which women, such as herself and her late mother, "were regarded as perpetual minors, incapable of making up our own minds" (5). That is, like Grey Owl, she is not quite at home in the world into which she is born.

Anahareo has been praised for being a more factual writer than Grey Owl. Donald Smith maintains that while her two memoirs are not as dramatic or as well written as *Pilgrims of the Wild*, they "rank much higher" as "historical records" (1990, 78). Yet Anahareo can be frustratingly frugal with crucial details about her life. Thus, in *My Life* she never provides us with her birth name, which is Gertrude Bernard. She also does not identify her birthplace, beyond stating that she was raised in "a wooden dwelling on the outskirts of a modern town" in "the Iroquois valley" (1940, 2). Although she hails from Mattawa, Ontario, a small town on the Quebec border some 300 kilometres north of Ottawa, she informs us that she was "born in the North" (1). This is rather imprecise, considering that her hometown is closer to the United States border than it is to Hudson Bay, to say nothing of the Arctic Circle.

One aspect of her story about which Anahareo can be quite expansive, however, is her relationship with Grey Owl, the mysterious stranger with whom she would be forever linked. Anahareo's meeting the future conservationist is the most fateful event in her life, and Anahareo describes the encounter with uncharacteristic precision: "I first met Grey Owl in 1925, when I was eighteen years old" (1940, 5). She relates that she had been spending her summer holidays with an aunt at Camp Wabikon, a bungalow resort on Lake Temagami. As her vacation neared its conclusion, one of the waitresses had to leave unexpectedly, and Anahareo persuaded her aunt to let her spend to rest of the summer working there. It was then that she first glimpsed what she terms "a rhapsody in brown" (14), "a tall, very lithe and strong woodsman, burnt a deep brown," sporting "moccasins and trousers of buckskin, a woolen shirt, and a highly-coloured Hudson's Bay belt around his middle," and gliding out of his canoe (5–6). From the moment Anahareo notices this "godlike male" emerge out of Lake Temagami like an apparition, she becomes determined to make him her "first conquest" (17, 16), and one has little doubt that she will. After all, the man who was "always" Archie to her, "just as I became Pony and not Anahareo to him" (6), is even more infatuated with her than she is with him.

When Anahareo describes Grey Owl, or more precisely Archie, she stresses that he is perceived by the people in the area as "a good trapper," which is noteworthy, since in fur country "praise of one man for another in that hardest of professions was given grudgingly" (1940, 18–19). But her fascination with Grey Owl has less to do with his aptitude as a woodsman, or even with his looks, than with his image, his reputation as an anti-authority figure who enjoys clashing with the police and who carries a revolver even in town. Initially at least, Anahareo falls in love less with the individual than with what he represents: "a gangster whose exploits at that time were more admired than they are today when International [*sic*] politicians have stolen their rôle" (7). As she elaborates,

> It was a strange coincidence that Archie should fit so well with the picture of a man that I was in love with at that time. Of course, that love of mine was a futile affair, as the object of my affection had been shot and killed fifty years before I was born. His name was Jesse James, a daring train-robber from Clay County, Missouri. Jesse James is the Robin Hood of America. Archie was no angel, but he certainly was no robber or anything like that. But there was no getting away from it that he gave the impression that he was liable at any time to sit right down and enjoy a good dish of human flesh. (29–30)

Grey Owl evidently is not the only member of the couple whose life is shaped by popular culture. Anahareo, too, allows Hollywood to decide her fate, including her choice of romantic partner.

Even though Anahareo was set "to attend a convent [school] in Toronto" (1940, 30), she alters her plans soon upon meeting Grey Owl. After her carefree summer at Camp Wabikon, formal education suddenly seems much less enticing than "the prospect of going into the depths of the frozen North with a real live Jesse James" (35). Still, it is apparent that Anahareo is not well prepared for life in the bush. For one, she is not used to the material privations that are part and parcel of trapping. Anahareo writes that when she was younger and accompanied her father "to make maple sugar or to pick berries in the autumn, he used to put up a royal lunch, and I expected, I was anxious, that this should be the same" (42). But she quickly discovers that Archie, like other trappers, travels very lightly. "Anyone who has always lived with a store near-by," she writes, "would starve on a trapper's diet" (42). Despite her background as a trapper's daughter, she clearly has little idea of what living in the wilderness entails.

No less significant than the material privations and the social isolation faced by Anahareo is the fact she does not seem to love Grey Owl the way he loves her. She is fascinated by the long-haired woodsman, especially because of his resemblance to her favourite outlaw, but he is enraptured by her. Early in the text, Anahareo states that she considers Grey Owl her "hero" (1940, 14) and, after she has to leave Temagami suddenly because of a death in her family and return home, she has the "urge to write and invite him down" (21). However, it is Grey Owl who takes the initiative and visits her, before he is asked to do so. It is also he who later sends her "a return ticket" so that she can join him in the bush, which she does after she promises her father to come back in a week and be "a good girl" (32). So thrilled is Grey Owl by the prospect of Anahareo being with him that he builds "a little cabin" just for her, which he names "Pony Hall" (35, 37). Before long, "very shyly, but with great determination," he professes his love for her (49). However, to his shock, she informs him that she does not share his feelings. As Anahareo explains to the reader—but apparently not to the man she has agreed to live with in the bush—although Grey Owl "had that Jesse James fascination still," the truth is that "I had never been in love before, nor was I in love with him then" (50). The situation between the two of them becomes so tense that Anahareo decides to fake her love for her companion. She says that every time Grey Owl leaves the cabin to go hunting, he tells her that he loves her. One day she determines to do the same and replies, " 'I love you, too,' " but Grey Owl is not persuaded. He shakes "his head sadly," and asks her " 'please not to say so until [she] really meant it.' " To which she adds, " 'It's beyond me how he could have cared for such a dumb-bell' " (51).

Anahareo's relationship with Grey Owl is further complicated by her religious beliefs and family obligations. Even though she is living in the wilderness with a man without the sanction of marriage, Anahareo continues to consider herself a dutiful Catholic. As well, she never forgets her father's warning that "if you come home now and not married to that man you will have a mighty lonely life here" (1940, 53). Her father assures her that his house will be "your home as long as I live," but he does not hide that whereas her brother "doesn't seem to mind" her lifestyle, her "sister is angry" (53), suggesting that Grey Owl may not be the only person who is pressuring her to marry him (see also McCall 2014, 200–1). Yet Anahareo remains unfazed, a reaction that at least one of Grey Owl's (female) biographers finds perplexing, given that it has not been that long since "couples who lived together before marriage were almost certain to create a scandal" (Gordon 2004, 59). In *My Life*, Anahareo states that she cannot see "what all the fuss [is] all about" and becomes even more opposed to the idea, telling Grey Owl that "I wouldn't go home nor would I marry him" (1940, 53). That is, her awareness of the opposition by the people around her just makes her more determined not to change her ways.

In fairness to Anahareo, it must be noted that her initial rejections of Grey Owl's marriage proposals are not determined solely by her feelings toward him; they also have a philosophical dimension. The reality is that Anahareo is sceptical about the idea of marriage as such. In their early days together in the bush, as she describes in *My Life*, she becomes irritated by the fact that when he talks to her it is usually to say that "he love[s] me," and that he keeps repeating the "same thing over and over again" (1940, 65). At one point, when Grey Owl declares his love for her for the umpteenth time, she replies bluntly, " 'I hate you,' " and acknowledges that at the moment "I actually thought that I did hate him" (68). But she then adds that soon after, she realizes that "each time that he went away my loneliness became more and more unbearable. And quite suddenly a most disturbing fact made itself known; the fact that it was lonesome, desperately so, for Archie" (69). She confesses that she begins to develop at least some empathy for Grey Owl, to strive to see the world from his perspective. Yet this new feeling is not enough reason to wed him. As they continue to live together, Grey Owl tells Anahareo, " 'I love you, and I mean it; and furthermore, I mean to marry you to-morrow' " (75). He even attempts to blackmail her by claiming, as Anahareo paraphrases him, that "he wouldn't take me North again unless I went as his wife" (76). Still, she will not be moved. She may feel that she has "written [her] own ticket to hell" by living with a man out of wedlock, yet as she informs him, "it didn't matter whether I cared for him or not, that I could never marry him or anybody else" (75). Again, her resolve not to marry Grey Owl reflects her rejection of the whole institution of marriage, even if her decision is coloured by her own apparent lack of passion for him.

Grey Owl gradually comes to accept that Anahareo does not feel about him the way he does about her. This seems to be underscored when she gently tells him that " 'I love you as much as I can' " (1940, 93). Anahareo even suggests that it is her consistent refusal to agree to "this splicing business" that leads Grey Owl to start "to drink" (104), which is unlikely, since he reportedly began indulging in alcohol soon after arriving in Temagami (Smith, 1990, 22). Nevertheless, he does not cease talking about his unrequited love for her. One time when she has been planning to move to a nearby town, she feels that she cannot leave him on his own because of his frequent inebriation. Grey Owl does not want her to stay, telling her, " 'You don't love me and it's plain that you don't want me. So why worry over what I do?' " (1940, 109). But at that moment, she realizes that "I wanted him more than anything in the world" and tells him that " 'I do want you.... And I love you' " (109), a response that seems to surprise her as much as it does him.

Following Anahareo's unexpected profession of love for him, Grey Owl takes her in his arms and the two at last appear to become one. Yet Anahareo's declaration remains a qualified one. Part of her reaction is probably informed by her finally becoming aware of the optics of living with a man to whom she is not married. As she writes, "I was light-headed to take the initial step of going into the woods with him without weighing in the balance what other people, not fully aware of all the circumstances, would think of such behaviour" (1940, 110). Still, she continues to be unapologetic about her actions, asserting that she has nothing to say about her role "in the strange adventures of those years," except to underline that "for the first time in my life I was free and in love. The life we were living seemed to me to be perfect, and marriage, from what I had seen of it amongst my own people, was a matter of cooking pancakes, making soup and wearing a chequered pinafore. I felt that I would die rather than submit to that state of bondage" (110). Again, even after she declares her love for Grey Owl, she admits that she does so, not because she believes in marriage, but in spite of the fact she does not.

Anahareo's transformation is nonetheless significant. Before long, she even begins "to think that to have a baby that looked exactly like Archie would be about the most heavenly thing to have," and draws "pictures of it by the hour" (1940, 115). Eventually, Anahareo and Grey Owl do get married. The two of them are invited the visit the Lac Simon band in Quebec, whose chief

and his wife happen to be celebrating "fifty years" of marriage (132). At the end of the ceremony, Grey Owl tells the chief, "Fifty years from to-day...,
Anahareo and I will celebrate our golden wedding," and so they get married (148). Needless to say, there is not a Catholic priest in sight.

Their marriage, though, does not eliminate the main problems that confront them. One of the challenges faced by Anahareo since moving to the bush is her isolation and loneliness. She observes that she is aware that solitude supposedly "holds a multitude of virtues" for some people, but clearly not for someone as sociable, and young, as she is. As she describes her early experience, "To young people, solitude is just another word for monotony. So the only lesson I learned during the lonely week at Pony Hall was that a person can practically choke with impatience without actually passing out" (1940, 59). Her loneliness is further exacerbated by her ambivalence about nature.
"I couldn't see anything in a tree," she writes in an unexpected confession for someone who would become renowned as an environmentalist, "except that it took a lot of them to make a forest, and what was a forest, anyhow? Just a lot of trees, nice to play in when you're a child, but now I was a grown up—phooey!" (67). She does not seem to be any more at home in the wilderness than she was in town with her family.

Given her solitude, it is not surprising that after they marry, Anahareo demands that Grey Owl let her to go to the neighbouring town of Rouyn, Quebec, "to work to help me forget my loneliness for him." But it is not until she threatens "suicide" that he agrees that "I ought to have something to occupy my time" (1940, 151). Before long, she joins Grey Owl on the hunt itself, an event that will have unanticipated consequences for both of them. Initially, Anahareo is excited about being out in the woods, stating that when they reach their first trap and notice "mink tracks circling all around but none going toward the set," she is terribly disappointed at the trap's "emptiness, for in those days I was ignorant of the tortures suffered by the animals caught in traps" (178). But she soon becomes aware of her growing aversion toward her partner's profession, a response that she believes is responsible for "the gap in our spiritual relationship" (178). Anahareo seems especially disturbed by the sight of a marten they catch, who has "clawed and gnawed" the trap house in a futile attempt to escape (178). She writes that she has never been able to forget the animal's "two unblinking eyes shining with pain and terror," which leads her to beg Grey Owl to spare the marten and "carry him home" (179). Grey Owl is "rightly puzzled at my inconsistency," she underlines; "one moment, as it were, I was all for killing; and the next I wanted to save a life." Thus, he ignores her pleas and, perhaps hoping that she will change her view again, strikes the marten. But as Anahareo writes, "the feeling of revulsion that overcame me was such as I cannot describe" (179).

Interestingly, Anahareo does not demonize Grey Owl for continuing to hunt, remarking that he is merely doing what every trapper does. She asserts that his decision not to spare the marten is to be expected, since "that is the way of the hunt. Killing is a business.... The main thing is that the hide must be preserved so that the value of it is not lowered" (1940, 179). While she regrets his choice, she understands it. Besides, Grey Owl is driven by economic considerations, even when she rescues two beaver kittens that become orphaned when their mother drowns in a pond after being caught in a trap. Anahareo thinks that the kittens will make "cute pets" but Grey Owl has other ideas, for "[l]ive beaver bring a larger price than dead ones" (183, 193). To her surprise, however, he will be no less affected than she already is by the two kittens, whom they later name McGinnis and McGinty. The extent to which Grey Owl is changed by the young beaver becomes evident when one of them, McGinnis, disappears. He frantically searches for McGinnis because he fears the kitten "wouldn't have a ghost of a chance if a hawk or an owl should spot him." The "concerned look" on his face as he speaks reveals to Anahareo that "it wasn't the price of the beaver that worried him, but that tiny handlike paws had begun to play a favourable tune on the good old heart-strings" (195). Grey Owl subsequently finds McGinnis by a creek but then refuses to sell the animal, even though he owes money to a dealer, who "can force us to turn the beaver over to him on that account" (206). In fact, so touched is Grey Owl by McGinnis and McGinty that he decides "never to trap beaver again" (211). This is of course a decision that will lead them to start "a small colony" so that they can "recolonise the country" with beaver (215), and which will change them forever.

Anahareo concludes *My Life with Grey Owl* with a rushed overview of her partner's life after he determines to rebuild in "Canada a magic forest where the hearts of man and beast might throb in harmony" (1940, 225). She notes his being hired as a conservationist by the National Parks Branch and the birth of their daughter Dawn. She also describes his success as a writer, notably with his memoir about their life together, which had "tremendous success...in nearly every country in the world" and elicited "thousands upon thousands of letters" from grateful readers (225). Yet she elects not to analyze how Grey Owl is influenced by McGinnis and McGinty, since "Archie has given so perfect a description of them in *Pilgrims of the Wild*, and his other books, that I have not the courage to writer further of their little personalities and to describe their moods" (185). Her own major insight into his conservationist epiphany is that it is linked not only to his coming to favour beaver over people but also to his great desire "to get as far away from the human race as possible" (224). For her, Grey Owl's conservationism would seem to be infused with a considerable dose of misanthropy.

There is something irredeemably anticlimactic about *My Life with Grey Owl*, not only because it necessarily ends with Grey Owl's death but also because, by then, the author had been "left far behind in the fight that Archie was waging" (1940, 226). Anahareo concedes that readers may feel that "there is something missing from my story," which she attributes to her having "crowded the story of our last few years into a few pages" (227). But she confides that there may be another reason for her abruptness toward the conclusion of her account of her days with Grey Owl, and that has to do with the fact her "story, if you would know, ended on a certain mid-summer night two years before he died" (227). In short, *My Life with Grey Owl* has a major structural flaw. The book revolves around Anahareo's relationship with the titular subject but, well before the end of his life, she is no longer part of his existence, an estrangement of whose "full cost" she would become acutely aware (Gleeson 2012, 174). Moreover, since Anahareo is supposedly the one who abandons the hero of her narrative, she likely fears that she is unable to tell the story without losing the sympathy of her readers. As she confesses, "How can I tell you of what happened without giving you the wrong impression?" (Anahareo, 1940, 228). Indeed, this apprehension seems to colour the whole narrative.

*My Life with Grey Owl* is a divided book. It is a memoir but, as the title suggests, it is less about the author than about her life with her more famous husband. In her very title, Anahareo acknowledges that her life is notable primarily because of her connection to someone else. No less important, she always had serious reservations about her writing skills, even stating that it was extremely difficult for any screenwriter to capture the essence of "a many-sided person" like Grey Owl when "all he has to go by is what he can glean from certain or uncertain biographies: The book 'My Life With Grey Owl' being the worst" (qtd. in Gleeson 2012, 214). But years later she became so outraged by an article on Grey Owl she read in a sensational magazine that she "threw the magazine across the room in disgust and said, 'that's enough of that bull-shit! I'm going to write a book and tell the truth about Archie'"

(qtd. in Gleeson 2012, 220), determined to achieve the second time around what she had failed to do the first time.

Anahareo's second memoir, *Devil in Deerskins: My Life with Grey Owl* ([1972] 2014), overlaps in many ways with her first one, as reflected in the fact that the latter's title has become its subtitle. But there are also notable differences between the two books both in emphasis and language, as is evident when one contrasts the opening of *My Life with Grey Owl* with that of *Devil in Deerskins*:

> Do you know the North, the land that is our land, the home of the Wilderness people? There are some who think it barren and monotonous. There is so much of it that perhaps it does seem depressing at first sight, especially if you see it from the windows of a train, and watch mile after mile of green and silver forest wall, broken only by an occasional lake, or by some outcrop of rock on which no trees can grow. (1940, 1)

> It was the Moon of the Windigo and the tamarack, sounding like rifle fire, cracked in the freezing night. The little black spruce were hunched and distorted, bent to the breaking point under their burden of snow. This was northern Quebec in midwinter, at midnight, and well below zero. ([1972] 2014, 1)

The writing in *Devil in Deerskins* is far more self-consciously Indigenous than in *My Life with Grey Owl*. Considering the author's turbulent relationships with her publishers, and their alleged interference, what remains unclear is which text, if either, captures the real Anahareo.

The most striking characteristic of *Devil in Deerskins* in relation to *My Life with Grey Owl*, as noted earlier, is that Anahareo emphasizes much more her championing of Grey Owl, downplaying her initial lack of interest in marrying him in particular and in marriage in general. There are other significant elements in her second memoir, though, not the least what can be at times rather critical accounts of Grey Owl's (and her own) trapping practices. For instance, early in *Devil in Deerskins,* Anahareo writes that "[m]ost trappers use strychnine to get wolves and foxes, and I regret to say that this included Archie and me" ([1972] 2014, 27). Strychnine is a highly toxic poison that can be fatal to both non-human animals and humans, and Anahareo knows well that "this is a dreadful thing to do," underscoring that "trapping is cruel." She further adds, "Those lovely ladies clad in their exquisite furs would faint if they were to see the pain and torture suffered by only one of the many creatures whose lives must be taken to make up that fur coat or stole" (27). But without referring to this passage, later in the text she notes that one of Grey Owl's earliest publications, "The Vanishing of the Wild," was written to lambaste a magazine article that advocated that "the Forestry Branch drop strychnine pellets from airplanes to destroy the wolves in Algonquin Park in Ontario" (101; see also Grey Owl 1930a, 321). It would seem that it was not only society ladies who were not always able or willing to examine the consequences of their practices.

Another compelling aspect of *Devil in Deerskins* is Anahareo's portrayal of Grey Owl's traditionalism about gender relations and his almost debilitating acrophobia. According to Anahareo, Grey Owl was so conservative that he did not allow her to carry even part of the load whenever they reached a portage. She writes that "Archie abhorred the sight of a woman doing a man's job. 'It's the surest way to emasculate a man,' he swore" ([1972] 2014, 77), articulating a view that later writers like M.T. Kelly would parody viciously in their representations of him, as we will see in the next chapter. Paradoxically, this most masculine of men also found it painfully trying to be a fire ranger. Fire rangers work out of small lookout towers and Grey Owl not only "hated being confined to that cubbyhole, as he called it," but "his fear of heights amounted to a phobia. It took all the willpower that he possessed to climb the 106-foot ladder, and he found it more frightening to climb down" (76). That is, Grey Owl's masculinity at times could be seen as an attempt to mask some deep insecurities.

Anahareo also details Grey Owl's practice of writing frequent—and long—letters. She states that during their courtship, there were periods when he sent her "a letter every day," and she now deeply regrets having "lost those letters," for "I would put them down here, and without doubt they would be the better part of this book" ([1972] 2014, 11). She amplifies that the letters "were all ninety or more pages—one was a hundred and four pages—and they were all interesting and imaginative" (12; see also Anahareo 1940, 31). Throughout his life, Grey Owl would remain an inveterate writer of letters to her, several of which Anahareo reproduces in her memoir. Tellingly, not only does she lose some of his letters, but she also acknowledges that she often did not reply to them, exposing the apparently asymmetrical nature of their relationship.

Perhaps most consequential, in her second book Anahareo claims that Grey Owl told her about his previous wives or lovers early in their relationship. She writes that soon after Grey Owl arrived in northern Ontario, he came in contact with the Bear Island Anishinaabe. On his way to the Cobalt silver rush, he ran out of food and water and was rescued by a white trapper, who took him to a nearby Anishinaabe village. There he was brought back to health by a "medicine man" named Old Ag-Nu and a "tall and slender" young woman called Angele ([1972] 2014, 44, 46). When Anahareo asks Grey Owl what happened to "Angele, the belle of Timagami," he replies, " 'I married her.' " Anahareo says that she was astonished at the news, since she "couldn't imagine Archie married" (49). But she must have recovered quickly, for he then informed her that Angele was not the only woman he had wedded. He disclosed that when he was "convalescing" from his war wound in Europe, he "met a dancer, fell in love, and married her" (52). Grey Owl supposedly even told Anahareo about his involvement with Marie Girard in Biscotasing and how he got her "to go into the Spanish River country with him for the winter" (53) the year the First World War broke out.

Anahareo's main purpose in writing that Grey Owl apprised her of his previous romantic relationships would seem to be either to emphasize the degree of intimacy between the two of them or to highlight her magnanimous attitude toward her husband's sexual history. She asserts that when Grey Owl told her that he had been married to a dancer, she was less hurt than impressed, since, as a teenager, she "had been as stage-struck as could be, and even now being with someone who had hobnobbed with a professional dancer was just too thrilling" ([1972] 2014, 52). While it is possible that Grey Owl confided in Anahareo about his serial marriages, the scenario does not sound too plausible. Even assuming that Anahareo was as understanding as she avers decades later, it is hard to imagine that Grey Owl would risk telling her about his earlier paramours and potentially reveal his English background. This is especially true in the case of Angele, who lived in the area and whom Anahareo could easily contact.

The more likely explanation for Anahareo's decision to have Grey Owl tell her about his previous wives is the book's structure. Although *Devil in Deerskins* is a memoir, Anahareo does not organize her second account of her life with the conservationist as she experienced it but in light of the posthumous revelations about his ethnocultural background. For instance, she relates that she first meets Grey Owl while she is "reading in the shade of the pines" at Camp Wabikon and spots "a man dressed in brown deerskins stepping with the speed and grace of a panther from a canoe" ([1972] 2014, 1). Anahareo is deeply affected by "this most striking man's appearance," and notes that it was "the first time that I set eyes on Archie Belaney, Englishman, trapper, and guide" (2). Her description of her future husband's nationality is curious, since she maintains throughout the book, as she does in her previous one, that she learned about his English background only after his death (176). So the real reason she fell for the wilderness Jesse James would seem to have had nothing to do with his (then unknown) Englishness.

Besides, there are other factors that suggest one should be sceptical about her openness regarding Grey Owl's sexual past. Despite her much vaunted un-conventionality, and ostensible lack of jealousy of her predecessors, Anahareo is extremely reluctant to describe the nature of her romantic relationship with Grey Owl, even after she joins him in the bush. Her frequent assertions that the two of them have "separate shacks" have led Gleeson to conclude that they lived chastely for two months (2011, 293), which is possible but appears out of character for such iconoclastic individuals. In any case, Anahareo is so reticent about her sexual relationship with Grey Owl that, in both of her books, it is difficult to discern when they become sexually intimate, making the appearance of their daughter, Dawn, a bit of a surprise.

There are actually indications that, by the time she wrote *Devil in Deerskins*, Anahareo had become quite concerned about social propriety. In her biography, Gleeson describes one telling episode. Following the publi-cation of her second memoir, a Toronto theatre company produced a play entitled *The Life and Times of Grey Owl* based on "material from Anahareo's book" (2012, 237). Anahareo was invited to the play's rehearsal and "watched the woman who played her as she sat, wearing a dress, with her legs apart. Dismayed, Anahareo strode up to the stage and closed the woman's legs. 'No lady would sit that way,' she explained, 'especially if she had on a dress.' Anahareo never wore a dress" (237). Even if Anahareo "didn't wear dresses, just slacks or breeches with boots," as her daughter Katherine Swartile testi-fies (ix), it seems evident that she came to see herself as a lady, which perhaps elucidates both some of the contradictions and the gaps in her memoir.

"Lady" is obviously a fluid term. But even Grey Owl, who was infatuated with Anahareo, does not tend to see her as genteel. On the contrary, he boasts in *Pilgrims* that his partner is so versatile that she "could swing an axe as well as she could a lip-stick" (1935, 17). There are certainly aspects of her behav-iour that do not appear to be exactly ladylike, starting with her propensity for alcohol. Anahareo and Grey Owl's daughter, Dawn, for example, wrote to the renowned Hollywood actor Ellen Burstyn that her mother "learned many things from her husband—she also learned that when you hit town, you painted it red" (qtd. in Gleeson 2012, 248). As well, after she met her future partner Bob Richardson, Dawn advised him not to have "too much booze around," since Anahareo "could be unpredictable with her words if she had been holding hands with Johnny Walker, or with Calona Royal

Red" (Richardson 2001, 17). Again, there is a discernible conflict between the Anahareo who writes *Devil in Deerskins* and her younger self, or selves.

Another aspect of her life that Anahareo likely finds difficult to reconcile with the more genteel image she wishes to project is her unorthodox social life, as befits "a spirited outsider who lived outside of the norms of social convention" (McCall 2014, 202). Gleeson tends to attribute any criticism of Anahareo's sex life to racism, for "any Aboriginal woman who exhibited behaviour unlike that of Euro-Canadian women was equated with a prostitute" (2011, 287). However, this interpretation is problematic, considering Gleeson notes that Anahareo's own sister, Johanna, did not approve of her sibling's "independent spirit and vigorous approach to life" (2012, 207), something Anahareo acknowledges in her first memoir (1940, 53). Gleeson is particularly dismissive of a newspaper story that insinuated that, while Grey Owl was doing his second British tour, Anahareo " 'had engaged in prostitution' " (2012, 168; see also Harvey 1965, 85; and Lavertu 2000, 78). Yet the fact is that Grey Owl himself expressed concerns about her public image.

In *Devil in Deerskins*, Anahareo admits that she knew her long absences were causing tensions with Grey Owl. First, she writes that during one of her extended prospecting sojourns, she took the advice of their mutual friend David White Stone "not to tell Archie what I was doing, because if he knew I was working with a bunch of men and living in the same camp, it would drive him crazy, and it was just as well that I didn't tell him" ([1972] 2014, 126–27). Later, she reproduces a letter from Grey Owl in which he leaves little doubt what he thinks her behaviour says about their relationship:

> Dear Gurdy, Your letter surprised me. After all, you've written only twice in five months.... Since you left without telling me that you were going, I should think that you'd have the grace to ask if you could come back...instead of telling me that you were.... I, too, would like nothing better than to drop everything and take off...but I have my responsibilities, and must face them, and I expect you to do the same. What I mean is, you've got to look after yourself, at least till I can catch up on my bills.... Your coming and going as you see fit puts me in an awkward position. I know exactly what they are thinking of me.... I used to think the same of John. His wife was an actress, who spent most of her time in New York, but she'd come and see John every once in a while, either between shows or to get her strength back (after all that city life). Anyway, we used to think that John was a sucker. ([1972] 2014, 160; ellipses in text)

In addition to underlining that Anahareo has not troubled to inform him of her whereabouts for months, Grey Owl appears to be suggesting that he has been forced to distance himself from her, since her actions indicate to him (and the world) that he is "a sucker." This view is reinforced when Anahareo receives another "long, sad, and reminiscent" letter from Grey Owl. It includes "a gift of twenty-five dollars, but…no invitation to return home" (165), at which point even she realizes that their relationship is terminally wounded.

No less significant, Anahareo concedes that it is not only Grey Owl who cannot compete with her desire to be a prospector; neither can their daughter. She writes in *Devil in Deerskins* that "I had the baby I had wanted so badly, whom I loved more than anything in the world, yet I had to fight an urge, almost unbearable at times, to go north again" ([1972] 2014, 156). Her awareness of the optics of her predicament even leads her to a rare moment of introspection. "Was I abnormal?" she asks. "I thought I was and worried till I was a nervous wreck—this is no exaggeration. The expression 'the call of the wild' is hackneyed and a joke with most people, but with me it was a disease, and by spring, 1934, I knew I would have to make one more trip— out there" (156). Richardson states that he and Dawn used to speculate that perhaps the reason Anahareo "didn't have a typical maternal nature" was that she "had been raised by her grandmother…a hundred years older than her" (98). Although her commitment to prospecting may show the extent to which Anahareo "defied the social norms of her time" (McCall 2014, 207), it also illustrates that ultimately, for her, prospecting trumped all, even motherhood.

Anahareo's lack of engagement with both her husband and their daughter highlights the key structural problems in *Devil in Deerskins*. Like *My Life with Grey Owl*, her second memoir is riven by her conflicting aims to be perceived simultaneously as an independent woman and as Grey Owl's "inspiration and his passion" (Cuthand 2007, 66), the woman who taught the great conservationist "to love the animals" (Gwendolyn MacEwen 1985, 76). It may be true, as the historian Grant MacEwan contends, that "without her convictions and influence, the world would not have heard of Grey Owl and he would have remained an obscure trapper in the Canadian backcountry" ([1975] 1995, 267). However, her own texts suggest that her influence was more as a muse than as a companion. As I have argued, Anahareo's prolonged absences during her prospecting expeditions call into question her commitment to the conservation of wildlife, notably the raising of iconic beaver like McGinnis and McGinty or Jelly Roll and Rawhide. But even her view of her role in Grey Owl's writing career seems contradictory. On the one hand, Anahareo claims that she encouraged her companion to write articles for various magazines, even threatening him that "if you don't send them, I will" ([1972] 2014, 99). Yet, on the other hand, she often complains how boring it is to live with a writer, "to be stuck with a zombie all winter" (144). Indeed, one of the reasons she gives for leaving Ajawaan for Prince Albert in the winter season is that she finds life there "indescribably dull" when Grey Owl is "wrapped up in his writing" (155). In other words, she simultaneously takes credit for making possible his writing career and bemoans that his writing keeps him away from her.

Some of the contradictions at the core of *Devil in Deerskins* are probably masked by the fact that, later in her life, Anahareo became a passionate defender of the rights of non-human animals. That is, she appears to have come to embrace the image that Grey Owl presented in *Pilgrims of the Wild*. As Grant MacEwan asserts, "Anahareo's finest hours" came long after the death of Grey Owl, "when she renewed with greater vigor her opposition to cruelty to animals" ([1975] 1995, 273). But those do not seem to have been her priorities during the period she lived with Grey Owl, when she was consumed by a rather different love: her determination to find deposits of gold and silver.

In her two memoirs Anahareo leaves little doubt that, throughout most of her life, her great passion was not conservation but prospecting. Thus, the question one has to address is why she would emerge as the champion of both Grey Owl and the beaver. The answer would appear to lie primarily in the portrait Grey Owl paints of her in *Pilgrims of the Wild*, as well as in the documentary films that he used to illustrate his lectures, which were strategically employed to convey the impression that he too was Indigenous. This would suggest that Anahareo as the world came to know her is, to no little extent, the creation of Grey Owl. After all, contrary to what many critics argue, Anahareo was not the source of Grey Owl's Indigenization but the opposite.

Anahareo remains a pivotal figure in Grey Owl's life and legend, but not for the reasons that are usually offered. It is true that Grey Owl became so closely identified with her in the mind of the public that it had a difficult time imagining him without her. No less significant, since Anahareo attempted to rediscover her cultural roots through him, she demonstrates that his ethnocultural persona was not evident to at least some Indigenous people, challenging the still widely held notion of Indigenous transparency. In the short poem that serves as the epigraph to this chapter, "John Tootoosis,

1936," Armand Garnet Ruffo writes, "An Indian can tell who's Indian./ Grey Owl can't sing or dance" (1996, 128). While it may be the case that Grey Owl could neither sing nor dance, Anahareo complicates the notion that Indigenous people can always identify who is and who is not Indigenous. Also, she appears to have been far from alone, since she writes that her own father not only thought Grey Owl "looked Indian" but "always called Archie the 'Wendigo'" ([1972] 2014, 9, 12). Thus, the fact some critics continue to insist that Grey Owl owes his "Native sensibility" to Anahareo (Relke 1999, 262) and that "Native peoples in Canada were certainly not fooled" by him (Egan 2004, 17; 2011, 73) suggests that they have not read her two memoirs. But then if most critics read Grey Owl rather than his books, this is even truer of Anahareo, notably those critics who profess to champion her.

# CHAPTER FIVE

# Life after the Death of the Author: The Posthumous Image of Grey Owl

*What do [the beaver] care who he married,*
*Where he lived, or of his people.*
*Whether he was Red or White man?*
*He belonged to no man's country*
*Save that of the Beaver People.*

—Sianu

Grey Owl died on 13 April 1938, but he would not be destined to simply join what, in *Sajo*, he had termed "the Great Majority" (xvii). Rather, he was about to start yet another life. Until his demise at the age of forty-nine, Grey Owl was known primarily for his metamorphosis from a trapper into a conservationist and for his nature writings. That, however, would all change early in 1938. No sooner had it been announced that Grey Owl had succumbed to pneumonia, possibly brought about by exhaustion from his demanding lecturing, than it was alleged that he was not of Scottish and Apache ancestry but "a full-blooded white man" (Smith 1990, 210). The North Bay *Nugget* newspaper had actually known about his true identity for some three years. Its reporter Britt Jessup had conducted an interview with Angele Egwuna in which she told him that Grey Owl was an Englishman named Archie Belaney and that she was "very definitely married" to him (Jessup 1971; see also Jessup 1973). Perhaps because the newspaper's city editor was "humanitarian and fair-minded," he filed Jessup's article and did not publish it until the day after Grey Owl died (Smith 1990, 210). The *Nugget's* revelations soon spread around the world, precipitating an international controversy that transformed Grey Owl from a beloved conservationist and nature writer into an impostor who had deliberately deceived his legions of readers and admirers.

The unmasking of Grey Owl seems to have been the materialization of J.C. Campbell's fears about the champion of the beaver. In a series of fascinating letters to his predecessor, M.B. (Mabel) Williams, the National Parks Branch publicist hints at some mystery about Grey Owl. On 20 March 1936, Campbell apologizes to Williams that "I cannot be as enthusiastic as you are over Grey Owl. There are things I know that I cannot write to you and my constant prayer is that there will be no outbreak that would cast discredit on the National Parks and those with whom he is associated" (1936b, 1). Then on 16 April 1936, Campbell confides that Grey Owl has informed him that "he had got practically above this beaver stuff" and that "from a National Parks standpoint you can count him out. The unfortunate thing about it is that while we know the truth now we will have to let him carry on if the Publishers [*sic*] so wish until such times as he meets his Waterloo" (1936c, 1–2). The suspicion is that "the truth" about Grey Owl that Campbell cannot share with Williams involves his ethnocultural background, but it may not have been. There were other secrets about Grey Owl that were being exposed, not the least his alcoholism and his polygamy. Instead of being the loyal mate of the beautiful Anahareo, he was now presumed to have had a series of wives, including an English one. As the London *Times* quipped in an editorial, "the strange bird seems to be acquiring as many birthplaces as Homer, as many wives as Solomon, and as many aunts as Sir Joseph Porter" (qtd. in Dickson 1938a, 37). So concerned were those close to Grey Owl about the never-ending stories circulating regarding his national origins and his romantic life that they decided to intervene in an attempt to counter them, none more passionately and assiduously than the redoubtable Lovat Dickson.

Horatio Henry Lovat Dickson was not merely Grey Owl's London-based publisher but also his main promoter; in fact, he probably had as much impact on the conservationist's image as Anahareo did (Eayrs 1938, xi). Although Dickson was born in Australia, his family had deep Canadian roots and relocated to Canada when he was a teenager, eventually settling in Alberta. He studied English at the University of Alberta, writing his MA thesis on the Renaissance English playwright John Lyly. Thanks to the support of his mentor E.K. Broadus, Dickson started teaching at both his alma mater and, during the summer holidays, at the University of California at Los Angeles. He appeared set for an academic career, especially after UCLA's president offered him a teaching position (Dickson [1959] 1975, 247). But there was one complication—the young lecturer discovered that he had "no vocation for teaching" (240). He neither enjoyed lecturing nor valued his scholarship, which he had begun publishing in academic journals. As well, Dickson had been dreaming for years of writing a great book, aspiring to be "a Dostoievsky or a Gogol of the Prairies" ([1963] 1976, 7). Consequently, when a Canadian mining magnate who had just acquired London's *English Review* offered him the position of "assistant editor" ([1959] 1975, 254–55), he promptly accepted.

Dickson arrived in London early in 1929, at the age of twenty-five, and immersed himself in the British capital's literary scene. He became friends with promising young writers, such as Charles Morgan, V.S. Pritchett, and the brothers Alec and Evelyn Waugh. Besides his editorial duties, he also started "writing book reviews," prompting a major U.S. publisher to hire him to look for important new books for the United States market (Dickson 1973, 2). Dickson proved adept at identifying new literary talent and, before long, his friends began suggesting that he open his own publishing house (Dickson [1963] 1976, 87). With considerable trepidation, given his knowledge of the financial risks involved, less than three years after moving to London, he resigned his position as a magazine editor and founded "Lovat Dickson Limited" (91). His company would become quite successful, publishing "nearly four hundred books" in its first seven years of existence (181). Not surprisingly, it did not have great sales right away. Indeed, while Dickson opened his publishing house in 1932, he felt he only "became a publisher" in 1934, which he came to see as his "*annus mirabilis*" (149, 156). The main reason for that turn of events was that Grey Owl sent him his memoir *Pilgrims of the Wild*, a book that Dickson boasted made him "a great deal of money" (163).

Dickson seems to have begun publicizing Grey Owl almost from the moment he agreed to become his United Kingdom publisher. Even before the appearance of *Pilgrims*, he printed an essay by Grey Owl in the December 1934 issue of his quarterly, *Lovat Dickson's Magazine*, titled "The Wilderness Awakes." In a footnote to the text, he informs readers that Grey Owl's memoir will be published the following spring and that the author is "a North American Indian" (qtd. in Grey Owl 1934, 670). Then, in a subsequent issue of the periodical, which styled itself "A Magazine for Thoughtful People," he publishes a laudatory review of Grey Owl's memoir. According to the text, *Pilgrims* is "a romantic book, and its very origin is a romance in itself…. If there is any parallel to this achievement of a half-breed Indian, writing under appalling difficulties hundreds of miles from civilisation, building on his vocabulary by listening to the wireless, I do not know it" ("Literary" 1935, 116). The piece's unidentified author, who is likely Dickson, adds that Grey Owl "has the sure touch of the born writer" and has "already won international celebrity of a fleeting kind" thanks to his numerous appearances in magazines, newspapers, and films. The writer further asserts that, "unless I am much mistaken, this book will give him fame of a more enduring nature, as the author of one of the most moving and delightful books about animals and humans ever written" (116). Yet in another issue of his magazine, Dickson includes an excerpt from Grey Owl's memoir, entitled "How Anahareo Had Her Way," in which he once more introduces his author, whom he describes as having been "a trapper, a guide, a sniper in the Canadian Army, and is now an officially-appointed Protector of Wild Life in a vast reserve in North-Western Canada" (qtd. in Grey Owl 1935a, 322). That is, Dickson's readers may be uncertain whether Grey Owl is of mixed race or Indigenous, but they are left with little doubt that he is not only an accomplished writer but also one whose work derives from a life full of achievement.

Moreover, Dickson's promotion of Grey Owl was not restricted to his own journals. In 1936, the year after the publication of *Pilgrims*, he wrote a comprehensive profile of his author for the prominent London magazine *Strand*. Titled "Grey Owl, Man of the Wilderness," the article focuses particularly on the subject's lack of formal education and on his Indigeneity. Dickson states that Grey Owl was born in "an Indian village in Mexico" to "a white man and an Apache woman." But while he is "part white, he never remembers this. He grows up an Indian in mentality and physique. The Indians teach him their way of life, and from his earliest youth he is hunting and trapping with the braves" (1936, 64). His education is fully traditional, which explains why, as a youngster, he is "completely uncivilized in the sense that he has never lived in a town, never been to a school, and for the greater part of his life has lived only under canvas or the open sky." Grey Owl is "no saint," though, and seemed destined to have ended his life as "he had begun, as a hard-living, reckless half-breed" (64). What transforms him is, of course, his meeting Anahareo, "the daughter of a line of Iroquois chiefs" and the catalyst for "the great revolution that was to change Grey Owl from a hunter and trapper into the Protector of Wild Life, which is the official title he has in Canada to-day" (73). Thanks to the impact of the regal Anahareo, writes Dickson, Grey Owl has become "the only Indian ever to have influenced thousands of people, and to have made a mark in the world of English letters. Fame and wealth are open to him, with his writing and lecturing, but he has chosen to return to that lonely spot in the wilderness" (74). So Grey Owl is notable both for his metamorphosis from a trapper into a conservationist and for his achievements as an "Indian" writer. His ostensible Indigeneity is crucial for Dickson. He contends that most people are searching for that something that gives their existence "meaning," and that "[t]he answer may be anywhere, but it is likeliest to be where man and animal and all natural life are closest in accord

with one another" (74). In short, the source of humanity's potential salvation is a return to nature, and no one is closer to the natural than Indigenous
people such as Grey Owl.

While Dickson would emerge as Grey Owl's greatest champion, the relationship between author and publisher was a symbiotic one. The burgeoning
man of letters often stresses the irony that he moved to London to become a
literary figure, yet the key event in his publishing career did not originate at
either Oxford or Bloomsbury, two places where he was spending much time,
but back in the Canadian Prairies. As he relates in *Wilderness Man*, "from the
adjoining province to mine in Canada, Saskatchewan, came a manuscript that
was indirectly to make my fortune and change the whole course of my life.
That script was *Pilgrims of the Wild*" (1973, 3). Dickson openly admits that
Grey Owl became his "first money-maker" (230), and that "the sales" of the
latter's books "had transformed Lovat Dickson Ltd. just as much as—perhaps
even more than—it had transformed Grey Owl" (247). The publisher's focus
on money may explain why Campbell questions his motivation for championing his author. In a letter to Williams on 2 December 1935, Campbell
charges that Dickson's activities really amounted to "a case of highly specialized commercialism, endeavouring to get all the benefits possible under the
guise of conservation and helping Canada" (1935, 1). Campbell also states
that he does "not believe for an instant that Grey Owl has any idea of the
game [Dickson and his people] are playing" (1). But by mid-April 1936, he
claims that "Dickson didn't understand Grey Owl and Grey Owl succeeded
in putting it over him like a tent" (2), making one wonder which interpretation is correct.

In any case, Grey Owl's books did not become international bestsellers
merely because they were compelling. The fact is that Dickson was instrumental in promoting both the author and his works. Hugh Eayrs, Grey Owl's
Toronto-based publisher and the individual who introduced Grey Owl and
Dickson to each other (Dickson 1973, 230), states that "Mr. Dickson's abili-
ties and expertise as a publisher and in matters of the lecture platform were
responsible not only for Grey Owl's extraordinary rise to best-sellerdom
but also for two personal lecture tours in the British Isles" (Eayrs 1938, xi).
Dickson even used Grey Owl as a bit of a guinea pig in an "experiment"
that revolutionized the way books are promoted. In the mid-1930s, he had
"discovered that the average life of a general book is only about two months.
After that time the demand for it sinks to a whisper. The book is crowded
out by hustling youngsters, most of whom are born only to suffer presently
a similar fate" (Horwill 1935, 23). Upon coming across "the program of an

American lecture agency," he deduced that "it might be worth while to adopt a similar method" in Great Britain and decided to ask Grey Owl to tour the country (Horwill 1935, 8).

In addition to his roles as Grey Owl's British publisher and lecture organizer, Dickson contributed tremendously to the promotion of Grey Owl through the numerous publications he devoted to the author. This is especially true after the latter's death. Dickson's unrelenting championing of Grey Owl actually became rather complicated in the aftermath of the revelations about the conservationist's European origins, since many people suspected that Dickson was "in on the hoax" (Dickson [1963] 1976, 179). Consequently, Dickson had to shift his strategy from promoter to defender of Grey Owl. He writes in "The Passing of Grey Owl" that for "ten hysterical days" immediately after the death of Grey Owl, the media seemed determined to utterly nullify the accomplishments of "a noble and self-sacrificing life" (1938b, 13, 14). Perhaps even more critical, the sales of Grey Owl's books dropped precipitously. As Dickson apprises Eayrs in a four-page letter dated 9 May 1938:

> I know you are right, Hugh, in thinking that eventually this will make no difference to Grey Owl's books as a property, and, as always, I am willing to take your advice. There is this point, however: if I had not put up the fight that I did and managed to bring it about that the final conclusion was that the question of Grey Owl's identity must always be left in doubt, I believe the books would have suffered. For the first week or two after his death the sales stopped absolutely dead. There was not a quiver from the trade. Aside from the loss that one suffers in the death of a successful author, I foresaw the devaluation of the large stocks of Grey Owl's books which we are carrying. I had to keep the ball rolling and not to let Grey Owl go out in a blaze of sensationalism in the press and marked as a fraud. (Dickson 1938c, 1–2)

Dickson adds that he is "not afraid of what the public would think, but of what the educational authorities would think…. If they suspect fraud they simply won't have the books, and that would mean not only the stoppage of the sales of Grey Owl's regular books in these quarters but also do great harm to the anthology we have planned" (2). Again, there is a strong pecuniary interest in Dickson's defence of Grey Owl.

Still, Dickson remained certain of Grey Owl's Indigeneity. As someone who claimed he "knew half-breeds," since he "had seen them and talked to them often in the Alberta foothills country" ([1963] 1976, 162–63), he was positive that Grey Owl was of mixed ancestry. So Dickson became determined to prove it, confidently proclaiming, "'The biggest hoax I ever heard is that Grey Owl was a hoax'" (qtd. in Halton 1938, 8). In 1938, he edited a collection of essays titled *The Green Leaf: A Tribute to Grey Owl*, which comprises a series of letters from Grey Owl; epigrammatic statements by him that supposedly constitute his philosophy; and his 1937 address to the children of Great Britain, which the BBC refused to broadcast. As well, the volume includes a long introduction by Dickson; excerpts of the press coverage following Grey Owl's death, and "The Lament of the Beaver People," the poem by Sianu from which I have borrowed the epigraph to this chapter. Dickson states in a prefatory note that since the volume is "a requiem for Grey Owl," he does not discuss "the question of his origins, except for one passing reference that the editor's indignation and the context of his sketch could not avoid" (1938a, 5). Once more, his reading of the public proved correct. Dickson writes years later that he "printed 100,000 copies of *The Green Leaf* as a pamphlet at, I think, threepence a copy: they melted away within a day or two" (1973, 268). Intriguingly, Dickson names his introductory chapter "The Passing of Grey Owl," which could refer either to the death of the conservationist or to his "passing" as a member of an ethnocultural group to which he was not biologically related.

At that point Dickson clearly must not have believed that Grey Owl had tried to "pass" as someone of mixed Indigenous and European ancestry, for the following year, 1939, he wrote a biography called *Half-Breed: The Story of Grey Owl*, a book designed to vindicate the author of *Pilgrims of the Wild*. To that end, as discussed in the previous chapter, Dickson even invited Anahareo to England to meet Grey Owl's mother in the hope that she "would, or could, detect in her a drop of Indian blood" (Anahareo [1972] 2014, 183). He almost certainly also had a hand in the telegram that Anahareo sent to the London *Times* in the early days of the controversy, meant to "help us all to be properly ashamed of the howls of 'hoax', 'fake', 'imposter', and the rest which have shattered the peace of a great man's newly made grave" (qtd. in Dickson 1938a, 38). However, Dickson's continued assertions that Grey Owl was a "half-breed" were firmly challenged by two elderly English women, Ada and Carrie Belaney, who contended that he was their nephew Archie Belaney and that they had raised him. Dickson, at first, ridiculed the Belaney sisters. But after they allowed him into their home and showed him numerous photographs of their nephew as a youngster, as well as copies of books and notebooks with his handwriting scribbled on them, he was forced to concede that Grey Owl and Archie Belaney were one and the same, and likely had no Indigenous ancestry.

*Half-Breed* is a highly problematic book. Like many other biographers, Dickson felt compelled "to make drastic excisions" in his manuscript "in order that the feelings of people still living might not be hurt by references that might have been taken to reflect on them" (1939, vii-viii). The book's most critical flaw, though, is structural. Dickson had designed his text as a defence of Grey Owl's account of his life but, by the time he finished writing it, he had been persuaded that Grey Owl and Archie Belaney were the same person. Thus, while he may still believe that Grey Owl's "achievement...is beyond comparison with anything except that of T.E. Lawrence who, by a coincidence, was born in the same month of the same year" (viii), he cannot help but entertain serious doubts about the veracity of crucial elements of the narrative he is assembling. This uncertainty probably explains Dickson's decision to attempt to make "a living picture of Grey Owl" by presenting "not a transcription but a dramatization of his life. While he stresses that "I have not introduced any event which has not a foundation in fact," he writes that "I have in some particulars, in order to round out my picture, dramatized the event by the use of dialogue and description" (viii). For a biographer, Dickson is just not convinced about the truth of some of the "facts" he presents.

Yet his ultimate discovery that Grey Owl was a white man from Hastings, England, does not lead Dickson either to question his accomplishments or to dissociate himself from him. In fact, in 1973, some thirty-five years after the death of his once prized author, Dickson produces another biography of him entitled *Wilderness Man: The Strange Story of Grey Owl*. In his new work, which one Grey Owl scholar describes as "spellbinding" (Mitcham 1981, 58), Dickson admits that *Half-Breed*, which was "written hastily in 1939 under the shadow of war..., was a lop-sided book," given that it was "a passionate defence of Grey Owl's integrity against the charges of 'fraud' and 'impostor', and in its single-mindedness, it missed the essential man" (1973, 268). Actually, the most significant aspect of *Wilderness Man* is not what it reveals about its subject but about its author: the fact that Dickson had misread Grey Owl.

Throughout his second biography of Grey Owl, Dickson dwells at some length on how one of the consequences of all the revelations about the conservationist's non-Indigenous past is that they were "destroying the whole myth on which his appeal to the English public had been based" (1973, 5–6). Furthermore, it is evident that it is not only Grey Owl's reputation that is being negatively affected by this development but also that of his promoters, notably Dickson. As he states, "The saint was fast being turned into a mountebank. I had so long been devoting myself to this man and his books that automatically I began to spend as much time in defending him as I had done promoting him. I became his sole champion. I could not believe that he had deceived me" (6). His recognition of Grey Owl's true identity is extremely painful to Dickson, since he had believed that "our relationship had been more than that of author and publisher. We had been brothers" (254). More than anyone else, Dickson had been the person who provided Grey Owl with an international stage to present his work as "a poet, recreating for us dreams of innocence," and to give "lectures [that] sang the glories of the past when the earth was untrammeled by the yokes by which men in search of wealth enslave their weaker kind and hold them captive to their jobs in cities" (241). Still, he finally cannot help but accept that he, too "had been duped. There was no Arcadia" (255), underlining that he did not really know Grey Owl.

The dilemma for Dickson is that he has always associated Grey Owl's conservationism and knowledge of wildlife with his reputed Indigeneity. For instance, in *Wilderness Man* he writes that the success of *Pilgrims of the Wild* "would depend on its having been written by a man of Indian blood, long inured to the woods and knowing very little about civilization" (1973, 200). Or, as he elaborates, "It was essential if his message was to be taken seriously that it should seem to come out of the Wilderness, to be the very voice of the Wilderness; and the figure he created for this purpose, simply to emphasize the message, was that of the untutored half-breed, who is now and then conscious of the presumptuousness of such a despised voice carrying so tremendous a message" (201). The social geographer Alastair Bonnett observes that in Dickson's writing "the term 'half-breed' was transformed over the generations into *Wilderness Man*" (2000, 95). Considering that Dickson had always depicted Grey Owl as the wilderness personified, on the assumption that the author was partly Indigenous, he is now compelled to argue that Grey Owl is able to capture the essence of Canadian nature, even though he possesses no Indigenous ancestry. To phrase it differently, the Indigeneity that supposedly was inextricably linked to Grey Owl's acute understanding of nature is now not essential at all. So Dickson has to reverse his stance on the connection between Indigeneity and ecologism, which explains some of the intellectual pyrotechnics in his two biographies.

Dickson's scholarship on Grey Owl has been largely eclipsed by the work of the historian and biographer Donald B. Smith, particularly his 1990 biography *From the Land of Shadows: The Making of Grey Owl*. Smith, whose research was widely used in *Wilderness Man*, as a grateful Dickson acknowledges (1973, 267), has emerged as the dean of Grey Owl scholars. All subsequent studies of the champion of the beaver—including this one—rely extensively on his meticulous research, not the least the numerous interviews he conducted with people who knew Grey Owl in an attempt to discern what motivated him to pretend to be Indigenous. Smith's eminence in the field is reflected not only in the frequency with which he is cited but also in the fact that he is often asked to introduce the work of other writers on Grey Owl and his associates (Billinghurst 1999, viii–ix; Richardson 2001, 3; Gleeson 2012, iii–iv). Still, even without taking into account their lively style, Dickson's writings on Grey Owl remain foundational. After all, Dickson does not merely document the life and work of the trapper-turned-conservationist. In a profound way, he shapes the author's image. Especially since so much of the discourse on Grey Owl has been influenced by Dickson, he has become an intrinsic part of the story of his most popular author.

❑     ❑     ❑

Like the biographies, the literary representations of Grey Owl began to appear during his lifetime, and they too were profoundly affected by the revelations that followed his death. As Gordon Snell captures the impact of the exposure, in a poem written at the turn of the twenty-first century, "those who'd praised him to the skies/Now scorned his masquerading lies" (2001, 219). Snell is not one of those individuals for, echoing the filmmaker Richard Attenborough, he contends that Grey Owl's ecological vision trumps his imposture. As Snell writes, "It was a worthy dream he dreamed:/ A peaceful world where Man would be/ To Nature, friend—not enemy" (219). That said, the death of Grey Owl is a pivotal point in his literary and cultural image, precipitating some vitriolic portrayals of the man who had struggled so valiantly to camouflage his British origins. Yet what is most striking about the representations of Grey Owl is that they have never been uniform, as negative and positive views of him always seem to coexist.

Grey Owl became the subject of both a literary work and a scholarly study as early as 1935. That year saw the publication of *Grey Owl and the Beaver*, a monograph by Harper Cory. A fellow of the Canadian Geographic Society, Cory travelled to Prince Albert National Park to meet Grey Owl and was enthralled by the conservationist, whom he describes as being "dressed in a suit of buckskin heavily fringed with leather laces, and with his long glossy hair braided," a "striking person [that] might have been conjured out of the pages of Fenimore Cooper's *The Deerslayer*" (1935, 21). But what he considers most significant about Grey Owl is not his romantic persona but his work, his uncanny ability to make people aware of the urgency of saving wild animals, especially the beaver. "Trapping will continue while there is a demand for furs," writes Cory, "but the public conscience has at last been awakened by Grey Owl: there will be little more callous trapping of animals during the breeding season, and, just in time, the Beaver People have been saved from extinction" (109).

Also in 1935, the Toronto writer and editor Eric Gaskell wrote a poem entitled "The Pilgrim (a tribute to Grey Owl)," which appeared in the influential (but now defunct) magazine *Saturday Night* and which makes little effort to camouflage its admiration:

> The silences rejoice for him: and where
> Green, undetermined leagues of forest spread
> Life moves with a primeval urge. O there
> No cringing law evokes the ancient dead.
>
> To laugh at Man's unfortunate estate!
> Blue vistas languish for the seeing eye
> Beyond the beaten trails; and there, elate.
> The proud stars, in their orbits, keep the sky. (B1)

As the poem concludes, "He has kept faith: cool forests, virgin streams/ Bequeath him the dark knowledge of their dreams" (B1). The Pilgrim Grey Owl has shown his fellow human beings how to live in nature. Now it is just up to the rest of us to follow his lead.

If there were any doubt how Gaskell felt about the conservationist, he dispels it the following year with his essay "Grey Owl: Pathfinder and Artist." Published in the *Canadian Bookman*, the magazine of the Canadian Authors Association, the essay posits that Grey Owl's books are not only "redolent of the soil of Canada," but for many readers they "have come as a strong voice crying in the wilderness, urging Canadians to take a more intelligent and far-seeing interest in their great heritage" (1936, 1). Gaskell describes Grey Owl as "a patriot," "the divinely gifted interpreter of the Northland, mystic and beautiful; the stalwart champion of the Little People of the Forest, who have found in him a friend" (5). Grey Owl is significant both because of the way he writes and of who he is. "The Voice of the Indian long silent in the land of his fathers," states Gaskell, "is at last raised in an impassioned plea for a better understanding of the red man's philosophy," for "a spokesman has arisen whose solemn duty is to interpret for us the saga of the Northland—'to convey to the White Man, before it is too late, something of the spirit of a vanishing race'" (2). Grey Owl's value as a writer is thus inextricably linked to what he (ostensibly) represents.

In retrospect, one is tempted to self-righteously dismiss assessments such as Gaskell's as being irreparably tainted by essentialist Eurocentrism. But it might be wise to bear in mind that Gaskell was hardly alone in linking Grey Owl's knowledge of the Canadian landscape and wildlife to his purported Indigeneity. On the contrary, reactions like his were the rule rather than the exception. For example, in 1936 the celebrated photographer Yousuf Karsh was so determined to photograph Grey Owl that, for the occasion, he organized a party in Ottawa to which he invited a group of prominent writers, journalists, and politicians. "At the appointed hour," Karsh relates, "they all turned up, in high expectations and hearty appetite—all, that is, except Grey Owl" (1978, 68). After the party, he found a drunken Grey Owl at his hotel bar. But that in no way lessened the celebrity photographer's desire to capture the conservationist's image for posterity, which he did by portraying him as a dashing but enigmatic desperado, with long hair under a broad leather hat. Some four decades later, Karsh conceded that his fascination with "the gaudy imposter" had been "a serious mistake" (68). Yet he rationalized his response by arguing that Grey Owl's disguise could not "diminish his achievements as one of Canada's earliest conservationists.... He did much to convince the nation that [the beaver] must be protected from man's greed and folly. In that sense he was an imposter but, I like to think, a prophet." Karsh further underlines that his subject's "chiseled features and lustrous black hair must deceive anybody ignorant of his real origins" (68; see also Tippett 2007, 120, 123). Again, whatever one may think of him now, Grey Owl looked the part.

Moreover, Karsh's visual representation of Grey Owl had already been preceded the previous year, 1935, by an equally adulatory work by the Belfast-born society painter Sir John Lavery. Titled *Portrait of Grey Owl*, the painting presents a severe-looking Grey Owl in full Indigenous regalia, including two eagle feathers in his braided hair and an intricately beaded buckskin jacket—it was used on the cover of a booklet that Dickson assembled to promote the second British tour, *Grey Owl: A Biographical Note and A Day at Beaver Lodge*. Then, in 1936, Grey Owl was sketched by Arthur Lismer, one of Canada's iconic Group of Seven painters (James 2006, 14). Lismer's drawing was part of the sketches he did of writers and other artists that he met at Toronto's Arts and Letters Club. But likely because Lismer mistook Grey Owl for the long-dead painter Tom Thomson (Grigor 2002, 39), there is an unmistakable sadness about him. It is as if Grey Owl is anticipating his death, or already feels that he is no longer among the living.

Also in 1936, Grey Owl was the subject of a comprehensive article by T.D.A. Cockerell, which appeared in *Natural History* and was illustrated with several photographs. An English-born zoologist, Cockerell was a long-time professor at the University of Colorado who is perhaps best known for his work on North American bees. "A Visit with Grey Owl" documents his circuitous trip from Boulder to Ajawaan Lake with his wife, the botanist Wilmette Porter Cockerell. As Cockerell explains, two years earlier his wife had "obtained one of the moving picture films, put out by the Canadian Parks Administration, showing Grey Owl and his beavers," which was exhibited "to many thousands of people, in Colorado, California, and Wyoming, and was very popular" (1936, 223). That film was followed by others, as well as by Grey Owl's books, which captivated the two scientists. After showing "Grey Owl on the screen innumerable times, we thought it would be very interesting and worth while to see him in his environment, and so have a more vital sense of his personality and work" (224). The Cockerells not only travel all the way to Grey Owl's sanctuary but even spend a "night in Anahareo's cabin, up on the slope of the lake." They see "the famous beavers, Jelly Roll and Rawhide, and [watch] them do some of the things we had shown so often in the pictures." In addition, they have "a delightful evening talking and telling stories, and discussing the prospects of Grey Owl's lecturing tour in England, for which he was getting ready" (225). Cockerell concludes that regarding "the purely scientific results of the journey, it is too early to say much" (226). Yet there is little question that he is fascinated by both the personality of Grey Owl and his experiments in conservation. Indeed, in the booklet promoting Grey Owl's second tour of Great Britain, the one bearing the Lavery portrait on the cover, Dickson includes a photograph of Cockerell reading to Grey Owl, Anahareo, and his wife at Ajawaan (see *Grey Owl: A Biographical Note* 1937).

While Cockerell does not dwell much on Grey Owl's ancestry, he fully accepts that the conservationist "had a Scotch father and an Indian mother" and that he was "adopted by the Ojibway Indians, to whom he owes his name Grey Owl, given because of his habit of traveling about at night" (1936, 223–24). The novelist L.M. Montgomery, similarly, fails to recognize Grey Owl's ancestral origins. In her journals, Montgomery describes a luncheon at Toronto's Press Club in November 1936 held in honour of Grey Owl, who looked "quite the Indian of romances, with his long black braids of hair, his feather head-dress, and a genuine scalping knife—at least he told us it was genuine" (Montgomery 2004, 112). Montgomery found herself sitting between Grey Owl, to whom she had not been introduced, and her nemesis, William Arthur Deacon. Arguably Canada's most influential literary critic at the time, Deacon openly disapproved of her work and during the function ignored her and talked only "to the lady on his left." Isolated between the two men, Montgomery ate in silence. Then, as dessert was about to be served, she "heard Grey Owl's voice at [her] shoulder. 'You are a woman after my own heart.'" When she inquired why, he responded, "'*You don't talk*'" (2004, 112). Grey Owl delivered "a very interesting talk on beavers," and Montgomery had the task of thanking him. As she did, she related hearing an "owl's laughter" in the town where she lived north of Toronto. At this point, "Grey Owl sprang up, and exclaimed: 'You are the first white person I have ever met who has heard owl's laughter. I thought nobody but Indians ever heard it. We hear it often because we are a silent race. My full name is Laughing Grey Owl'" (112; see also Rubio 2008, 486). In another entry just over a year later, Montgomery writes: "'Grey Owl' is dead—and the papers are full of an exposure of his 'fake.' He was not an Indian at all but a Cockney Englishman! I always felt certain he was not pure-bred but I did think he had some Indian blood in him. He was certainly clever to hoodwink the world as he has done. And his love for animals was real" (2004, 247). Incidentally, Montgomery's date is incorrect; the entry says 12 April 1938, but Grey Owl died the following day, 13 April.

Montgomery's description of her encounter with Grey Owl is noteworthy not only because of the playful manner in which it conveys the bestselling novelist's view of the conservationist and author but also because it clashes dramatically with another well-known writer's depiction of a literary party with Grey Owl at the time. In "Grey Owl: Language of the Eyes," a chapter in his memoir *A Literary Life: Reflections and Reminiscences 1928–1990*, the novelist Morley Callaghan writes about meeting Grey Owl at Toronto's York Club in the 1930s, when he reportedly was able to divine the latter's true identity through what he terms "the language of the eyes" (2008, 61). Callaghan notes that today we know that "Grey Owl, a remarkable man, had become an Indian in thought, word and deed, although he was an Englishman without a drop of Indian blood." But this was not the case in the 1930s, when he was allegedly turned into "a nine-day wonder" and "was accepted as a native Indian, his book was widely read, and there was great local pride in him" (62). Callaghan's characterization of Grey Owl as "a nine-day wonder" is curious, given that he became the most popular Canadian writer of the decade, "both at home and abroad" (Lucas 1965, 376; see also Smith 1971, 162). No less perplexing is his suggestion that Grey Owl had published only one book. Grey Owl began to be feted only after he became associated with Lovat Dickson with the publication of *Pilgrims of the Wild*, his second book.

126126 Apostate Englishman

*126*     *Apostate Englishman*

Moreover, the same year *Pilgrims* was released, he also published *Sajo and the Beaver People*, a text that as we have seen at least one established critic—E.K. Broadus—compared favourably to Callaghan's own work. In other words, perhaps there were more personal reasons why Callaghan was compelled to forget how prolific Grey Owl had become.

In any case, Callaghan relates that his epiphany about the beaver man's identity occurred during the dinner. As Grey Owl turned his head to talk to his neighbour, he appeared to become aware that he was being observed by Callaghan, who describes the scene in detail:

> His eyes met mine in just one glance, a swift but full meeting of the eyes. My own eyes shifted away. I can't know what went on in him; but for me—just for me—there came a moment of certainty; it came from reading the language of the eyes, a thousand words in the exchanged glance. For me, there was recognition of him. Inwardly, though surprised, I was satisfied with my private recognition: there was no Indian blood in him. He was an Englishman.
>
> When the dinner party broke up Hugh Eayres [*sic*] said to me, "Well, what do you make of Grey Owl?"
>
> "An interesting man. But he's not an Indian."
>
> "He is an Indian. Don't say that."
>
> "His eyes."
>
> "His eyes?"
>
> "Our eyes met." (2008, 63)

Callaghan's account of what transpired that night at the York Club would be considerably more persuasive if it had been published before the revelations of 1938, as opposed to seventy years later, in 2008. Still, even then, his response would seem problematic, for Callaghan is opposing Indigenous essentialism with another kind of essentialism, an ocular one. After all, how is it that he is able to identify that Grey Owl has English eyes, as opposed to Canadian, American, or especially British? Considering that Grey Owl/ Archie Belaney was of mixed Scottish and English ancestry, should not his Scottish heritage manifest itself somewhere? Indeed, in light of his ethnocultural background, Grey Owl would appear to be Sean Connery's worst nightmare: a bona fide Brit.

Besides its belated publication, Callaghan's version of his discovery of Grey Owl's true ethnocultural background through eye language is not convincing because, as Callaghan remarks, "Why should an Indian have it written on his skull and in his face that he is an Indian?" (2008, 63). Besides, the main reason that Callaghan's "Grey Owl: Language of the Eyes" invites scepticism is that such insights proved so rare during the conservationist's life. The only two recorded exceptions were the Winnipeg critic W.T. Allison, as discussed earlier, and the Oxford ethnologist Geoffrey Turner. A "lifelong student of the North American Indian," Turner was flabbergasted when he attended a lecture by Grey Owl at the Oxford City Hall and he greeted the audience in Sioux rather than his adopted Anishinaabe or his native Apache (Smith 1990, 125). Yet even Turner would soon be won over by the visitor. "My heart sank," Turner wrote in his diary about his introduction to Grey Owl. "But as he got going the Hiawatha stuff vanished and we got down to the real Grey Owl—a man of acute perception, poetic feeling & whimsical humor, and an ardent faith in his mission of wild life conservation...fascinating" (qtd. in Smith, 1990, 125). One cannot help but speculate what might have been the ethnocultural and political factors that led so many people in the 1930s to believe that Grey Owl was able to capture the essence of Canadian nature because he was of Indigenous descent. But judging by the textual records, believe it they did, none more passionately than the journalist and writer Lloyd Roberts.

The son of the renowned poet and animal story writer Charles G.D. Roberts—who himself not only made a pilgrimage to Riding Mountain National Park in 1931 but even had his photograph duly taken with Grey Owl and Anahareo (Grey Owl 1932a, 91; Smith 1990, 108–9)—Lloyd Roberts became familiar with Grey Owl through the latter's early writings in *Forest and Outdoors*, to which he was also a contributor. The younger Roberts actually paid a direct role in the conservationist's writing career. Through a friend who worked at the National Parks Branch, he became aware of a book manuscript by Grey Owl—almost certainly the text that became *The Men of the Last Frontier*—for which his friend "wanted advice on...its publication" (Roberts, 1937, 2). Roberts learned that Grey Owl had already submitted the manuscript to a British publisher and it "had been accepted on terms that Shylock might have blushed to offer." When he read the contract, "with the audacity born of sad experience," he decided to take "the law into my own hands and cabled repudiation of the contract, signing it 'Grey Owl.'" Roberts then wrote "a long letter to the publishers, demanding fair royalties for book rights and reserving all other rights, and enclosed it with an explanatory letter to Grey Owl." As he underlines, he "breathed easier" after he "received his reply" (2). Grey Owl was so grateful for the stranger's unsolicited intervention that he invited Roberts to visit him and Anahareo at their new abode on Lac Témiscouata, solidifying what would become a mutually prized friendship.

Roberts was a correspondent for the *Christian Science Monitor*, and his trip to Témiscouata resulted in "Beaver Finds Visitor 'All Right' and Demonstrates Logging Art," a *"delightful account of Grey Owl and Gertie Grey Owl and Jelly-Roll and Rawhide and the rest,"* which introduced the Boston newspaper and its readers to the "unknown and unassisted" Grey Owl, who was "waging a defensive warfare on behalf of the few remnants of the once powerful beaver people" (1931, 1; italics in text). Later, he paid another visit to Grey Owl and Anahareo at their "commodious two-roomed log cabin in the heart of Riding Mountain National Park," which was quite a change from the "deserted lumber shack" the couple had occupied in Quebec (1). Roberts does not merely talk with his "friend" Grey Owl about his work with the beaver, but takes part in it. Grey Owl asks Roberts to join him on a past-midnight jaunt to feed the beaver and then informs the journalist that he believes " 'you are the first white man to watch a wild beaver working at night' " (2). Thanks to Grey Owl, Roberts thus becomes directly engaged in wildlife conservation.

The closeness of the relationship between the two men is reflected in the fact that Grey Owl would include an excerpt from a poem by Roberts as the epigraph to the "Mississauga" section of *Tales of an Empty Cabin* ([1936] 1999, 115) and Roberts would write a thirteen-part radio series for the Canadian Broadcasting Corporation (CBC) called "My Friend Grey Owl." But Roberts's most compelling account of his association with the champion of the beaver is "Grey Owl—the Man," a fascinating essay that was rejected by the *University of Toronto Quarterly* in 1937 for not falling within the journal's "scope" (Brown 1937), and which to my knowledge has not yet appeared in print. Roberts opens "Grey Owl—the Man" with the observation that occasionally one meets "someone who stands up" above the crowd, "like a steeple over houses." One such individual, he writes, is "Archie Belanie [*sic*], 'Grey Owl' the Indian half-breed, my latest discovery" (1937, 1). While Grey Owl has meanwhile become well-known, when Roberts "first met him, in the Temiscouata wilderness, he was entirely unfamous, little more than just another bush Indian." Their encounter was a propitious one, since it occurred soon after Grey Owl had "renounced hunting and trapping—his chief means of livelihood—and, like Saul, had seen a great light and suddenly become the ardent champion of those he had persecuted to the death. Like Paul too he took up the pen in their defence" (1). From the moment he starts to read the work of Grey Owl, Roberts is intrigued by both his "style and subject matter."

As he explains, "The style was, and still is, a bit ornate and sentimental, his sentences sometimes ungrammatical and smacking of the backwoods (which I rather liked), but the art of capturing and holding the reader from beginning to end—the rarest and most essential of all the arts—was there in fullest measure" (2). For Roberts, Grey Owl has the uncanny ability to create the impression that he is "a voice crying in the wilderness to dull ears and money-blinded interests" (2). His is a natural voice, arising out of the land itself.

If Grey Owl's writing seems authentic to Roberts, this is even truer of his persona; he is natural man incarnate. In "Grey Owl—the Man," Roberts describes the first time he sees Grey Owl in Témiscouata, in a much-cited passage that reveals more about him than it does about Grey Owl:

> He was waiting on the station platform and I instantly recognized him, being the first Indian that really looked like an Indian—an Indian from those thrilling Wild West days of covered wagons, buffalos and Sitting Bulls. The stamp of his fierce Apache ancestors showed in his tall, gaunt physique, his angular features, his keen eyes, even in his two braids dangling down his fringed buskskin [*sic*] shirt. (1937, 3)

Considering that Roberts was born in New Brunswick in 1884, and spent most of his life in the eastern half of the continent, his idea of what constituted a real Indian likely owed more to the popular media than to any first-hand knowledge of Indigenous people. So it becomes immensely ironic that his meeting with Grey Owl leads him to conclude that "[f]ew whites feel that kinship with nature that is innate in the Indian" (5). Even though Grey Owl tells him that he is "neither white nor red, only a half-breed," Roberts insists that because of his host's Indigeneity, "[t]o him animals and birds are as much entities as are humans, and in many ways higher in the scale of being" (5, 6). Needless to say, such impressions could not help but be profoundly shaken by the revelations that this voice that had supposedly emerged naturally from Canada's wild soil was born in Hastings, England, not to an Indigenous family but to parents of English and Scottish stock.

▫  ▫  ▫

Once Grey Owl was exposed following his death, writers and other commentators inevitably had to address his ethnocultural imposture as they pondered his legacy. In "The Lament of the Beaver People," her contribution to *The Green Leaf*, the pseudonymous poet Sianu writes that the hearts of all "Beaver People" are "sad and lonely/ At the news of Grey Owl's passing." But she stresses that they do not care about his origins or how many wives he had, since "He belonged to no man's country/ Save that of the Beaver People" (1938, 8). Sianu's sentiments, though, were not universally shared. People's outrage at being misled by Grey Owl was real. His readers clearly felt betrayed, deceived by an author they had come to love, given that most of them seem to have linked his ecological insights to his ostensible ancestral background. Yet this sense of injury, as we have seen with Dickson and Montgomery, was often tempered with admiration for his achievement as a conservationist, especially considering that he was not Indigenous.

One person who was not very forgiving toward Grey Owl was the Nova Scotia novelist Thomas Raddall. Also a native of England, Raddall migrated with his family to Canada as a child. In his short story "Bald Eagle," which was first published in the *Saturday Evening Post* in 1940 under the title "Bald Eagle 'Iggins," he portrays the transcultural metamorphosis of one Grey Owl–like character named Selby Higgins. A London orphan, Higgins early on develops a taste for "the penny shockers," particularly "tales of the Wild West." Thus, when at the age of eighteen he happens to attend a recital by the poet Pauline Johnson, in which the "handsome red Indian woman recited poems that breathed the air of the Canadian woods," he is deeply affected. Higgins leaves "the hall filled with visions of a savage and delightful life in the woods beyond the sea" (Raddall 1945, 26) and decides to move to Canada to live with Indigenous people. His plan is to travel to Western Canada. But after he lands in Halifax, he realizes that he does not have enough money for the train fare and settles for a nearby "green forest" (28). He eventually attaches himself to a group of Mi'kmaq people, speedily learning their "ancient tongue," and transforms himself into Bald Eagle (30). Since trapping is no longer economically viable, he builds a cabin in the woods and starts to write "Indian" poetry, which gains him international fame.

The characterization of Selby Higgins is openly satirical, but Raddall seems to be even more critical of Bald Eagle's audience than he is of the rhymester. As he writes early in the text, "Selby never stole a thing in his life, and if he practiced to deceive it was a charming deception, a rather magnificent deception, and the public had good value for its money" (1945, 26). Like Grey Owl in his books, in his early days in Canada Higgins does not usually declare that he is "an Indian. People looked at him and his wares and jumped to the obvious conclusion. One might almost say the deception was thrust upon him, but there is no denying he played up to it and revelled in it" (31). That is, the audience is complicit in the imposture. Raddall's narrator suggests as much when he states that, years later, Bald Eagle told him that "white people are easily deceived anyhow. The truth is that they know nothing of Indians. After three centuries of white contact the Micmac remains as aloof and mysterious as ever" (31–32). The general lack of knowledge of Mi'kmaq culture perhaps explains why people around the world would come to perceive Bald Eagle's "Lament for Summer" as authentically Indigenous:

> *On Blomidon behold the hunter's moon!*
> *This night is pricked with frost, and crisp the leaf*
> *Dies underfoot, and Kwemoo the mad loon*
> *Disturbs the shadowed water with his grief*
> *At summer's passing.*

> (Raddall 1945, 36; italics in text)

By the end, as the narrator reflects on the curious career of Bald Eagle, he remarks that "this is the most amazing thing about him—that man could be so blind" (46). Again, one should be more incensed with the multitude of readers who turn someone like Bald Eagle into a literary phenomenon than with a writer who simply takes advantage of people's gullibility and lack of cultural literacy.

One of the most dramatic scenes in the story occurs during the poet's tour of England. Bald Eagle gives a recital at a London theatre, where he declaims a dozen of his compositions. The show, in which he is accompanied by "the most brilliant young pianist" in the British capital, is "a tremendous success." But as Bald Eagle reaches the conclusion of his sensational "Warpath Song," there is much commotion in the hall, as a woman shouts: "'That's 'im! That's my 'usband, Selby 'Iggins! I'd know 'im in a million!'" (Raddall 1945, 42). The woman, who stands between a boy and a girl, charges that Bald Eagle married her "durin' the war, 'e did, and went orf and left me with two children on me 'ands, and not so much as a soldier's farewell!" (43). Magnanimously, the poet tells the audience to let the woman approach the stage and speak to him. When she does, he says serenely, "'I am *Wo-bu-lot-pa-jit*, Bald Eagle,'" and then asks if she believes he is anyone else. Interestingly, the woman suddenly becomes confused and responds, "'I-I dunno,' she faltered. 'You don't look the same, some'ow…. Not you. You're a bloody Injian all right. I never saw you before'" (44). In other words, even the woman Bald Eagle possibly married during the war, and with whom he had two children, appears to concede that he has undergone not just a major cultural metamorphosis but also physical one.

Still, it is hard not to notice the animus toward the protagonist in the story. Raddall fails to convey what is Higgins's motivation for transforming himself into an Indigenous bard and sage, beyond showing that it is not money. But he leaves little doubt about the "Indian" poet's hypocrisy. Bald Eagle cultivates the image of being someone who is at home only in the wilderness, far from people. Yet the text tells us that his rustic "cabin of peeled pine logs" not only overlooks a series of "Indian huts" but can be seen from "the motor road" (1945, 34)—something that, in truth, is far more reminiscent of Henry David Thoreau's *Walden* than of Grey Owl's cabins. Similarly, when Bald Eagle travels around North America, he likes to visit Indigenous communities with "press photographers and newsreel men" in tow, so that they can witness him "bestow[ing] largess on his less fortunate brothers with a generosity that was real if rather public. But once, in the Oklahoma oil fields, he found Indians richer than himself and left in disgust" (38). Again, Bald Eagle does not stand for anything; he is definitely not the champion of either Indigenous people or animal rights. With him, it is all for show.

Admittedly, the name of Raddall's protagonist is not Grey Owl but Bald Eagle. However, there are so many parallels between the lives of the two characters that it is hard not to believe that Bald Eagle is a stand-in for Archie Belaney/Grey Owl (Dudar 1991, 120–21). Even the fact that Bald Eagle writes sentimental nature poetry, as opposed to autobiographical and documentary prose, seems designed to undermine Grey Owl's literary achievement by association. Moreover, Raddall has confessed that Bald Eagle is really Grey Owl. In response to a query by a CBC research assistant about the background of his story, Raddall replies that it was only because of "libel" that he was forced "to deny that 'Bald Eagle' has anything whatever to do with 'Grey Owl,'" since the law "places an author utterly at the mercy of anyone, scrupulous or otherwise, who chooses to identify himself or herself with a supposedly fictitious character." In that letter he also asserts that when Grey Owl arrived in Canada, "he came to Nova Scotia, took to the Indian life, and was living amongst the Micmacs near Bear River when the First World War broke out" (1947, n.p.). These are claims that he revisits in "Grey Owl," a monograph-length article he writes in the 1960s (1968, 101–3, 154), but for which there is no persuasive evidence.

A few figures like Raddall notwithstanding, Grey Owl appears to have largely vanished from the world's consciousness between the late 1930s and the early 1960s. As the journalist and writer Gordon Winter jests, "The establishment, in England as in Canada, does not enjoy being taken in" (1988, 235). It is only in the Decade of Love that interest in both the man and his writings resurfaces, and it has not abated since. But even in the 1960s, this recovery is gradual, as we can see in Alice Munro's 1968 collection *Dance of the Happy Shades*. The title story has the protagonist relive her experience with one Miss Marsalles, a piano teacher who every year presents her pupils with "stiff-backed, unread" books that she must have found in "the basements of second-hand stores," tomes such as "*Northern Lakes and Rivers, Knowing the Birds, More Tales by Grey-Owl, Little Mission Friends*" (216). Margaret Atwood notes that by this time "Grey Owl was no longer even a scandal, but had dwindled into an outmoded prop of shabby gentility" (1995, 51). He seems to have simply vanished from popular discourse.

One of the works responsible for the rediscovery of the conservationist was "Grey Owl: Mysterious Genius of Nature Lore," by the U.S. novelist Robert Cantwell. Published in 1963 in *Sports Illustrated*, of all places, the long essay reveals a certain laxity with details about Grey Owl, including usually referring to his "Irish" beaver, not as McGinty and McGinnis but McGinty and "McGuiness" (114, 116). But Cantwell is rather perceptive when it comes to Grey Owl's impact as a writer, both in terms of his style and his sales, reflecting the fact he generated "exceptional reader response." As he stresses, such sales "were remarkable figures for books on two counts: Grey Owl's were nature books, which rarely approach bestseller status, and they were selling in the early 1930s, when the world-wide depression was at its worst" (113). For Cantwell, Grey Owl's popularity was especially surprising, since his "reaction to success was to head for the woods. Probably no author in the history of literature ever showed such a marked distaste for publicity, parties, interviews, flattery and the other rewards that go with writing bestsellers, as did Grey Owl at that time" (113). No less significant than his sales is his style. Cantwell contends that Grey Owl's greatest achievement is "the individualizing of wild animals." While there are "false notes and flat passages" in his writings, even those seem "appropriate and rather touching," given the author's constructed background. That is, Cantwell considers Grey Owl's work as a whole "a bold and original creation" (119), suggesting that it is time to go past the controversy about his imposture and reappraise him as a writer.

In his short 1965 essay "Hommes et bêtes" (Men and animals), the aforementioned Quebec man of letters Jean-Charles Harvey also leaves little doubt that he deems Grey Owl an important writer. Harvey first met Grey Owl in

Témiscouata in 1930 when he was the editor of the Quebec City newspaper *Le Soleil* and, by 1937, he had dedicated his short story "La mort de l'orignal" (The death of the moose) to Grey Owl and Anahareo (28). He is clearly proud of his connection with the "*très cher et très sympathique imposteur*" (very dear and very nice impostor) (85), boasting that he was the first journalist who introduced the conservationist to the world. Yet what really matters to Harvey about Grey Owl is that he is the author of "*livres inoubliables*" (unforgettable books) (85). In short, the conservationist deserves to be remembered not because of the controversy surrounding his life but because of his writings.

The appreciation of Grey Owl's writing continued into the 1970s, as reflected in Donald Smith's essay " 'Grey Owl,' " his initial contribution to a field in which he would attain eminence. " 'Grey Owl' " was published in the journal *Ontario History* in 1971, and the first thing one notices about it is that throughout the piece the then doctoral student Smith places the name of his subject between quotation marks, as if he is not certain whether Grey Owl has the right to his chosen name. Still, regardless of how Smith may feel about the legitimacy of Grey Owl's claim to his moniker, there is little doubt what he thinks about the writer behind the name. He opens his essay with the declaration: "It seems strange that young dissenters in Canada have not yet caught on to 'Grey Owl' " as one of their national "folk heroes," along with the revolutionary doctor Norman Bethune and the political mystic Louis Riel (1971, 161). Smith finds this state of affairs both perplexing and regrettable, since he believes that " 'Grey Owl,' English-born or not, was a great Canadian. His defence of the Indian people, and his concern for our environment, merit him a respected position in our history" (175–76; see also Lucas 1965, 376–77). Smith holds Canadian literary scholars largely responsible for what he considers the severe underestimation of Grey Owl. "Until very recently," he maintains, "he was totally dismissed as a serious Canadian writer, and today is usually omitted from University [*sic*] English Canadian literature courses" (1971, 175). His assessment is echoed years later by A.W. Plumstead, who claims that the most conspicuous example of the way "the Canadian academic establishment" has ignored Grey Owl is that he is "not represented in Bruce Litteljohn's and Jon Pearce's 1973 anthology, *Marked by the Wild: An Anthology of Literature Shaped by the Canadian Wilderness*" (1997, 55; see also Litteljohn and Pearce 1973, 11). This is obviously a situation that Smith wishes to rectify, closing his essay with what appears to be a battle cry to other scholars to pay attention to the fact that " 'Grey Owl' is Canada's greatest Northern writer" (1971, 176), to say nothing of his achievement as a conservationist.

Whether Grey Owl is "Canada's greatest Northern writer" is debatable, since many critics would not consider him a Northern author. He certainly does not write about the High North, only the Near North of Ontario and Quebec and, to a lesser degree, the Prairies, what have been called the "provincial Norths" (Simpson-Housley and Williams 2002, 15)—although in 1914 the editors of his native town's newspaper introduced his article "An Old Hastonian amongst the Indians," by stating that "Bellaney [sic] is a forest-ranger" in Canada, "and seems to be snowed up for most of the year somewhere in the Arctic Circle" (1914, 6). That said, considerably fewer people would dispute his achievements as a chronicler (or mythologizer) of life in the Canadian wilderness. Thus, in 1972, James Polk includes Grey Owl among the three authors to whom he devotes his book *Wilderness Writers*—the others being Ernest Thompson Seton and Charles G.D. Roberts. Polk explains that the creator of McGinty and McGinnis deserves to appear in such a study, for "Grey Owl's incredible story, as an English boy who grew up to be a world-famous Indian author, lecturer, and champion of the Canadian beaver, is itself a modern legend of the wilderness" (1972, 15). No less important, that same year the filmmaker Nancy Ryley produced *Grey Owl*, a fascinating one-hour television documentary about the conservationist's life and career, which was broadcast on the CBC. Written by Dickson, using Smith's research, the film presents a series of interviews with people, both Indigenous and white, who had known Grey Owl. It notes at the outset that "within twenty-four hours of his death" the subject "was accused of perpetrating the greatest hoax of this century," but the focus remains very much on his accomplishments as a conservationist and writer. As we are told twice by the narrator in the opening section, Grey Owl was "the best-known Canadian Indian of his day" and "the most celebrated Indian of his day." His disguise, suggests Ryley's " 'documentary mystery' " (Page 1979, 130), simply seems to have been necessary in order for him to be able to accomplish his mission.

The most unusual portrayal of Grey Owl during this period, however, is unquestionably Robert Kroetsch's novel *Gone Indian*. Published in 1973, the same year as Dickson's *Wilderness Man*, Kroetsch's text is a satire of the quest novel. It details the ribald misadventures of one Jeremy Sadness, a PhD student at an upstate New York university who flies to Edmonton for a job interview at the University of Alberta, "that last university in that last city on the far, last edge of our civilization" (5)—and, incidentally, the institution where this study was produced. While Sadness arrives at the Edmonton International Airport, he never shows up at the interview. Part of the reason may have to do with the fact he is a professional student who has been in graduate school for almost a decade and has not yet managed to complete his dissertation. Even more likely, he appears to have little interest in an academic career. Thus, when he is asked by a Canadian customs officer why he is travelling to Edmonton, he does not mention the potential job. Instead, he responds, " 'I want to be Grey Owl.' " Or, as he elaborates, " 'Grey Owl. I want to become—' " (6). We gradually learn that Sadness has been obsessed with the conservationist since he was a boy growing up in New York City and a neighbour, a tailor who lived across the hall from his mother's apartment, introduced him to the "books of Grey Owl; one by one, he brought them. Unfolded them. Unveiled them. He gave me his dream of the European boy who became... pathfinder...borderman...the truest Indian of them all" (99; ellipses in text). As he later confides to his PhD supervisor, the only issue in the world that captivates him is, "Why did Archie Belaney become Grey Owl?" His own view is that Belaney was someone "who died into a new life." The conservationist may have "faked" his death, Sadness argues, but "he woke up free nevertheless" (65). In short, the metamorphosis of Archie Belaney into Grey Owl suggests not only the possibility of self-transformation but also of mental awakening and emancipation.

Kroetsch is best known for his postmodernism, being described by the influential critic Linda Hutcheon as "Mr Canadian Postmodern" (1988, 160). His novels usually eschew such realist conventions as linear narratives and reliable narrators. *Gone Native* is no exception. To begin with, Alberta is not Grey Owl country; it only borders it. More important, while the text focuses mainly on Sadness, it is mediated through a third party, R. Mark Madham. A native of "those wind-torn prairies, on the ripped edge of that northern forest" (Kroetsch 1973, 13), like Kroetsch—who also taught for years in upstate New York—Madham would seem to possess a certain degree of authority. This is especially true since he is Sadness's supervisor, and it was he who "arranged for him the job interview" (5). But this is not necessarily an act of mentorial solidarity, for Madham makes little effort to camouflage the fact that he is having an affair with his student's wife, Carol. In the very opening section of the novel we are told that, during Sadness's absence in distant Alberta, Madham likes to drive Carol to the local zoo. Sometimes, they simply watch the caged bison. Other times, though, they imitate the "great beasts" and begin "to frolic...on all fours" (2). As well, it is implied that Madham himself may be an impersonator, who abandoned his wife and daughter in Canada and assumed a new identity in the academic world of New York. So readers have valid reasons for being sceptical about the truthfulness of the narrative. As

Madham quotes Sadness after he arrives in Canada, "This is a peculiar land, Professor. Illusion is rife" (8), a statement that is true of the novel as a whole.

Nevertheless, there is one aspect of Kroetsch's novel that is difficult to ignore, and that is how Sadness is treated in Alberta because people believe he is Indigenous. Following a series of increasingly improbable situations after his arrival in Edmonton, Sadness heads away from the city and ends up at the 27th Annual Notikeewin Winter Festival. Later, he is swarmed by a group of white men because they suspect he is from "the Hobbema Reserve" (1973, 95), an actual Indigenous community south of Edmonton now named Maskwacis. Sadness says that he does not quite know why one "guy hit me," but the text leaves little doubt about the reason: " 'You fucking Indian,' a voice said." This is repeated: " 'You fucking Indian,' he said. He swung again. 'You come in here you want trouble, you fucker, I'll give you some fucking trouble' " (97). Significantly, a Cree musher he has befriended not only confirms that the strangers beat up Sadness because "[t]hey took you for an Indian" but even adds, "You look like an Indian" (99). Regardless of what one may think of Sadness's desire to become Grey Owl, "the truest Indian of them all" (84), it is evident that his aim is not without negative consequences, making one wonder why anyone would elect to place himself in such a position.

In light of his postmodern playfulness, it is difficult to discern how Kroetsch feels about Grey Owl and his supposed ethnocultural transformation. But that is not usually the case with most writers on the subject, whether they approve of or loathe him. In a long 1978 essay called "Grey Owl," the novelist Howard O'Hagan writes that his eponymous subject was, "quite literally, a 'self-made' man" who "had four wives and was probably a three-time bigamist" (100). In his felicitous phrase, "Marriage, instead of binding" him to a "place, propelled him away from it" (105). Yet O'Hagan contends that there was justification for Grey Owl's "masquerade," which was "purely beneficent in its purpose and effects. He not only impersonated an Indian, he became one to such a degree that his true identity was lost in the process. Until, finally, he *believed* himself to be one. He was a man with a message. Only by being an Indian could he speak forthrightly for them and for their 'little people,' the beaver" (101). O'Hagan does not deny that Grey Owl misled people about his origins, especially his wives or common-law partners, but he remains convinced that a real transformation did occur. As O'Hagan encapsulates his position: "An actor? Of course. Playing a part? He was living it. He *was* Grey Owl. No Indian would speak of 'illimitable forests.' He would take them for granted. Few white men would have the effrontery to use 'us' in such a context. But the speaker was neither red nor white. He was Grey Owl, Archie Belaney's imaginary man" (117). O'Hagan, who wrote mostly about the Rocky Mountains borderland between Alberta and British Columbia but who travelled widely around the world, considers Grey Owl not only separate from Archie Belaney but as the latter's imaginative creation. This is the reason he states that on 13 April 1938, a man died "who had never, in fact, been born" (99). More important, for O'Hagan, the ability of Archie Belaney/Grey Owl to fashion a literary landscape of his own is the most incontestable proof of his triumph.

In sharp contrast, the following year, 1979, the literary critic Colin Ross produces an essay in which he not only is unable to see anything positive about Grey Owl but completely demonizes him. The opening sentences of "The Story of Grey Owl" give a fair idea of how Ross feels about both the conservationist and his place in the Canadian imaginary. "Once upon a time," he writes, "there was a pervert called Grey Owl, who lived in the Canadian woods. He is famous because he came to Canada and learned how to imitate the Indians—he wore a disguise and grew his hair long" (79). Ross seems more troubled by the way Canadians supposedly view Grey Owl than by the beaver man himself. He maintains that the reason Grey Owl is admired in Canada is not only that "Canadians have so few heroes" but also that "[h]is books are such a relief for them. When they read his books then they're not afraid of nature anymore—Archie makes them feel that nature is tame and friendly and safe" (79, 80). According to Ross, Grey Owl is particularly popular with "Canadian ladies," who "may live in Canada, but they don't like Canada—they don't like the cold, they don't like the bears, they don't like the lonely prairies, they don't like the forest" (79). Therefore, the appeal (and sin) of Grey Owl is that he makes natural Canada safe for Canadians, something Ross presumably deems some kind of perversion.

A far more favourable portrait of the conservationist is sketched by Allison Mitcham in her 1981 book *Grey Owl's Favorite Wilderness*. A novelist and literary scholar, Mitcham clearly admires her subject, whom she considers a "Canadian Thoreau" (7; see also Mitcham 1983, 24, 30). She asserts that rather than being a mere imitator of the author of *Walden*, Grey Owl had a much deeper engagement with the wild than did his American antecedent. As she emphasizes, in clear juxtaposition to Raddall, "Grey Owl's Wilderness was hundreds of miles from civilization, instead of a stone's throw from Concord or later Bangor" (10). Perhaps even more significant, Mitcham appreciates Grey Owl as a writer. She describes his four books as "delightful and memorable" (9), which perhaps explains why she intersperses copious quotations from his writings throughout her monograph. Also, in a footnote, she remarks that when she "taught briefly some years ago in Edinburgh's famous Royal High School, the school which Sir Walter Scott and so many other famous men once attended, Grey Owl was the only Canadian writer on the curriculum! And with the boys of the first form (aged 13), he was perhaps the most popular" (15). Ross notwithstanding, an international bestselling author must have appealed to more than nature-fearing Canadian ladies.

Like other scholars, Mitcham maintains that, even though Grey Owl wrote most of his books during his sojourn in Prince Albert National Park, the landscape that most affected him was that of northern Ontario, "the land radiating from Temagami and Bear Island, as well as that emanating from Biscotasing" (1981, 19). Grey Owl's love of northern Ontario seems to be reciprocated by its inhabitants. During her travels through the region, Mitcham discovers that not only are various commercial enterprises named after the conservationist, but some locals go as far as to claim that his grave is there. "Even our Indian guide," she writes, "informed me solemnly that this was indeed where Grey Owl was buried" (23–24), despite the fact it is common knowledge that he was interred at Ajawaan Lake. One especially compelling section of Mitcham's book is her interview with Grey Owl's oldest child, Agnes Belaney Lalonde. Not surprisingly, Agnes is ambivalent about "her remarkable and unpredictable father," a man "whose talents and teasing, happy visits and prolonged absences evoked in this daughter feelings of pride and love interspersed fleetingly with sadness and even exasperation" (51). Still, she testifies to her English-born progenitor's immersion in Anishinaabe culture, asserting that Grey Owl "watched everything my mother and the rest of our people did very closely—watched unblinking like an owl" (qtd. in Mitcham 1981, 55). In particular, he made remarkable progress learning the Anishinaabe language. Agnes states that she was told by her mother, who "did not speak English at all" when she met her future husband, that "they did not talk much at first—of course. But soon my father learned to speak the Indian language fluently—so fluently that he spoke it better and faster than most Indians!" (qtd. in Mitcham 1981, 55). Again, unless one dismisses the testimony of his and Angele Egwuna's daughter, it would appear that Grey Owl's Anishinaabe transculturation was far from being superficial.

This perceived acculturation perhaps explains why a respected literary scholar like Leslie Monkman considers Grey Owl "a living successor to [Pauline] Johnson as 'Indian' littérateur" (1981, 99), which is striking, given that Johnson had Indigenous ancestry and he did not. But then Monkman suggests that Grey Owl appealed to Canadians both because of his purported Indigenous heritage and his ecological consciousness. "Canadians of the thirties knew that the wilderness existed," he writes. "In Grey Owl, they found a potential guide who could also tell them how to save it" (99). Monkman further asserts that we should not downplay the extent to which the author's allure lay in his authenticity, not as an Indigenous person but as someone who was intimately familiar with the world about which he was writing. "By basing his narratives on his own experience," states Monkman, "Grey Owl became a questing knight in this romantic landscape and offered his readers and audiences the vicarious thrill of sharing his adventures" (99). This is especially true since he has such a positive view of the human relation to nature. After all, "Grey Owl the conservationist speaks for harmony rather than control and manages to add to ecological theory the promise of 'wild romantic beauty and adventure'" (100).

Gwendolyn MacEwen, too, offers a sympathetic depiction of the conservationist in her 1985 short story "An Evening with Grey Owl," which appears in her book *Noman's Land*. One of Canada's most admired poets, MacEwen mixes prose and poetry in her text. The story takes place in Ontario's emblematic Algonquin Park during the last night of a camping trip by the protagonists, Kali and Noman. It opens with Kali reading an untitled poem by "an obscure Kanadian poet" (72), who turns out to be MacEwen herself, considering that she later published it separately as "Grey Owl's Poem"—along with two other related poems—in her collection *Afterworlds* (1987, 71–73). In the poem, MacEwen notes the foreignness of the landscape that Grey Owl encounters in Canada, yet she stresses that he is not looking so much for the wild as for himself:

> *There is no chart of his movement through the borrowed*
> > *forest,*
> *A place so alien that all he could do with it*
> > *was pretend it was his own*
> *And turn himself into an Indian, savage and lean,*
> *A hunter of the forest's excellent green secret.*
>
> *For all his movement through the forest was*
> *In search of himself, in search of Archie Belaney.* (1985, 74)

MacEwen adds that Grey Owl may not find solace even in the forest, since "*the beaver [are] all laughing at him*," being aware of "*the savage secret—if there ever was one—/ Never revealed to him*" (74; italics in text). In short, there is really no place in which he can hide from himself, not even in his cherished Canadian woods.

In the prose section of her story, MacEwen focuses largely on the relationship between Grey Owl and Anahareo and on their inability to "discover their histories in one another," because of what their ancestors have done (1985, 75). Grey Owl says that "only natives had a memory" and that "the white man suffered from a permanent amnesia brought about by his first glimpse of vast and horrifying expanses of snow," but Anahareo realizes neither that he is "speaking of himself" nor that he is "jealous of her" and her hereditary connection to the land (75). For when Grey Owl "looked inside himself, he discovered an imposter," which is perhaps why he is driven to embrace her forebears (75). Toward the end of the story, Kali tells Noman that, some other time, she will read to him from Anahareo's memoir about her consternation when she discovers that he was English and "for all those years I had been married to a ghost—that Archie never really existed" (78; see also Anahareo [1972] 2014, 184). To this, Noman responds that Anahareo is being "unfair" to Grey Owl. " 'Of course he existed,' insists Noman. 'As surely as you or I. He was only looking for his soul, or for God, or whatever' " (78). Once more, the key to understanding Grey Owl is to recognize that his journey is really an internal one.

There has always been some interest in Grey Owl in Quebec, especially regarding his activities in Témiscouata. This interest was evident again in the late 1980s when the cartoonists Toufik and Zoran serialized their graphic biography of the conservationist in the Sunday edition of Montreal's largest newspaper, *La Presse*, between 3 September and 8 October 1989. Titled "Grey Owl, l'Indien Blanc" (Grey Owl, the white Indian), Toufik and Zoran's biography opens in 1906 with the teenager Archie Belaney leaving England for Canada, a great country where, his teary-eyed aunt tells him, he will make his fortune: "TU PROSPÉRERAS" (3 September 1989, C5). But Archie is less interested in the silver deposits that have just been discovered around North Bay than he is in the area's forests. Once he comes in contact with the Anishinaabe, he not only decides to learn their language and way of life but also begins to transform himself, growing his hair long and trading his tailored clothes for buckskin outfits. However, in 1914, war breaks out in Europe and Archie (as Toufik and Zoran erroneously claim) enlists in the English Army, "L'ARMÉE ANGLAISE" (10 September 1989, C5); he, in fact, joined the Canadian Army (Smith 1990, 52–61). For Toufik and Zoran, his war experience is clearly a turning point for Archie. In addition to being wounded physically, he turns not only against the war but against European civilization in general, and by the time he comes back to Canada he has undergone a complete transformation. As they have him explode in a pub,

"JE DÉTESTE LA GUERRE ET LE MONDE DES BLANCS!!!" 17 September 1989, C5), His outburst is not well received by one of his fellow drinkers, who pounds him, but Archie remains unrepentant.

After he returns from fighting in the First World War, Archie becomes increasingly convinced that his salvation lies in the Canadian forests and their Indigenous dwellers. This seems to be confirmed when, soon after he resumes his life as a trapper and begins to fashion himself as Grey Owl, he meets the beautiful Anahareo, with whom he has a "VÉRITABLE HISTOIRE D'AMOUR" (TRUE LOVE STORY) (24 September 1989, C5). Anahareo appears to be not only Grey Owl's only wife but his only love. She also precipitates his other great transformations, first into a conservationist and then into a writer, before departing on one of her prospecting expeditions. He becomes obsessed with the idea of spreading his message that nature is not inexhaustible and, to that end, agrees to give a public lecture in Métis-sur-Mer, a resort town on the Lower Saint Lawrence River. That initial lecture, combined with his writings, leads him to be hired by the National Parks Branch to start a beaver colony in Prince Albert National Park and to disseminate his message about conservation around the world. Toufik and Zoran acknowledge that the revelations following their subject's death generated a "LONGUE CONTROVERSE" (8 October 1989, C5). But the authors leave little doubt about Grey Owl's ultimate triumph, as reflected in the fact that his cabin on Ajawaan Lake has been declared a national historical site.

The year 1990 also saw the publication of several works on Grey Owl, including Kenneth Brower's long essay "Grey Owl," which appeared in *Atlantic* magazine. Brower is a respected non-fiction writer and environmentalist whose family is closely associated with the Sierra Club. He underscores why Grey Owl is less known in the United States than in much of the world, a relative invisibility that is not so much related to him as to the Canadian dimension of his story. As Brower notes with "a certain embarrassment[,] Americans know so much less of Canadian history than Canadians know of American" (74). In his words,

> I had grown up in a California household where environmentalism and its poets and heroes made most of the table talk, yet before coming to Manitoba I had never heard of Grey Owl. No man was more important to Canadian environmental consciousness, or to the environmental consciousness of the entire British Commonwealth, for that matter. If his deeds had been done at a slightly lower latitude, we all would have heard of him. In the pantheon

> Grey Owl belongs with Henry David Thoreau, John Muir, Aldo Leopold, and Rachel Carson—or perhaps with Lewis Mumford and Joseph Wood Krutch, on the level just below. (1990, 74)

Brower does not mention that one factor that may explain the relative lack of interest in Grey Owl in the United States could be his presumed Indigenous heritage, given the country's troubled history with the First Peoples. In any case, it is revealing of his initial lack of knowledge of Grey Owl that Brower decides to honour him with a trip that is "part hike and part pilgrimage" to the conservationist's cabin, not at Ajawaan Lake, but at Riding Mountain National Park (74), where he lived only briefly.

Brower provides an excellent overview of Grey Owl's career as a public speaker, noting that during his first British tour he became "a sensation," giving "two hundred lectures to more than a quarter million people," but he is particularly perceptive in his analysis of his literary achievement. "As a writer," he asserts, "Grey Owl had many voices—too many voices, some might argue" (1990, 78). At least, he did until he wrote *Pilgrims of the Wild*, his "best book." According to Brower, it is in his memoir about his life with Anahareo that Grey Owl "finds a single voice, one that seems to be his own. There is a nice symmetry to his cast of characters: two human beings and two beavers. Grey Owl is at his best when writing about the beaver" (79). Brower further contends that, retrospectively, it is curious that audiences did not detect Grey Owl's true identity, something he says seems to have demanded "a willing suspension of belief in the laws of genetics" (83). Interestingly, he does not mention how he feels about Anahareo's claims that she never suspected her partner had no Indigenous ancestry. More germane perhaps, Brower argues that the notion of "Grey Owl as an Indian required, as well, considerable naiveté about the nature of literary art," since he finds it impossible to believe that a youngster "taught his three R's by an Apache aunt in dusty Indian encampments on the Mexican desert" could possibly "learn to write in the several mannered styles of Grey Owl" (83). Yet, judging by the archival record, almost no critics questioned that someone with so little formal education could write the way Grey Owl did.

Of course, 1990 was also the year when Donald B. Smith published his book *From the Land of Shadows: The Making of Grey Owl*. Since, throughout my study, I have relied extensively on what is the definitive biography of Grey Owl, I will not analyze Smith's book at any length here. The only point that I wish to stress is that, despite unmasking and dissecting the myriad contradictions in his subject's life, Smith remains extremely sympathetic toward the man first known as Archie Belaney. He maintains that the conservationist was "one of the most effective champions of the Canadians wilderness in [the twentieth] century. As a popularizer in the 1930s of Canada's forests, lakes, rivers, and wildlife, Grey Owl has no equal" (7). Smith is especially prescient about the Englishness of Grey Owl's story, how his unstable family life leads him to seek "refuge in a warm, friendly fantasy world" among the First Nations of North America (215). Yet, as he does in his early essay, Smith insists that Grey Owl is "a Canadian folk hero" and that his "magic story… will live on as long" as there is a Prince Albert National Park (217). Indeed, perhaps, as long as there is a Canada.

Even Smith, however, could not redeem his hero for everyone, as the Toronto novelist M.T. Kelly demonstrated the following year, 1991. Kelly's short story "Case History" is only indirectly about Grey Owl, yet the portrait it paints of the conservationist and canoeist makes it patently clear that he does not deserve to be in the pantheon of Canadian heroes, or possibly in any human pantheon. Kelly's story describes a canoe trip in northern Ontario by three male friends from Toronto: Gallegar, Jones, and Mick, the narrator. The three men have been canoeing together for years. But this particular summer's trip is different because they have responded to an advertisement in the magazine *Wildculture* in which a nature writer named Allison advertises for companions to join her "on a canoe journey 'down the historic Mississagi, a naturalists' trip, following Grey Owl's route'" (129). For Mick and his friends, Allison does not merely emulate Grey Owl, but may be his reincarnation. They are reading one of Grey Owl's books and have much fun with the latter's references to "pale emasculates" (129, 130). Unlike most critics, such as Cantwell and Brower, they even dismiss his writings, since "[t]he guy can't write. It's shit" (131). R.E. Rashley, for instance, contends that "Grey Owl's limitations as a writer are great," not the least the "lack of power of language" (1971, 63). At the same time, he remarks that "[h]is ability as a writer is easily underestimated. He knew very well what he wanted to do and how to go about it" (58). That is, Grey Owl's language may have been designed to achieve a specific aim, but this is something that Kelly's characters either do not recognize or refuse to consider.

Mick and his male friends are particularly critical of the conservationist's character and his politics. As Mick explains,

> I parodied with revulsion Grey Owl's greeting to the King of England. I tried to keep in mind that Grey Owl was an early conservationist, but then I let myself go: another tall, twisted, imperial

> phoney, a Brit who "seeded" native women, then abandoned the
> children, a violent sociopath only concerned with himself, *his*
> reactions to the country, *his* feelings. I saw a six-foot child in a
> canoe acting willfully, turning aside from the things he'd done
> to other people, turning away. (Kelly 1991, 131; italics in text)

Mick knows that there is "something wrong" about standing in the middle of
the wilderness "hating a man dead fifty years" (Kelly 1991, 131), yet he cannot
help himself. For him, Grey Owl represents everything that is repellent about
Canada's colonial past. But considering the ease with which Mick transfers his
hatred of Grey Owl to Allison, who is not only of another gender but bears
no physical resemblance whatsoever to her ostensible archetype—she is "a
short woman, a little stocky" (134), where he was a tall, lean man—one cannot
help but wonder why the one-time trapper can still elicit such raw animus.
"Symbols matter," Mick states toward the end of the story, as he reflects on
the disastrous canoe trip (144). So the question is what sort of symbol is Grey
Owl for Canadians like Mick and his friends? Perhaps he is not so much a
remnant of a long outgrown past but an indication that the past may continue
to live in the present. Or that the past is not quite past.

⊡ ⊡ ⊡

Such is the interest in Grey Owl in the 1990s that, for a while, he is not merely
"Canada's most famous Indian impostor," but "Canada's most famous Indian"
(Dewar 2002, 258). The extent to which Grey Owl reenters the Canadian cultural consciousness during that decade is reflected in the fact that he comes
under the scrutiny of some of the most popular writers and scholars in the
country, such as Margaret Atwood and Daniel Francis. In his 1992 book *The
Imaginary Indian: The Image of the Indian in Canadian Culture*, the historian
Francis presents Grey Owl as just another example of "plastic shamans,"
which he describes as "non-Natives who appropriate an Indian persona and
claim to have special insight into the Indian way of life" (109). Yet he then
proceeds to argue that, despite his deception about his identity, Grey Owl
perceived Indigenous people as being "supremely suited to be the guardians of
the wilderness," and "sought to end the marginalization of aboriginal people
by giving them a key role to play in the development of the country" (139). For
Francis, "The greening of the Indian begins with Grey Owl. To him belongs
the credit for affirming, if not creating, the image of the Indian as the original

environmentalist, an image which has gained strength in the years since he expressed it" (140). More important, by the end of the book, Francis comes to see the conservationist as nothing less than a national hero, someone all non-Indigenous Canadians ought to emulate if they wish to be at home in their country and continent. "Grey Owl was the archetypal Canadian," he posits, "shedding his European past and transforming himself into an Indian in order to connect through the wilderness with the New World" (223), a claim that he repeats in his subsequent book *National Dreams: Myth, Memory, and Canadian History* (1997, 143). Francis's thesis is not unproblematic. For one, it seems that even if non-Indigenous Canadians followed Grey Owl's example, they would merely succeed in becoming "plastic shamans." Also, as I will discuss in the conclusion, the impetus for Archie Belaney's ethnocultural metamorphosis preceded his arrival in Canada, and thus had to be motivated by non-Canadian identity concerns. That said, it is remains fascinating how such an "extravagant act of self-definition" (Hayman 1944, 44) can come to embody the non-Indigenous experience in Canada and North America in general, if not the Americas as a whole.

Grey Owl's curious place in the Canadian imagination again is what the poet and novelist Atwood explores in the chapter she devotes to the conservationist in her 1995 book *Strange Things: The Malevolent North in Canadian Literature*, which is based on a series of lectures she delivered at Oxford University four years earlier. In a chapter titled "The Grey Owl Syndrome," Atwood refers to the desire of non-Indigenous people to Indigenize themselves, a yearning that she says "becomes entwined with a version of wilderness itself, not as a demonic ice-goddess who will claim you for her own, but as the repository of salvation and a new life" (35). Atwood does not gloss over the fact that Grey Owl pretended to belong to a different ethnocultural group than the one into which he was born. Yet she is less interested in what he and "his avatars" did than in their motivation for doing so. As she asks, "Why did they do it? Imitation, after all, is the sincerest form of flattery. What was it that the Indians had—or were thought to have—that the imitators wanted?" (37; see also Hulan 2006, 43). That is, people like Grey Owl must have reached the conclusion that Indigenous cultures possessed something theirs lacked and, for that reason, they were willing to forsake the world in which they were raised.

The matter of what Grey Owl believed the First Nations offered him is examined with much depth, and considerable sympathy, by Armand Garnet Ruffo in his 1996 poetic biography *Grey Owl: The Mystery of Archie Belaney*. Ruffo's long poem has been praised for making "a significant intervention in Canadian historiography" by "inviting readers to think seriously about the significance of the past in Native societies" (Hulan 2006, 40). But it is of special interest because its creator is not only Anishinaabe but is actually a great-grandson of Annie (Ruffo spells her name differently from Smith) and Alex Espaniel, the Biscotasing couple who invited a drunken Archie into their house and enabled him, at least temporarily, to come to terms with his demons. In his subsequent essay "Writing the Water," Ruffo goes as far as to state that his great-grandfather became so close to "the Englishman turned Indian" that he "hid" him "from the law" in his trapping cabin (2000, 186). In light of the poet's background, critics have always been perplexed that someone like Ruffo would suggest that "Grey Owl may not be guilty of deception, at least of most Aboriginal people he knew, since they were not only aware of his true identity but were instrumental in his metamorphosis" (Braz 2001–02, 172). Thus, instead of the First Nations being deceived by Grey Owl, they appear to have been complicit in his ethnocultural masquerade in order to further their own causes.

One of the most surprising aspects of *Grey Owl: The Mystery of Archie Belaney* is the poet's choice of epigraphs. In the first one, Ruffo uses a passage from *The Men of the Last Frontier* in which Grey Owl states, "The Trail, then, is not merely a connecting link between widely distant points, it becomes an idea, a symbol of self-sacrifice and deathless determination, an ideal to be lived up to, a creed from which none may falter" (1996, n.p., citing Grey Owl [1931] 1973, 78). More unusually, for his second epigraph, Ruffo cites part of "The Man Made of Words," the canonical essay in which N. Scott Momaday asserts that "an Indian is an idea which a given man has of himself. And it is a moral idea, for it accounts for the way in which he reacts to other men and to the world in general. And that idea, in order to be realized completely, has to be expressed" (n.p., citing Momaday 1970, 82). In other words, before we get to the poem proper, we have already been conditioned to accept that both the trail and "the Indian" are ideas, and therefore that different individuals can embody them.

No less significant, in contrast to most other writers on Grey Owl, Ruffo structures the conservationist's story chronologically. The poem opens in Hastings, and from the outset there is never any doubt about the subject's true identity. This is something that is further reinforced by the numerous photographs that Ruffo reproduces in his text, starting with a full-page picture of a rather Caucasian-looking teenaged Archie posing formally in what appears to be a prosperous sitting room, sporting a formal jacket and bow tie, with a gold chain across his vest. Moreover, the poet seems to approve of the protagonist's desire to escape "the collar of Edwardian England/the cackle of his spinster aunts" (1996, 7) and fashion a new identity on the other side of the Atlantic:

> His father, his mother,
> his grandmother (who dies on him)
> and finally his classmates, including
> his best friend, Hopkin, who prefers
> the pursuit of girls to animals,
> all abandon him.
>
> And so, with no one, he creates himself
> companionship and dreams for hours
> of the life he will lead
> among his brethren in America.
> Though, never, not once,
> despite an ache for someone as big as a country,
> does he ever imagine
> four or five wives. (1996, 7)

While Grey Owl's journey to the New World may be an unusual one, Ruffo suggests, it follows a logic of its own. The poet certainly appears to understand why someone growing up in such a stultifyingly ordered universe might fantasize about a less restricted life among North America's First Nations.

Furthermore, Ruffo implies that Archie Belaney has already become extensively acculturated to Indigenous life, particularly Anishinaabe culture, by the time he transforms himself into Grey Owl. Throughout the text he underscores how different Indigenous individuals help the young Englishman to adjust to a new way of being and seeing. First, it is Angele Egwuna, the Belle of Temagami, who notices "him struggling with himself" after he comes in contact with her people, and attempts to "make him/ one with them" (Ruffo 1996, 19). Later, it is Anahareo, "his true wife,/ the heroine of his pilgrimage" (205). Critically important, in between, there are the Espaniels. Noticing how damaged Archie has become by "the beast of war," they realize that the only way "the pitiful thing" can be helped is if he "get[s] back into the bush" (33). Besides, the Espaniels do not merely help Archie return to the wild. They make him "part of the family," welcoming him into their home "for nearly three years" (36). Not surprisingly, Grey Owl gratefully acknowledges that the Espaniel patriarch, Alex, is the one man whom he is "proud to call 'Dad'" (162). Thanks to the Espaniels, he has been able to discover not only a new culture but a new family.

Ruffo seems to rationalize even Archie Belaney's transformation into Grey Owl. The poet's apparent affinity with his protagonist reflects the belief that, regardless of his deceptions about his identity, Grey Owl cares deeply about the welfare of the First Nations. As mentioned earlier, Ruffo has the Saskatchewan Cree leader John Tootoosis state that Indigenous people know that the conservationist is not one of them, since an "Indian can tell who's Indian" and "Grey Owl can't sing or dance." Yet Tootoosis promptly adds that, despite his lack of rhythm, Grey Owl is "doing good" (1996, 128). Or, as he elaborates later in the poem, "We know Wa-Sha-Quon-Asin is not born of us, and we say nothing" because he "flies for us true and/sharp, and we are thankful he has chosen our side" (145, 146; see also Goodwill and Sluman 1984, 167–68). As well, Ruffo makes it explicit that the fact Grey Owl has no Indigenous ancestry does not preclude him from being mistreated like a real Indigenous person, such as when some people in Quebec "call him *Sauvage*, a name he detests" (70). So it becomes relatively easy to understand why Archie would not only start to identify with Indigenous people but desire to be one of them. In any case, his transformation does not seem to be completely premeditated:

> I begin by signing my name Grey Owl,
> and saying I was adopted by the Ojibway,
> and that for 15 years I spoke nothing but Indian;
> then, before I know it, I have Apache blood.
> Finally I'm calling myself an Indian writer. (Ruffo 1996, 71)

Grey Owl contends that he has become so different since he arrived in Canada and came to live among the First Nations that he can no longer even relate to Archie Belaney. As he says of his old English self, "That was someone else, some Englishman named Belaney/who died and was reborn. Grey Owl. A name I've earned" (Ruffo 1996, 97), suggesting that he has undergone a real cultural transformation.

Ruffo does not ignore the less pleasant aspects of Grey Owl, notably the deceptions or half-truths that are required by his ethnocultural metamorphosis and his treatment of his romantic partners and his children. In the words Ruffo gives to the conservationist's son, Johnny Jero, who declares that his mother was Marie Girard but "my father, I never met,/ Archie Baloney" (1996, 82). Still, one cannot help but be struck that, "rather than vilifying his subject for pretending to be Native, Ruffo praises him for championing Aboriginal causes" (Braz 2001–02, 172). Critics like Carrie Dawson have remarked that because Ruffo is both Anishinaabe and an academic, "there is a temptation to respond ironically to passages in which the writer/narrator identifies most strongly with the would-be indigene who learned Ojibwa from Longfellow, but there is nothing remotely ironic about this biography" (1998, 131). The first point one would have to make is that Ruffo does not show his protagonist learning Anishinaabe from Longfellow but from the Anishinaabe themselves, notably his Espaniel ancestors. Indeed, the general absence of irony in *Grey Owl: The Mystery of Archie Belaney* simply underscores the fact Ruffo "uses Grey Owl to celebrate his own family" (Braz 2001–02, 172), which indicates that he has a very different view of the English-born conservationist than do many contemporary critics.

The publication of Armand Ruffo's poetic biography is obviously a turning point in the cultural representations of Grey Owl, a text that started to reverse what has been perceived as the systematic neglect of the author by the Canadian academy. In his 1997 essay "What's the Matter with Grey Owl?" A.W. Plumstead lists a series of ways in which "to bring the writings of Grey Owl into the mainstream of Canadian Literature." The most important of these is to "try to swing Grey Owl studies around to recognizing him as a literary artist rather than a misinformer and raiser of beavers, to consider him as an imaginative craftsman of a high order rather than merely the man with a mission to save the woods and its creatures" (57). That is, he should be treated as a writer. Plumstead maintains it is imperative that scholars place Grey Owl in his proper cultural and literary context, so that they will be able to identify the tradition to which he belongs, and his departures from it. He further argues that as one reads Grey Owl, one notices an "American connection," notably to writers like Fenimore Cooper and Longfellow (58). Yet he observes that in "*Pilgrims of the Wild*, the narrator-pathfinder brings along a woman—a no-no in the classic American frontier adventures of Leatherstocking, Huck Finn, Davy Crockett, Mike Fink, Paul Bunyan, Johnny Appleseed and even the Harvard graduate translating his Aeschlus [sic] and planting his beans by Walden pond" (57). In other words, while Grey Owl has major affinities with classic American writers, he does not always belong with them. For Plumstead, the key is to try to ascertain what is the tradition into which Grey Owl inserts himself, something that Ruffo is obviously willing to do.

Another significant aspect of Ruffo's poem is that it paints a largely positive portrait of Grey Owl, a trend that has continued since then. One of the most interesting of these works is Jane Billinghurst's 1999 book *Grey Owl: The Many Faces of Archie Belaney*. The author of several non-fiction works, Billinghurst is receptive to the idea of someone who attempts to escape his family and culture. This is especially true of a boy, like Archie Belaney, who is growing up in Edwardian England with "no mother or father at home, an unusual situation for the times and one that he needed to explain, both to himself and to his friends" (2). Billinghurst shows Archie plotting to escape "the matriarchy" in which he is being raised. More precisely, he resists "his Aunt Ada's attempts to turn him into a better man than his father had been," something which he does by immersing "himself in a life of private adventure" by reading as much as possible about North American Indigenous peoples (6). Like Ruffo, Billinghurst illustrates her biography with numerous photographs of Grey Owl and his friends and acquaintances. Unlike him, though, she intersperses her biographical text with long passages from Grey Owl's own writings. So the reader is not only able to follow her analysis, but may actually encounter the subject's own texts for the first time and discover the vitality of those writings.

Also in 1999, Peter Unwin published his long essay "The Fabulations of Grey Owl" in the appropriately titled magazine *The Beaver*, which since then has been renamed *Canada's History*. A Toronto journalist and writer with a special interest in the Canadian North and the frontier, Unwin was born in Sheffield, England, and migrated with his family to Canada as a child. In his essay, he focuses mainly on Grey Owl's controversial identity, being particularly interested in how someone from an English coastal town manages to transform himself into "the most famous Red Indian in the world" in the interwar period (13, 19). For Unwin, Grey Owl's ethnocultural metamorphosis is "one of the most remarkable stories in Canadian history. It is the story of a man who, for a brief time, spanned the two great solitudes of North America. He was both immigrant and native" (14). Unwin adds that Archie Belaney "*went* native—not by accident—but on purpose, knowing it was essential for his survival. He was at the same time civilized and 'savage,' European and non-European. In the course of this extraordinary balancing act, he became something that never existed before" (14). Needless to say, what exactly Archie became when he turned himself into Grey Owl is a question that has never been adequately answered, and he was definitely not the first white Indian. Still, for Unwin, as for Francis, Atwood, and legions of other Canadian writers and scholars, there is little doubt that his transformation is not merely about Grey Owl; it stands for a much larger phenomenon, one that is inextricably linked to the citizenship of not only non-Indigenous Canadians but also non-Indigenous people in the whole of the Americas and probably in other so-called settler societies.

In the preamble to Unwin's essay, we are told that the reason it is so timely to explore "the complexity and contradictions of the Indian who wasn't" is that Hollywood is preparing "to bring Grey Owl's story to the big screen" (1999, 13). The movie to which Unwin alludes is Richard Attenborough's 1999 film *Grey Owl*, which starred Pierce Brosnan as the title character and the young Algonquin actor Annie Galipeau as Anahareo. Attenborough became rightly famous for his films about historical figures, such as Winston Churchill (*Young Winston*, 1972), Mohandas Gandhi (*Gandhi*, 1982), Steve Biko and Donald Woods (*Cry Freedom*, 1987), and Charlie Chaplin (*Chaplin*, 1992). He also had been fascinated with Grey Owl since he was a child, along with his younger brother David, the celebrated naturalist and broadcaster. In an article on the genesis of his film, Attenborough writes that in 1936, when he was thirteen and David was ten, they attended a lecture by Grey Owl in Leicester, England. They even managed to get the "real 'Redskin' " to autograph their copy of *Pilgrims of the Wild*, a prized book that, after they "fought" for its possession with a bet, his brother won (Attenborough 2000; see also Braz 2013, 177). The magnitude of the impression that Grey Owl made on the future filmmaker is reflected in the fact that when Attenborough and his long-time friend Bryan Forbes started a movie production company in the 1950s, they named it "Beaver Films" (Castell 1984, 13). No less telling, Attenborough's "picturesque Queen Anne house" in London is called "Beaver Lodge" (Macnab 2003), the name of Grey Owl's cabin in Prince Albert National Park. So Attenborough would appear to have been the ideal director to translate to the screen the intricacies and contradictions of the story of the man who became Grey Owl. Instead, he produced what has been described as "one of the dullest films of 1999" (Bonnett 2006, 322), something for which he bears no little responsibility.

There are two main problems with Attenborough's *Grey Owl*, one visual and verbal and the other structural. The most conspicuous flaw in the film involves the casting, notably Brosnan as Grey Owl. While some critics contend that the choice of the former James Bond as the champion of the beaver was "oddly appropriate" and that he delivers "a surprisingly strong performance" (Johnson, with Oh 1999, 53; Johnson 1999, 54), many others feel otherwise. As Alastair Bonnett writes, the decision to have the Irish actor "play the lead role instantly rendered Grey Owl a ludicrous figure. Brosnan's imitation of an Englishman imitating a Native Canadian falls back on Grey Owl's basic facial trick: rigidity, no smiling; a mouth so straight and tight that words, if they come at all, seem to be being forced painfully through the lips" (2006, 322). Or, as the canoeist and wilderness guide Hap Wilson describes his reaction upon learning that Brosnan got the role, "I felt nauseous. Remington Steele, James Bond *for Christ's sake*, playing the part of the man who inspired me to live a life in the canoe" (2010, 102; italics in text). Like Bonnett and Wilson, who subsequently became involved with the making of the film, I must confess that I remain sceptical about Brosnan's acting ability. The extent of the conservationist's Canadianization is reflected in the fascinating description of one of his London lectures by the Canadian foreign correspondent Gladys Arnold, who states that "it gave me a pang of homesickness to hear Grey Owl's Canadian drawl accent" (1935, 4). Brosnan, however, is never able to convey the impression that his "Grey Owl is Canadian, much less an Indigenous Canadian" (Braz 2013, 172). Galipeau presents other challenges. Judging by her appearance, there is no questioning either her Indigenous ancestry or her beauty. As Gilbert Oskaboose gushes in his review of the film, Galipeau is "as pretty as a Spring morning. One could only fall in love with her, along with Grey Owl. She [is] the beautiful, intelligent and nurturing native woman personified. Thank you, Lord Attenborough" (2000, para 4). Unfortunately, like Brosnan, Galipeau is not the most versatile of actors.

The other major problem with Attenborough's *Grey Owl* is its structure. As I have asserted elsewhere, it is not only "a historical film with an ahistorical premise" (Braz 2013, 169) but also one that refuses to acknowledge its authorial debt to Grey Owl. The film claims to be "based on a true story," yet it never identifies its source, or sources. The sole screenwriter listed is William Nicholson, but anyone familiar with the conservationist's writings will recognize that *Grey Owl* borrows extensively from *Pilgrims of the Wild*. The film itself draws much attention to the 1935 text, to the point of creating the impression that Grey Owl wrote, not four books, but a single one. Thus, it is quite perplexing why Attenborough (or Nicholson) would conceal the eponymous subject's authorial contribution to the work. One possibility may have to do with the fact that the film is divided against itself. On the one hand, Attenborough sanitizes the story of Grey Owl by focusing almost exclusively on his relationship with Anahareo, downplaying his serial marriages and his chronic substance abuse. Yet, on the other hand, Attenborough severely undermines Grey Owl by suggesting that his transformation from an Englishman into someone of mixed Scottish and Apache ancestry is transparent, a view that is contradicted by none other than Anahareo. My suspicion is that the most likely reason Attenborough fails to acknowledge his extensive borrowing from Grey Owl is that cinema is a director's medium, and directors like to cultivate the myth that they are always the real authors of the narratives they film, a task in which they are often assisted by screenwriters (Braz 2013, 180).

Like several other of Attenborough's films, such as *Gandhi* and *Chaplin*,

*Grey Owl* is structured as a flashback. It opens with a journalist inquiring of Grey Owl if he knows one Archie Belaney. After a pregnant pause, Grey Owl says yes. Then, as if he has been waiting for this moment for some time, he asks the journalist, "What took you so long?" Contrary to what Attenborough's film implies, when a reporter for the North Bay *Nugget* "mentioned the name Archie Belaney" during an interview, Grey Owl did not admit that he was Belaney. Instead, he promptly " 'brought the interview to a definite close' " (Smith 1990, 171). Therefore, the idea that the intervention by the journalist led Grey Owl to bare his soul—and his upper body—during what would turn out to be his last lecture is an invention of Attenborough or Nicholson, or both. *Grey Owl* is much concerned with matters of ethnocultural authenticity, the flashback being triggered by the journalist asking him if anyone suspected that he was not the person he pretended to be. Without condoning the protagonist's actions, the film ultimately suggests that the prescience and urgency of his environmental crusade trump any deception about his identity. The film's central motif is actually that "men become what they dream." So for the rest of the action we see how a white English boy named Archie Belaney, who dreams of living in the wilderness, relocates to Canada as a teenager, moves to northern Ontario, and becomes a trapper. After undergoing a major personal crisis, he emerges as a conservationist, determined to save the beaver from imminent extinction. Equally significant, in the meantime, he metamorphoses from a white man into someone of mixed Indigenous and European ancestry.

Other than the protagonist's confession about his origins, which Attenborough later admitted is a "distortion" and one that was done "consciously" (qtd. in FFWD 1999), the most unusual feature of *Grey Owl* is the unswerving focus on Anahareo, an emphasis that calls into question the script's authorship. Anahareo, as we have seen, was not instrumental in the conservationist's Indigenization, a role that was played by his first wife, Angele Egwuna. But in the discourse on Grey Owl, including Attenborough's film, Anahareo has emerged almost as his only wife. Grey Owl of course was chiefly responsible for this development, since he not only credited Anahareo with being the catalyst for his conversion from a trapper into a conservationist and then into a writer but, more important, turned her into the heroine of both his memoir and the documentary films that he used to illustrate his lectures. Also as discussed earlier, there is another critical reason why Anahareo is pivotal to the narrative Grey Owl has fashioned for himself. Unlike someone such as Angele, who was aware of his origins, Anahareo proves that his ethnocultural transformation was accepted not only by whites but also by some Indigenous people. So by having Grey Owl confess to Anahareo that he is "a fake," Attenborough seriously undermines the figure he is purportedly celebrating. In addition, by not acknowledging that the story of the love affair between Anahareo and Grey Owl is largely constructed by the latter, he also fails to credit him for being one of the creators of the film known as "Richard Attenborough's *Grey Owl*" (*Grey Owl*, 1999).

It is not evident what impact the Attenborough film has had on the image of Grey Owl. After all, its concentration on his relationship with Anahareo is already a reflection of an old trend in the representations of the conservationist, starting with those by Grey Owl himself. Another trend that has reemerged since the 1990s is a focus on the ecological Grey Owl, notwithstanding his deceptions about his ostensible Indigeneity. This approach frequently involves a pilgrimage to Beaver Lodge at Ajawaan Lake, which has emerged as a semi-sacred site. In the foreword to his 2001 collection *Portraits from Life*, which includes "The Life of Grey Owl," the cartoonist David Collier writes that, in January 1992, he made a three-day "ski [trip] to Grey Owl's cabin," an outing that he says seems to have changed "[e]verything—the style I drew my comics in, my outlook on life" (n.p.). Although it is not clear whether Collier's transformation has to do with the physical rigours of marathon skiing in bitterly cold weather or with the site itself, which he depicts in another text he includes in *Portrait from Life*, called "Pilgrimage," there is little doubt that his journey affects the way he comes to perceive Grey Owl. Collier, who was then living in Saskatoon, emphasizes the local aspects of the story. His approach is self-reflexive, but humorous. He shows a male cartoonist discussing the life of Grey Owl with a male friend as he writes his text, and his initial impetus seems to be the fact that it is "ABOUT A GUY FROM **HERE**, FROM **NOWEHERESVILLE!**" (n.p.; bold in text). Indeed, the most fascinating aspect of the text is its exploration of the local angle.

Collier opens "The Life of Grey Owl" with the death of his protagonist. But instead of ruminating on the implications of his masquerade, he shows four park wardens dropping his coffin through a hole in the ice of Kingsmere Lake, saying in unison, "SO LONG ASSHOLE, WE NEVER LIKED YOU ANYWAYS!" (2001, n.p.). Collier's panel reflects (unsubstantiated) rumours that the wardens of Prince Albert National Park loathed Grey Owl so much that they never bothered to transport his body to Ajawaan for a proper burial—sometimes the story is that the wardens lost the body during the trip (Dorell Taylor 1984, 39–40). Furthermore, Collier does not use the image of the coffin being dropped through the ice merely for its shock value but rather to contextualize the story. As the cartoonist's friend responds after he hears about the episode, "I GUESS HE WASN'T THOUGHT OF TOO HIGHLY AT HOME, DESPITE BEING AN INTERNATIONALLY KNOWN AUTHOR!" Or, as the cartoonist adds, people in the area neither knew much nor cared about Grey Owl. For them, he was "'JUST ANOTHER DRUNK INDIAN'" (2001, n.p.), which renders quite ironic the posthumous recovery of the conservationist, including perhaps by the cartoonist.

Like most other writers on Grey Owl, Collier is fascinated by the conservationist's relationship with Anahareo. Yet even here his perspective is unique, underscoring the paradox of "A TOWN-REARED CANADIAN NATIVE BEING TAUGHT BUSHCRAFT BY A GUY BORN AND RAISED IN **ENGLAND!**" (2001, n.p.). Still, Collier cannot avoid some of the contradictions about her presumed centrality in Grey Owl's career and life. For instance, he portrays Anahareo both as being instrumental to his becoming a writer, showing her "PUTTING [HIS] WRITING TOGETHER TO SEND TO A MAGAZINE!" (n.p.), and becoming increasingly alienated from him because of his writing. As he states, "FOR ANAHAREO, A CABIN WITH ARCHIE WRITING IN IT WAS HELL MANIFESTED!" (n.p.). Echoing her self-portrait in *Devil in Deerskins*, Collier's Anahareo simultaneously encourages Grey Owl to write and deeply resents the fact he has to take time away from her in order to write. The most compelling aspect of Collier's graphic biography of Grey Owl, though, is not so much what it says about the conservationist but what his story reveals about the society in which he lived. As Collier writes after depicting Grey Owl and Anahareo being insulted on a train and told to "BEHAVE LIKE CHRISTIANS," it was "A GOLDEN AGE FOR RACISTS AND ASSHOLES!" (n.p.). The two figures in the graphic text seem to believe that they live in more emancipated times, or at least less "**GULLIBLE**" ones (n.p.). Yet there is remarkably little in "The Life of Grey Owl" to support that conclusion.

In "The Grey Wizard," a chapter in his 2009 book *Lakeland: Journeys into the Soul of Canada*, the journalist and nature writer Allan Casey describes another trek to Beaver Lodge, but this time on foot. Casey, who was raised in Prince Albert, states that his wife, Marlene, does not share his love of long backpacking trips through the woods. But she makes an exception for "journeys of the soul" (41), such as the forty-kilometre walk to Ajawaan Lake. Like Collier, Casey is interested in the perception of Grey Owl in north-central Saskatchewan. He writes that while the conservationist was "a celebrity in the wide world, at home he was a desperate alcoholic who patronized bootleggers. Local people did not buy Grey Owl's Indian act" (42). Furthermore, the antipathy toward Grey Owl does not appear to have been restricted to the region. Casey adds that his "grandfather Allan knew Archie Grey Owl from former days in northern Ontario and had nothing kind to say of him—he was a drunk, an impostor, and a bigamist, and that was that" (42). Yet Casey then makes one wonder if Grey Owl's negative image in the Prince Albert area is related to either his imposture or his association with bootleggers, which must have been hardly exceptional at the time, or to some other factor, contending that "it was not the charade itself, but the role he played, that drew indignation. Western Canada was effectively an apartheid society in Grey Owl's day and long after; to pretend to be Aboriginal was an affront to the establishment in a time and place of systemic racism" (42).

Casey's view of the racial relations in Saskatchewan during the time Grey Owl lived there is strongly supported by Maria Campbell in her classic memoir about growing up Métis in Canada's breadbasket—in *Halfbreed* she incidentally states that her grandfather was "a good friend of Grey Owl, an Englishman who came to our land and lived as an Indian" ([1973] 1983, 11–12). It is also widely documented in the historian Bill Waiser's book on Prince Albert National Park. In *Saskatchewan's Playground*, Waiser traces Grey Owl's poor relations with the people with whom he worked in the park. He asserts that most of the park wardens "had little use" for the conservationist, and especially resented his frequent "drinking escapades," which "were overlooked by the department" and invariably necessitated that they "retrieve him from Prince Albert" (1989, 82). Waiser alleges that such was "the disdain" for Grey Owl that "many wardens who joined the service after his death and had never known him personally continued to describe him as that 'bastard Grey Owl' or 'Hoot Owl.'" More significant, he notes that a "curious thing about Grey Owl's tenure at the park" was that, despite his growing popularity with tourists, he was "virtually a nonentity in Prince Albert," where to many of the locals "he was 'just another Indian'" (82). Again, the fact that Grey Owl had no Indigenous ancestry did not seem to preclude him from being treated like a real "Indian," as a non-citizen.

For Casey, the cultural image of Grey Owl clearly says at least as much about the society in which he lived as it does about him. Still, he considers Grey Owl an ecological model worth emulating in the twenty-first century. It is because Casey believes the conservationist's "message is perennially worthwhile" that he undertakes his trek with his wife to Beaver Lodge, a "pilgrimage" that hundreds of people make every year and one which he himself had made "a few times before" (2009, 43). Admittedly, his admiration of Grey Owl's ecologism appears to be inextricably linked to his fascination with the personalities of Grey Owl and Anahareo, whom Casey deems "one of the most enigmatically glamorous couples of the 1930s" (31). He particularly appears to have fallen under the spell of Anahareo, describing her as Grey Owl's "true-Iroquois wife…, who shaped him into a brand that sold throughout the British Empire" (41). More problematically, he claims that if Grey Owl "was the actor, she was the impresario," alleging that "she got him to stop trapping and supplied him with the conservationist ideas that later made him famous" (45). Yet, for the Caseys, whether Grey Owl developed his conservationism or borrowed it from Anahareo, he "changed the way people felt about nature, and that is not an easy thing to do" (54). Thus, it is not surprising that, decades after he died, people continue to make pilgrimages to the site where he did most of his work.

As might be expected of a work aimed at a children's audience, Lori Punshon's 2006 book *He Who Flies by Night: The Story of Grey Owl* does not have the complexity of texts like Collier's or Casey's. The book, which is sumptuously illustrated by the landscape artist Mike Keepness, also bears a foreword by Tanyann Grey Owl Belaney, in which the subject's great-great-granddaughter, like Richard Attenborough, exhorts readers, "Always remember that people become what they dream" (n.p.). The fantasy that Punshon depicts, and Keepness illustrates, is that of "a little boy in England," who "dreamed of living in Canada's wilderness" (9), and came to realize his goal. Paradoxically, considering Anahareo's ubiquity in the discourse on Grey Owl, she is not even mentioned by Punshon. The text relates that the Englishman married "a beautiful Ojibwa woman," who not only teaches him her language but also "named [him] Grey Owl" (10, 11). Soon after that, realizing that the beaver faced imminent "extinction" (13), he decided to dedicate his life to their preservation. But there is no evidence of any woman being around; certainly not Anahareo. All indications are that, as befits an ecological hero, he dedicated himself completely to preserving nature and wildlife.

In contrast to Punshon and Keepness, in her 2007 painting *Grey Owl and Anahareo at Beaver Swamp*, the visual artist Diana Thorneycroft presents a considerably less salubrious view of the conservationist and his fourth wife. *Grey Owl and Anahareo at Beaver Swamp* is part of the *Group of Seven Awkward Moments Series*, in which Thorneycroft parodies the work of Canada's most iconic painters, the Group of Seven. At first glance, her canvas seems historical, showing Grey Owl standing in a front of a cabin by a lake, surrounded by wild animals, and with a canoe partly visible. But then one notices that Anahareo is not communing with either the wild animals or with her partner but is, rather, pointing a rifle at him. While Thorneycroft may wish to celebrate Grey Owl and Anahareo, she is clearly aware of the volatility in their relationship. "Grey Owl was an ambiguous character," she notes in an interview. "The fact that he disguised himself his entire life as a First Nations person is an awkward stain on our history. People don't quite know what to make of him" (2009, 53). Yet, after describing Grey Owl as "an embarrassment because he was a fraud," as well as "a womanizer and a drunk," Thorneycroft contends that he was "also one of Canada's first conservationists; and he brought attention to the decline of the beaver population. Our ambiguous feelings towards our heroes are very Canadian-like" (53). Whether ambiguity is truly a Canadian response is open to debate, but there is no question that Grey Owl invites an equivocal response.

Perhaps it is because so many aspects of the story of Grey Owl have become politically problematic that current writers interested in him often emphasize his prowess with a canoe. In their 2002 book *In the Footsteps of Grey Owl: Journey into the Ancient Forest*, Gary and Joanie McGuffin document a 1,900-kilometre canoe trip through Grey Owl country in northern Ontario. The book is divided into two parts: "The Journey in Words," written by Joanie, and "The Journey in Pictures," in which lush photographs of rivers, lakes, and forests are accompanied by excerpts from the works of Grey Owl. Gary becomes interested in canoeing and the wilderness through an "elderly prospector" and former school teacher who has an immense library of wilderness books, including all of Grey Owl's (13). Gary and Joanie, who grew up in different parts of Ontario's cottage country, are both avid canoeists. So one day they decide to "paddle a route across Ontario from the places of our childhood summers all the way to the Algoma Highlands, the very route that Grey Owl traversed in his wandering between Lake Temagami and the Mississagi River." As they explain, "the idea was to create an adventure story through which people could learn about the complete forest landscape and realize how fast the roadless, self-sustaining wilderness Grey Owl described seventy years ago was disappearing. We could be a voice for the forest and its inhabitants" (15). The McGuffins declare that their primary objective is "to save the ancient forests" of Ontario (16). Yet it is fascinating that the figure they use for inspiration is Grey Owl, someone who is now widely perceived as an impostor but who clearly still has the power to compel people in the twenty-first century to undertake such an arduous journey.

The degree to which Grey Owl continues to be a living presence is never more evident than in the writings of the wilderness guide, canoeist, and nature writer Hap Wilson. Born in the outskirts of Toronto, Wilson is not satisfied to emulate Grey Owl but wishes to become him, or possibly his reincarnation. The conservationist's influence is evident throughout Wilson's work, including his 2005 book, *The Cabin: A Search for Personal Sanctuary*, in which Wilson appears unable to determine whether Grey Owl is "famous" or "infamous" (12, 52). But it is particularly conspicuous in his 2010 collection of essays, *Grey Owl and Me: Stories from the Trail and Beyond*, in which Wilson shows the myriad ways his life has been shaped by the experiences of the former Archie Belaney.

Wilson opens *Grey Owl and Me* with a brief essay titled "Grey Owl: Scoundrel or Champion? A Short Biography," which concludes with the following observation: "Posthumous recognition for his environmental work and poignant writing about the disappearing Canadian wilderness raised Archie Grey Owl's reputation as a great Canadian" (2010, 15). Ironically, Wilson first learned about the champion of the Canadian wild in that ultimate repository of civilization, grade school. In *The Cabin* he writes that he was introduced to Grey Owl through a certain Frank McConnaghy, who was "our High School math teacher, and a very poor one at that. He was as enthusiastic about teaching us math as we were in learning it" (2005, 52). McConnaghy, however, loved nature and "took our coterie of misfits in as his own boys, feeding us stories about his own woodland travels, of having actually met the infamous Grey Owl in the 1920s, about this wonderful place called Temagami" (52). Still, McConnaghy did not simply decide to expose Wilson to Grey Owl's books because he realized that the teenager (and his friends) had never heard of either Grey Owl or Temagami, which is less than 500 kilometres north of the city. As Wilson quotes McConaghy in *Grey Owl and Me* (he spells the name differently in the second book), " 'He wanted to be an Indian, like you, and wrote about his experiences masqueraded as an Indian,' he went on, talking as if he knew him personally. I was captured" (2010, 18).

In his introduction to *Grey Owl and Me*, Wilson states that "I can't remember that I had any heroes when I was growing up. The male members of my family were anything but high-quality role models, unless of course I was to follow a path of self-indulgence, narcissism, bigotry, and heavy drinking" (2010, 17). He later becomes convinced that he was not only born into the wrong family but the wrong ethnocultural group. Thus, when he discovers Grey Owl's books, and subsequently the northern landscape of majestic rivers, lakes, and forests that he writes about, it is as if he is born again. Wilson explains, "I passed through a portal into another world—Grey Owl's world—and I knew I had found my home. Having read all of Grey Owl's books, I was primed to discover the very places he paddled and lived, to meet the people who taught him his skills, and perhaps live as he lived in the Canadian hinterland" (18). He adds that he is "astonished" when he becomes aware of "the similarities to Grey Owl that might parallel our lives," yet he maintains that "Archie Grey Owl was never my hero." While Wilson admires his predecessor's "pithy form of writing" and is "smitten wholeheartedly by the lifestyle he lived and by the places he had been," he cannot ignore his "many flaws and shortcomings" as a human being, notably his womanizing and his drinking (20). Toward the end of the book, he even asserts that it is evident the conservationist "suffered internally. In today's terms and behaviour patternology, Grey Owl may have been labelled a sociopath, or as having DPD—dissociated personality disorder" (235). Nevertheless, it is this polemical figure that Wilson uses as a model to escape his urban life and find some purpose in the universe.

Wilson's life as a canoeist and wilderness guide takes him not only across Canada, especially the Canadian Shield, but around the world. Through most of these experiences, as he relates in *Grey Owl and Me*, he is joined by the spirit of the man he considers "Canada's first wilderness advocate and wildlife conservationist" (2010, 21), whom he often addresses directly as if he were a living being. Wilson claims that Grey Owl possesses the uncanny ability to materialize "every time I [feel] guilty about doing something" (89). Grey Owl actually becomes a sort of alter ego that Wilson consults whenever he faces either troubling or ironic situations, which can lead to some rather interesting dialogues. One of these situations is detailed in the chapter Wilson titles "007 Grey Owl—The Movie," which concerns his participation in Attenborough's film, especially his conflicted relationship with the main star, Pierce Brosnan. Wilson was hired "to teach Brosnan the Ojibwa or guide-stroke—the method of paddling Grey Owl" used (102). As mentioned earlier, he felt disgusted when he first learned that the former James Bond had been hired to play the conservationist, telling Grey Owl that he feared the movie would make "*a mockery of two Canadian icons—you and the canoe*" (104; italics in text). Wilson's view of Attenborough's film never really changes. He eventually concludes that "the movie lacked any pith, any character flaws, or mystery; it was devoid of the drama that defined Grey Owl's true personality" (117). This is a sentiment that seems to have been shared widely by moviegoers, who largely stayed away from the film.

Wilson, however, does develop one close relationship during the shoot, with Brosnan. He flies out to California to teach the actor to canoe at Malibu Lake, and confesses that "007 was a quick learner, and eager to be good at paddling a canoe" (2010, 110). Wilson even appears to have had some fun on the set, such as witnessing the cast and crew's reaction when a "scene had to be cut because Brosnan forgot to take off his Ray Bans," which made him rather "frustrated" (114). His reservations about the star's acting, though, are soon compounded by his suspicion that the fact Brosnan is determined to represent a famous conservationist does not necessarily mean that he shares the latter's values. As Wilson cites Brosnan's response when he tries to enlist his support on behalf of the Temagami forest conservation: " 'Time out...I'm a one-issue environmentalist; the whales are my only interest. Anyway, I'm in the process of buying a rainforest logging company. What do you think about that?' " (116; ellipsis in text). Wilson infers that Brosnan is probably playing with him with the talk about his investment in rainforest logging, but he is not quite certain. Still, the damage is done, and things will only get worse. After he criticized Brosnan's acting in an article for a Canadian magazine, his "name was removed from the credits" (117). That is, while he was not able to save the blockbuster movie about Grey Owl, at least he is not officially associated with it.

Hap Wilson's writings on Grey Owl, not the least his playful account of his involvement with the Attenborough film and Brosnan, raise as many questions as they answer about the literary and cultural significance of the Hastings-born Archie Belaney. But one thing Wilson clearly demonstrates is that Grey Owl remains very much a usable figure in today's culture. For better or for worse, he can be appropriated by almost anyone, especially by those people who vociferously proclaim to share his causes but may in fact know very little about him and his work.

# Grey Owl as a Caucasian Apostate

*If people get tired*
*Of being in the same place,*
*Why shouldn't they tire*
*Of having the same self?*

—Fernando Pessoa

Grey Owl's image in the early part of the twenty-first century remains as conflicted as it has ever been since the revelations that followed his death in 1938 when, in Allan Casey's graphic words, his reputation "went down like a drowned muskrat" (2009, 42). In the aftermath of the publication of Armand Garnet Ruffo's long poem *Grey Owl: The Mystery of Archie Belaney* in 1996, numerous sympathetic representations have appeared of the trapper-turned-conservationist, notably Richard Attenborough's feature film and Hap Wilson's collection of essays, *Grey Owl and Me*. Yet, despite the adulation showered on him in certain circles, he continues to invite much opprobrium. As recently as 2006, the environmental historian Tina Loo condemned Grey Owl for articulating an "anthropocentric and anti-modern conservation message" and even expressed her disapproval of the fact his vision requires that people "see animals as 'fellow dwellers on this earth'" (2006, 113; see also Grey Owl 1938c, 84). As Loo encapsulates her critique, seemingly failing him for his lack of scientific progressivism, "He was not an ecologist or even an amateur naturalist, but rather, as Lovat Dickson recalled, 'a poet, recreating for us dreams of innocence'" (116; Dickson 1973, 241). Writing in 2011, the historians Mark Cronlund Anderson and Carmen L. Robertson character-ized Grey Owl as "a poster boy for Canadian colonialism" and "a perfectly authentic colonial stooge" (116, 136), which seems an odd description for someone who in "My Mission to My Country" claimed that one of his "great ambitions" was "to persuade the people of Canada that the rightful and effective place of the Indian is as the supervisor and custodian of the wilderness itself" (Grey Owl 1938e, 52). Also in 2011, the geographer Bruce Erickson accused Grey Owl of being "complicit in preserving the whiteness of the [Canadian] nation" (2011, 22). That is, instead of deserving to be celebrated for his nature writings and his conservationism, he should be castigated for his anti-modernism, his colonialism, his imperialism, his sexism, and his alleged racism.

Despite the proliferation of such negative assessments, there are compelling reasons for believing that Grey Owl is not likely to vanish from contemporary discourse any time soon. First and foremost, because of the acute (and growing) concerns about the health of the planet, his ecological message continues to resonate. For instance, the naturalist David Attenborough considers Grey Owl a foundational figure in the ecological movement. His regret is that the controversy about the latter's identity, "plus the outbreak of war, meant that all his warnings were ignored. The great tragedy is that if people had acted on what he was saying, the whole ecological movement would have been advanced by at least 30 years" (qtd. in Attenborough 2000). Similarly, the painter and illustrator Graham Ward praises him for "actively promot[ing] the concept of environmentalism and nature conservation" in all his work (2009, para. 6). The writer Vicky Shipton, in turn, has reservations about the way he fashioned his public self. Yet she maintains that "a lot of people [now] agree with Grey Owl's message. They know that many animals are in danger in the world. We should protect them. We should not cut down all of our forests" (2008, 3). The writer Thomas Everitt too contends that, regardless of Grey Owl's "deceptions," the fact remains that his "views on the conservation of fur-bearing animals and the habitats that surrounded them proved decades ahead of their time" (1999, para 4). Finally, the non-fiction writer Kurt Caswell confesses that we may need "the bureaucrats, the lawyers, and the lobbyists" to persuade the masses of the urgency of the environmental fight, "but we need Grey Owl too. Or at least, I need Grey Owl" (2013, para. 38). In other words, for a sizable number of people of all ages, Grey Owl the conservationist has never lost his relevance, which may explain why his books continue to attract readers.

Perhaps not surprisingly, Grey Owl's place seems especially secure in Canada. To begin with, there is the obvious love of the land, and its human and non-human denizens, that is evident throughout his writings. While it is disputable whether Grey Owl is "the most colourful character in Canadian history," there is no question that he is "the greatest public relations spokesman the Canadian wilderness [has] ever had" (Kettle and Walker 1968, 171). Lovat Dickson, for one, claims that he "could think of no [other] writer in Canada who had caught so truly the essential boom-note of this huge, rocky, monolithic land. He made pure Canada, the Canada outside the concrete urban enclosures, come alive" (1973, 239). More significantly, a celebrated novelist like Howard O'Hagan praises him for creating what is now called "'Grey Owl country'" ([1978] 1995, 117), a sentiment shared by both Wilson and his teacher Frank McConnaghy (Wilson 2005, 53, 124). The verdict by O'Hagan, in particular, underlines the magnitude of Grey Owl's contribution to Canadian letters and culture in general, a contribution that is both sustained and deliberate. Indeed, along with Robert Service and Louis Hémon, Grey Owl stands among an elect group of foreign-born writers who have succeeded in creating lasting images of Canada, images that have found enormous audiences around the world and have helped shape the perception of the country both domestically and internationally.

Another reason that Grey Owl is likely to remain a living presence for Canadians has to do with matters of citizenship, notably the relations between non-Indigenous Canadians and the First Nations. The young Archie Belaney's fervent desire to escape Edwardian England and come to Canada clashes with the surprisingly popular Canadian notion that no one chooses Canada. This is a view promulgated by such prominent authors as Margaret Atwood and Jane Urquhart, who contend that, with the exception of "escaped slaves" from the United States, "Canada [has] rarely been seen as the promised land" (Atwood 2004, 9), or that Canada possesses "an entirely different sensibility" than other countries precisely because it is "a place that was never chosen" (Urquhart qtd. in Richler 2006, 11). Needless to say, Archie Belaney/Grey Owl chose Canada. Actually, one of the reasons Casey maintains his "message is perennially worthwhile" is that he is "a figure who stood apart from Margaret Atwood's literary survival motif, who wrote about nature as a trusted ally" (2009, 43). In short, Grey Owl embodies an alternative vision of Canadian nature, one that is not shared by a significant portion of the country's current cultural elites.

It must be noted, however, that Grey Owl did not select Canada as such but only "natural" Canada, the land of endless forests, rivers, and lakes. This is a (vast) part of the country that is sparsely populated, and that most Canadians do not know well. It is also a region with a significant Indigenous populace, the very ethnocultural group that attracted the young Belaney to Canada and with whom he had close interactions from the day he arrived until he died. In fact, many Canadian writers and scholars have come to see the Englishman's metamorphosis into Grey Owl as symbolic of a process of Indigenization that all non-Indigenous Canadians must undergo, at least psychologically, if they are to become at home in their country as well as their continent (Sheridan 2001, 419–20). Atwood herself identifies what she terms "The Grey Owl Syndrome" as "that curious phenomenon, the desire among non-Natives to turn themselves into Natives" (1995, 35). Without minimizing the ethical issues involved in pretending to belong to another ethnocultural group, Grey Owl simply appears to have dramatized an experience that is not uncommon to people with no Indigenous ancestry in Canada and across the Americas.

Through his so-called masquerade, Grey Owl also exposes some of the major fissures in Canadian society, particularly the still problematic place of Indigenous people in the country. In her discussion of the heyday of "Indian impersonators" in Canada in the early decades of the twentieth century (Atwood 1995, 45), Atwood remarks that it is ironic that it occurred "during a period of intense but concealed guerrilla warfare conducted against Indians—when the North was being increasingly invaded by the forces of commercialism, when treaties were being violated, lands appropriated, rights denied" (1995, 47). The fact that Grey Owl could elicit so much xenophobia, if not outright racism, on the part of non-Indigenous Canadians merely because they (wrongly) believed he was partly Indigenous clearly suggests that the wider Canadian society has not yet managed to come to terms with the country's Indigenous populace.

For example, in an essay entitled "Let's Bury the Noble Savage," the influential cultural journalist Robert Fulford describes being told by the Macmillan of Canada editor John Gray, Hugh Eayrs's successor, about an incident involving Grey Owl in the 1930s. Gray and his author were walking across the lobby of Toronto's ritzy King Edward Hotel, on the way to a banquet, when Grey Owl was recognized by a group of drunks, one of whom "shouted, 'Where's your squaw?'" An incensed Grey Owl reached for the knife he carried strapped to his belt before Gray persuaded him that he should not allow such people to get to him. Grey Owl agreed with Gray, but with resignation, saying "'you see how it is. In this country I'll never be anything but a *god-damned Indian!*'" (Fulford 1992, 31; italics in text; see also Gray 1978, 215–16). For Fulford, the moral of the episode is that it "summarized perfectly the way whites deal symbolically with natives," since the scene "had all the necessary elements—anger, bigotry, nobility, and the presence of a man with a powerful image. It had everything but a native" (31). But there is another way of interpreting the incident. It also reveals that a famous white writer and conservationist with no Indigenous ancestry whatsoever can be insulted in public merely because people believe he is Indigenous, something that says much about the way the dominant Canadian society perceives Indigenous peoples. Tellingly, in her response to Fulford, the Anishinaabe writer Lenore Keeshig-Tobias asserts that *"it's too late"* to bury the noble savage *"because we, Aboriginal peoples, have embraced the noble stereotype, adopted him, and he is now one of us, and has been for a very long time. So, back off"* (2005, xvi; italics in text). While Keeshig-Tobias is being somewhat ironic, it is significant that Indigenous people seem more comfortable with the image than do non-Indigenous ones. Perhaps their experiences suggest that the dominant society cannot yet always differentiate between stereotypes and the real thing.

The idea that Canadians harboured reservations about the champion of the beaver is reinforced by his domestic book sales. Even though Grey Owl became an international bestseller, he did not fare nearly as well in Canada, something that Eayrs took personally. Eayrs made "extraordinary efforts to penetrate the Canadian market with Grey Owl's books" and, for him, the "weak sales…were a source of constant disappointment" (Panofsky 2012, 101). Yet while he blamed Grey Owl's limited appeal to Canadians on " 'the churlishness of the Canadian public to our own [writers]' " (qtd. in Panofsky, 101), it is possible that there is something foreign about both his conservationism and his fascination with the First Nations. It is hard to deny the fact that in New World countries where the overwhelming majority of the populace is of diasporic origin, there is a profound need to Indigenize oneself. At the same time, we should not forget that the young Archie Belaney's fascination with Indigenous people preceded his arrival in Canada. Therefore, it cannot have been precipitated by a Canadian—or New World—anxiety about not being at home in one's homeland, what the Hopi and Miwok poet Wendy Rose terms the non-Indigenous "wants for roots" (1994, 22). As Alastair Bonnett observes, "Grey Owl's veneration of nature and his identification with 'Red Indians' were not learned in Canada but in Hastings" (2000, 91). In other words, there is a critical portion of the story of Grey Owl that is not Canadian at all. Rather, it is English—or British—and we will never be able to understand what may have precipitated his journey unless we come to terms with his early years on the other side of the Atlantic.

Of Grey Owl's three major transformations—from a trapper to a conservationist, then to a writer and lecturer, and finally from an Englishman into either someone of mixed European and Indigenous ancestry or a North American Indian—the last is clearly the most controversial; it is the event that colours every other aspect of his life. Yet it is also the one metamorphosis that he conceals. As Gordon Snell writes in the poem he produces in collaboration with the cartoonist Aislin:

> He made sure nobody recalled
> That his real name was Archibald,
> Pretending that it wasn't true
> That he was English through and through. (2001, 217)

Perhaps the reason Grey Owl does not talk about his Englishness is that even he is not persuaded that he has escaped it. No less a student of the conservationist than Donald B. Smith asserts that "[t]he key to his creativity and his genius lies in his childhood in England. A combination of circumstances led him to enter into a fantasy world of his own making, one which would totally devour him" (1990, 7). Clive Bloom, similarly, states that Canada appealed to Archie Belaney because it not only provided him with "the freedom he craved" but also enabled him to be "far away from the Englishness that had come to suffocate him" (2013, 235–36). At one point, Grey Owl himself admits that he is partly European, at least culturally. In a 1935 letter to Dickson, in response to a "critic of *Pilgrims* (and one only)" who "cast a slight aspersion at the 'Transatlantic flavour' of the book," he confesses, "Well, I am transatlantic; and I do not have to take my cue from the English craftsman. He writes his way, and I write mine. That is my style and I am entitled to it, and will always use it" ([1934–35] 1938a, 72). Still, what is most notable about Grey Owl's early life in England is that he never seems to have felt at home in his native culture.

The fact someone is not at peace in the place where he was born of course does not mean that it is not some kind of home, even if in a negative manner. As that other complicated Englishman, the horror and fantasy writer Clive Barker, reflects on belonging, "Home? No, never that. Never home. And yet what other word was there for this place he'd fled from?" (1997, 366). Even Grey Owl's own dream of going native in another culture seems to be a rather English yearning. As the explorer Percy Harrison Fawcett once declared, "The English go native very easily.... There is no disgrace in it. On the contrary, in my opinion it shows a creditable regard for the real things in life" (qtd. in Thorpe 2004). But not everyone is as generous about the apparent English propensity to disappear into other cultures as Fawcett, who himself is believed to have gone native in his elusive search for the Lost City of Z in Mato Grosso, Brazil. Thomas Raddall, for example, states in a 1947 letter to Margaret Vollmer, "For some reason the notion of living amongst Indians and posing as one of them seems to have a peculiar appeal for a certain type of Englishman. Apart from 'Grey Owl' I know of two who have done it quite successfully." Raddall does not identify the two other Englishmen who have passed as Indians, but one senses that he does not approve of the trend. Similarly, Colin Ross contends, "When Archie writes a book, he writes just like an Englishman," and "[i]nside Archie Belaney was an Englishman who got lonely for his aunts" (1979, 82, 83). The notion that Grey Owl writes like an Englishman is historically unpersuasive, since prior to his posthumous exposure there is remarkably little evidence of readers or critics who expressed their scepticism that a half-Indigenous person could have written such texts. Likewise, the idea that the career of Grey Owl is explained by his longing for his aunts is contradicted by his own writings, in which he does not convey much love for his biological family.

Furthermore, the purported English inclination to go native is probably not unrelated to the phenomenal mobility that the English people have enjoyed over the last few centuries. The fact that until recently they were at the centre of a global empire made it relatively easy to move to other countries. This is certainly true of Grey Owl. When he migrated to Canada, he was not only able to continue to live in his native language but even under his own monarch, who also happened to be Canada's head of state. That said, Grey Owl's desire to escape his early self is neither anomalous nor are impulses such as his restricted to the English. As the Portuguese poet Fernando Pessoa writes in the stanza that serves as the epigraph to this chapter, considering that many people get tired of being in the same location, "Why shouldn't they tire/ Of having the same self?" (2006, 315). The solution for Pessoa, who was born in 1888 and died in 1935 and is Grey Owl's almost exact contemporary, was to create a series of autonomous poets, or heteronyms, the way other writers fashion characters. In contrast, Grey Owl does not attempt "to flee" his early self (315) by embracing multiples selves but by adopting another culture.

Although Grey Owl's odyssey has a European dimension that predates his arrival in Canada, it is part of an archetypal New World experience. Ever since the Europeans crossed the Atlantic and landed on American shores, there have been numerous instances of individuals—usually young men—who have preferred the Indigenous cultures they encountered to their own and joined them. Two of the best known cases are the Spaniard Gonzalo Guerrero in Mexico and the Frenchman Étienne Brûlé in Canada. But scholars like James Axtell and Philippe Jacquin have shown that the phenomenon was widespread across the continent, and that it had no equivalent of Indigenous people fleeing their communities for white ones (Axtell 1979, 7–8). The motivations for such decisions had to be diverse. Yet, as Jacquin argues in his 1996 book *Les Indiens Blancs* (The white Indians), the Europeans who chose to "go Indian" inevitably bore "*le sceau de l'infamie*" (the mark of infamy) (208). By embracing what were supposed to be less advanced cultures, those individuals called into question the value of their own cultures, especially when those cultures were at the zenith of their economic, political, and military power.

That is also what Grey Owl did: he forsook British culture for Anishinaabe culture—and North American Indigenous culture in general—at a time when the British Empire was one of the dominant powers in the world. What his journey entailed remains open to debate, but there is little doubt that it involved some kind of rejection of the culture into which he was born and of his European self. Jeremy Sadness, Robert Kroetsch's protagonist in *Gone Indian*, says of his hero, " 'He killed himself…. He killed Archie Belaney. Then he became an Indian' " ([1973] 1999, 106). Other scholars and writers, though, have argued that Archie Belaney's metamorphosis into Grey Owl was not just about self-transformation but also about cultural apostasy. Some have even suggested that, in addition to their misreading him, the reason many non-Indigenous critics are so disturbed by the revelations about his identity is precisely the implication that he forsook European civilization for an alien one.

For R.E. Rashley, writing in 1971, Grey Owl is a "drop-out from European culture," who "sets up his own concept of a superior culture, the woodsman's culture, the culture in which man accepts and adjusts to his environment instead of manipulating and re-creating it" (61). Rashley maintains that Grey Owl reduces man "to an alert and capable animal, a creature of nature, a big brother to the other creatures, inhabiting the same house in much the same way," yet he asserts that Grey Owl's "rejection of European civilization is a rejection of the whole man-created western culture" (63). James Polk agrees. In his book on Canadian nature writers, he states that the controversy that followed Grey Owl's death "seems stupid and unfair today," and suggests that what really troubled the media was "his whiteness" (1972, 146). While a few people tried to draw attention to "the man's contribution to conservation and literature" and "his wide knowledge of Indian customs and language," he continues, it did not make any difference. This peculiar reaction leads Polk to ponder, "Perhaps deep down, people were disturbed by the thought that a white man would actually prefer a more primitive culture to his 'advanced' society" (146). In short, the problem with Grey Owl appears to be not so much his masquerade as his cultural apostasy, a view that is shared by an increasing number of Indigenous people.

Among Indigenous people, Grey Owl's image is as uneven as it is with the general public. For the Anishinaabe playwright and novelist Drew Hayden Taylor, Grey Owl is a cultural appropriator. He is someone whose adopted name, "He-Who-Flies-By-Night," says all we need to know about his relations with the First Nations (1999, 120). But other Indigenous people hold rather different views of Grey Owl. Following his posthumous exposure in 1938, one of the more puzzling questions that surfaced was why Indigenous people had not unmasked him. The reason, as the case of Anahareo illustrates, would appear to be that there were individuals who did not know that he had no Indigenous ancestry. But it has also been postulated that even though some Indigenous people were aware of the conservationist's ethnocultural identity, they remained silent because they approved of his work. The Saskatchewan Cree leader John Tootoosis, for instance, claimed that when he met Grey Owl in Ottawa and saw him play drums, he immediately knew that he was "not an Indian" (Goodwill and Sluman 1984, 168). Yet Tootoosis elected not to say anything to anyone, since "he respected the work Grey Owl was doing in conserving the beaver, and more beavers meant more dams to hold back the water and that in turn meant better conditions for the muskrat and waterfowl population" (169). Similarly, in his essay "Writing the Water," Ruffo imagines a conversation with his great-grandfather years after the latter has "passed on" (2000, 193). During a visit to his great-grandfather's trapping cabin, where his forebear is believed to have given refuge to the newcomer, Ruffo inquires about the Indigenous silence regarding Grey Owl's identity:

> "Why didn't you say anything?"
> "Because he'd learned good and was doing good and that was good enough for us."
> "That's what it was about, wasn't it?"
> "That's all it's ever about. Besides he made us laugh, all that hooting of his!"
> "There were reporters who wanted to expose him."
> "Sure there were, but nobody asked us. Back then we didn't exist. Least not in a real way." (200, 192–93)

Besides the fact that few journalists seem to have been interested in what Indigenous people may have had to say about Grey Owl, Ruffo's great-grandfather suggests that some Indigenous people had no desire to expose the conservationist, since they approved of his actions. Actually, even Drew Hayden Taylor seems to have reversed his view of Grey Owl. He now not only praises him for becoming "fluent" in Anishinaabe, but even states that, "[i]n some ways, he did a lot more for Native culture than a lot of Natives did." As Taylor adds, "you can thank God and his sense of Irony" (2014, 229).

Moreover, there is at least one other reason why some Indigenous people did not reveal Grey Owl's true identity to the media—the fact that they did not merely applaud his advocacy on their behalf but also appreciated his preference of their culture to his own. One of Gilbert Oskaboose's criticisms of Richard Attenborough's film is that it shows so little of its protagonist's engagement with the Anishinaabe. "Grey Owl has walked out onto the Wind to be with the Grandfathers," concludes Oskaboose, "but his spirit lives on in the hearts of the Ahnishnawbek people. He will always be with us, a part of the First People, a shining beacon of great strength and Hope for a better future" (2000, para 7). For someone like Oskaboose, Grey Owl's ethnocultural transformation does not necessarily have to be perceived as a negative act from an Indigenous perspective; quite the opposite. The same is true of the Cree actor Nathaniel Arcand, who plays Grey Owl's best friend in Attenborough's film. Arcand asserts that for "a white guy like Archie Belaney to come to Canada on a dream to become an Indian by choice is sort of admirable in our culture—that someone would want to protect the forest and do the things that natives do." As he underscores, "A lot of native people back then didn't want to be native" (qtd. in FFWD 1999). Again, for some Indigenous people, Grey Owl was an outsider who championed Indigenous culture at a time when not too many people prized it. So rather than being a fraud, he is someone who should be praised for his identification with the First Nations. Perhaps more significant, as noted in the introduction, the Anishinaabe leader Gary Potts (2001) claims that what troubles white people the most about Archie Belaney's transformation into Grey Owl is precisely that he favoured Indigenous ways over European ones. That is, he commited cultural apostasy. This is something that many of his critics can neither understand nor forgive. Thus, they accuse him of cultural appropriation.

# Works Cited

## Books by Grey Owl

Grey Owl. 1937. *The Tree*. First published in essay form in *Tales of an Empty Cabin*. London: Lovat Dickson.

_____. 1938. *A Book of Grey Owl: Pages from the Writings of Wa-Sha-Quon-Asin*. Toronto: Macmillan.

_____. [1931] 1973. *The Men of the Last Frontier*. Toronto: Macmillan.

_____. [1935] 1977. *Sajo and the Beaver People*. With sketches by the author. Toronto: Macmillan. Published in Great Britain as *The Adventures of Sajo and Her Beaver People*.

_____. [1935] 1990. *Pilgrims of the Wild*. Toronto: Macmillan.

_____. [1936] 1999. *Tales of an Empty Cabin*. Toronto: Stoddart.

## Articles, Interviews, and Letters by Grey Owl

Grey Owl. 1914. "An Old Hastonian amongst the Indians." *Hastonian*, 10 July, 6–7. Smith Papers. Glenbow Archives. M 8102, Box 3, Folder 30.

_____. [H. Scott-Brown pseud.]. 1929. "The Passing of the Last Frontier." *Country Life*, 2 March, 302–5.

_____. 1930a. "The Vanishing Life of the Wild." *Illustrated Canadian Forest and Outdoors*, June, 312–23, 361–64.

_____. 1930b. "Little Brethren of the Wilderness." Part One. *Illustrated Canadian Forest and Outdoors*, September, 499–501.

_____. 1930c. "Little Brethren of the Wilderness." Part Two. *Illustrated Canadian Forest and Outdoors*, October, 573–74.

_____. 1930d. "The Fine Art of the Still Hunt." *Illustrated Canadian Forest and Outdoors*, November, 624–26, 666.

_____. 1930e. "King of the Beaver People." Part One. *Illustrated Canadian Forest and Outdoors*, December, 683–86.

_____. 1931a. "King of the Beaver People." Part Two. *Illustrated Canadian Forest and Outdoors*, January, 13–15.

_____. 1931b. "Who Will Repay?" *Illustrated Canadian Forest and Outdoors*, March, 119–22.

_____. 1931c. "A Day in a Hidden…Town." *Illustrated Canadian Forest and Outdoors*, April, 177–80.

_____. 1931d. "The Indian's Side of the Question." *Illustrated Canadian Forest and Outdoors*, April, 195.

_____. 1931e. "Comments on Mr. Godsell's Article." *Illustrated Canadian Forest and Outdoors*, July, 343–44.

_____. 1931f. "Indian Legends and Lore." *Illustrated Canadian Forest and Outdoors*, October, 23, 32.

_____. 1931g. "And a Little Child Shall Lead Them." *Illustrated Canadian Forest and Outdoors*, October, 40.

_____. 1932a. "'Unto…the Least of These.'" *Illustrated Canadian Forest and Outdoors*, March, 89–91, 94.

_____. 1932b. "Re-builder of the Wilderness." Part One. *Illustrated Canadian Forest and Outdoors*, August, 289–92, 304.

_____. 1933. "The Beaver Family Migrates." *Illustrated Canadian Forest and Outdoors*, September, 229–31, 256.

_____. 1934."The Wilderness Awakes." *Lovat Dickson's Magazine* 3, no. 6, 670–75.

_____. 1935a. "How Anahareo Had Her Way." *Lovat Dickson's Magazine* 4, no. 4, 322–38.

_____. 1935b. "The Indian's Code of the Wild." *Illustrated Canadian Forest and Outdoors*, June, 883–84.

_____. 1935c. "The Fine Art of the Still Hunt." *Illustrated Canadian Forest and Outdoors*, November, 1048–50.

_____. 1936. "Grey Owl Speaks His Mind." *Illustrated Canadian Forest and Outdoors*, September, 269–70, 282.

_____. [1934–35] 1938a. "Grey Owl's Letters." In *The Green Leaf: A Tribute to Grey Owl*, edited by Lovat Dickson, 53–80. London: Lovat Dickson.

_____. [1937] 1938b. "Grey Owl's Farewell." In *The Green Leaf: A Tribute to Grey Owl*, edited by Lovat Dickson, 103–109. London: Lovat Dickson.

_____. 1938c. "Grey Owl's Precepts." In *The Green Leaf: A Tribute to Grey Owl*, edited by Lovat Dickson, 83–85. London: Lovat Dickson.

_____. 1938d. "Grey Owl Pleads for Wild Life (*Excerpts from Grey Owl's Letter to 'Forest & Outdoors'*)." *Illustrated Canadian Forest and Outdoors*, January, 397.

_____. [as told to Robson Black]. 1938e. "My Mission to My Country." *Illustrated Canadian Forest and Outdoors*, February, 37–38, 52.

_____. [1935] 1988. Letter to W.A. Deacon, 10 May. In *Dear Bill: The Correspondence of William Arthur Deacon*, edited by John Lennox and Michèle Lacombe, 162–66. Toronto: University of Toronto Press.

_____. [1931] 1995. "The Great Adventure." *Manitoba History* 29: 46–51.

Grey Owl, with Tony Lascelles. 1931. "A Philosophy of the Wild." *Illustrated Canadian Forest and Outdoors*, December, 15–17.

## Other Texts

"The Adventurous Career of GREY OWL (wa-shee-quon-asier)." 1931. *Illustrated Canadian Forest and Outdoors*, March, 118.

Allison, W.T. 1932. "'Beaver Man' Reveals Secrets of Mother Nature." Review of *The Men of the Last Frontier*, by Grey Owl. *Winnipeg Tribune*, 16 July.

Altmeyer, George. 1976. "Three Ideas of Nature in Canada, 1893–1914." In *Consuming Canada: Readings in Environmental History*, edited by Chad and Pam Gaffield, 96–118. Toronto: Copp Clark, 1995.

Anahareo. 1940. *My Life with Grey Owl.* London: Peter Davies.

———. 1972. *Devil in Deerskins: My Life with Grey Owl.* Toronto: New Press.

———. 2014. *Devil in Deerskins: My Life with Grey Owl*, edited by Sophie McCall. Winnipeg: University of Manitoba Press.

Anderson, Mark Cronlund, and Carmen L. Robertson. 2011. "Disrobing Grey Owl: The Death of Archie Belaney, 1938." In *Seeing Red: A History of Natives in Canadian Newspapers*, 116–36. Winnipeg: University of Manitoba Press.

"The Annual Forest Convention." 1931. *Illustrated Canadian Forest and Outdoors*, February, 93, 95.

*Annual Report of the Commissioner of National Parks, Fiscal Year Ended March 31, 1934.* 1935. Ottawa: J.O. Patenaude.

Arnold, G.A. 1935. "Grey Owl and His Beavers London Sensation." *Regina Leader-Post*, 27 November, 4.

Attenborough, Richard. 1999. "Grey Owl." *BFI*. http://www.bfi.org.uk/features/atten-borough/greyowl.html. Accessed 5 May 2009.

———. 2000. "Animal Magic." *Guardian*, 27 October. http://www.guardian.co.uk/film/2000/oct/27/culture.features1/print. Accessed 5 May 2009.

Atwood, Margaret. 1995. "The Grey Owl Syndrome." In *Strange Things: The Malevolent North in Canadian Literature*, 35–61. Oxford: Clarendon.

———. [1972] 2004. *Survival: A Thematic Guide to Canadian Literature.* Toronto: McClelland and Stewart.

Auden, W.H. 1962. "Writing." In *The Dyer's Hand and Other Essays*, 13–27. New York: Random House.

Axtell, James. 1979. *White Indians of Colonial America.* Fairfield, WA: Galleon.

Barker, Clive. 1997. *Sacrament.* New York: HarperPaperbacks.

Bates, M.U. 1930. "'Survival of the Fittest?'" *Illustrated Canadian Forest and Outdoors*, March, 137–38.

Belaney, Tanyann Grey Owl. 2006. Foreword to *He Who Flies by Night: The Story of Grey Owl* by Lori Punshon. Regina: Your Nickel's Worth.

Billinghurst, Jane. 1999. *Grey Owl: The Many Faces of Archie Belaney.* Vancouver: Greystone.

Bloom, Clive. 2013. *Victoria's Madmen: Revolution and Alienation.* Houndmills, UK: Palgrave Macmillan.

Bonnett, Alastair. 2000. "Escaping Whiteness? Primitivism and the Search for Human Authenticity." In *White Identities: Historical and International Perspectives*, 78–118. Harlow, UK: Prentice Hall.

_____. 2006. "Pale Face, Red Mask: Racial Ambiguity and the Imitation of 'American Indian' Facial Expressions." *Cultural Politics* 2, no. 3: 319–38.

Braz, Albert. 2001–02. "The White Indian: Armand Garnet Ruffo's *Grey Owl* and the Spectre of Authenticity." *Journal of Canadian Studies* 36, no. 4: 171–87.

_____. 2005. "The Modern Hiawatha: Grey Owl's Construction of His Aboriginal Self." In *Auto/biography in Canada: Critical Directions*, edited by Julie Rak, 53–68. Waterloo, ON: Wilfrid Laurier University Press.

_____. 2007. "St. Archie of the Wild: Grey Owl's Account of His 'Natural' Conversion." In *Other Selves: Animals in the Canadian Literary Imagination*, edited by Janice Fiamengo, 206–26. Ottawa: University of Ottawa Press.

_____. 2012. "Beaver Voices: Grey Owl and Interspecies Communication." In *Experiencing Animal Minds: An Anthology of Animal-Human Encounters*, edited by Julie A. Smith and Robert W. Mitchell, 51–62. New York: Columbia University Press.

_____. 2013. "The Director's Medium: Richard Attenborough's De-Authorization of Grey Owl." In *Double-Takes: Intersections between Canadian Literature and Film*, edited by David R. Jarraway, 169–82. Ottawa: University of Ottawa Press.

Broadus, E.K. 1936. "Fiction (List III)." *University of Toronto Quarterly* 5, no. 3: 368–88.

Brower, Kenneth. 1990. "Grey Owl." *Atlantic*, January, 74–84.

Brown, E.K. 1937. Letter to Lloyd Roberts, 18 August. Lloyd Roberts Collection of Grey Owl Papers. Thomas Fisher Rare Book Library, University of Toronto. Box 1, Folder 11.

Callaghan, Morley. 2008. "Grey Owl: Language of the Eyes." In *A Literary Life: Reflections and Reminiscences 1928–1990*, 61–64. Toronto: Exile.

Campbell, J.C. 1935. Letter to M.B. Williams, 2 December. In *MB: Living and Writing the Early Years of Parks Canada*, edited by Alan MacEachern, Luvneet Rana, and Adam Crymple. http://mbwilliams.academic-news.org. Accessed 23 December 2013.

_____. 1936a. Campbell, J.C. Letter to M.B. Williams, 4 January. In *MB: Living and Writing the Early Years of Parks Canada*, edited by Alan MacEachern, Luvneet Rana, and Adam Crymple. http://mbwilliams.academic-news.org. Accessed 23 December 2013.

_____. 1936b. Campbell, J.C. Letter to M.B. Williams, 20 March. In *MB: Living and Writing the Early Years of Parks Canada*, edited by Alan MacEachern, Luvneet Rana, and Adam Crymple. http://mbwilliams.academic-news.org. Accessed 23 December 2013.

_____. 1936c. Campbell, J.C. Letter to M.B. Williams, 16 April. In *MB: Living and Writing the Early Years of Parks Canada*, edited by Alan MacEachern, Luvneet Rana, and Adam Crymple. http://mbwilliams.academic-news.org. Accessed 23 December 2013.

Campbell, Maria. [1973] 1983. *Halfbreed*. Halifax: Goodread.

Cantwell, Robert. 1963. "Grey Owl: Mysterious Genius of Nature Lore." *Sports Illustrated*, 8 April, 113–26.

Casey, Allan. 2009. "The Grey Wizard." In *Lakeland: Journeys into the Soul of Canada*, 41–57. Vancouver: Greystone.

Castell, David. 1984. *Richard Attenborough: A Pictorial Biography*. London: Bodley Head.

Caswell, Kurt. 2013. "Getting to Grey Owl's Cabin." *Terrrain.org: A Journal of the Built and Natural Environments.* http://terrain.org/2013/nonfiction/getting-to-grey-owls-cabin/. Accessed 3 March 2014.

Chapin, David. 2000. "Gender and Indian Masquerade in the Life of Grey Owl." *American Indian Quarterly* 24, no. 1: 91–109.

Cockerell, T.D.A. 1936. "A Visit with Grey Owl." *Natural History*, March, 223–30.

Collier, David. 2001. "The Life of Grey Owl." In *Portraits from Life*, n.p. Montreal: Drawn and Quarterly.

Compton, Wayde. 2010. "Pheneticizing versus Passing." In *After Canaan: Essays on Race, Writing, and Region*, 19–59. Vancouver: Arsenal Pulp.

Cory, Harper. 1935. *Grey Owl and the Beaver.* London: Thomas Nelson.

Cuthand, Doug. 2007. *ASKIWINA: A Cree Word.* Regina: Coteau.

Dawson, Carrie. 1998. "Never Cry Fraud: Remembering Grey Owl, Rethinking Imposture." *Essays on Canadian Writing* 65: 120–40.

_____. 2007. "The 'I' in Beaver: Sympathetic Identification and Self-Representation in Grey Owl's *Pilgrims of the Wild*." In *Five Emus to the King of Siam: Environment and Empire*, edited by Helen Tiffin, 113–29. Amsterdam: Rodopi.

Deacon, William Arthur. 1988. *Dear Bill: The Correspondence of William Arthur Deacon*, edited by John Lennox and Michèle Lacombe. Toronto: University of Toronto Press.

Dean, Misao. 2007. "'The Mania for Killing': Hunting and Collecting in Seton's *The Arctic Prairies*." In *Other Selves: Animals in the Canadian Literary Imagination*, edited by Janice Fiamengo, 290–304. Ottawa: University of Ottawa Press.

Deloria, Philip J. 1998. *Playing Indian.* New Haven: Yale University Press.

Dewar, Jonathan R. 2002. "Fringes, Imposture, and Connection: Armand Garnet Ruffo's *Grey Owl: The Mystery of Archie Belaney* and 'Communitist' Literature." In *Creating Community: A Roundtable on Canadian Aboriginal Literature*, edited by Renate Eigenbrod and Jo-Ann Episkenew, 255–73. Penticton: Theytus/ Brandon: Bearpaw.

Dickinson, Adam. 2000. "By the Shape of a Canoe," review of *Tales of an Empty Cabin*, by Grey Owl. *Fiddlehead* 203: 108–10.

Dickson, Lovat. 1936. "Grey Owl, Man of the Wilderness." *Strand*, May, 64, 73–74.

_____, ed. 1938a. *The Green Leaf: A Tribute to Grey Owl.* London: Lovat Dickson.

_____. 1938b. "The Passing of Grey Owl." In *The Green Leaf: A Tribute to Grey Owl*, edited by Lovat Dickson, 9–33. London: Lovat Dickson.

_____. 1938c. Letter to Hugh Eayrs, 9 May. Macmillan Fonds. William Ready Division of Archives and Research Collections, McMaster University. Box 100, File 6.

_____. 1939. *Half-Breed: The Story of Grey Owl (Wa-Sha-quon-Wasin).* London: Peter Davies.

_____. 1973. *Wilderness Man: The Strange Story of Grey Owl.* Toronto: Macmillan.

_____. [1959] 1975. *The Ante-Room: Early Stages of a Literary Life.* Don Mills, ON: Totem.

_____. [1963] 1976. *The House of Words.* Don Mills, ON: Totem.

Diefenbaker, John. 1975. *One Canada: Memoirs of the Right Honourable John G. Diefenbaker: The Crusading Years 1895–1956.* Toronto: Macmillan.

Dudar, Judith. 1991. "The History of a History: Tracing Thomas H. Raddall's Research into Grey Owl." *Time and Place: The Life and Works of Thomas H. Raddall*, edited by Alan R. Young, 120–29. Fredericton: Acadiensis.

Duffus, R. L. 1932. "Grey Owl, a Scotch-Indian Half-Breed Trapper, Tells of the Last Frontier." Review of *The Men of the Last Frontier*, by Grey Owl. *New York Times*, 22 May, 4.

Eakin, Paul. 1999. *How Our Lives Become Stories: Making Selves*. Ithaca, NY: Cornell University Press.

Eaton, Anne T. 1936. "The New Books for Boys and Girls." Review of *Sajo and the Beaver People*, by Grey Owl. *New York Times*, 13 December, BR 11.

Eayrs, Hugh. 1935. Foreword to *Pilgrims of the Wild*, by Grey Owl. London: Lovat Dickson.

———. 1938. Preface to *A Book of Grey Owl: Pages from the Writings of Wa-Sha-Quon-Asin*, by Grey Owl. Alberta ed. Toronto: Macmillan.

Egan, Susanna. 2004. "The Company She Keeps: Demidenko and the Problems of Imposture in Autobiography." *Australian Literary Studies* 21, no. 4: 14–27.

———. 2011. *Burdens of Proof: Faith, Doubt, and Identity in Autobiography*. Waterloo, ON: Wilfrid Laurier University Press.

Erickson, Bruce. 2011. "'A Phantasy in White in a World That Is Dead': Grey Owl and the Whiteness of Surrogacy." In *Rethinking the Great White North: Race, Nature, and the Historical Geographies of Whiteness in Canada*, edited by Andrew Baldwin, Laura Cameron, and Audrey Kobayashi, 19–38. Vancouver: UBC Press.

Everitt, Thomas R. 1999. "The Helpful Fraud." Review of *Grey Owl: The Many Faces of Archie Belaney*, by Jane Billinghurst. *January Magazine*, November. http://www.januarymagazine.com/nonfiction/greyowl.html. Accessed 14 February 2010.

FFWD Staff. 1999. "Film." *FFWD Weekly*, 30 September. http://www.ffwdweekly.com/Issues/1999/0930/film.html. Accessed 4 May 2009.

Francis, Daniel. 1992. *The Imaginary Indian: The Image of the Indian in Canadian Culture*. Vancouver: Arsenal Pulp.

———. 1997. *National Dreams: Myth, Memory, and Canadian History*. Vancouver: Arsenal Pulp.

Fraser, John. 1975. "A Widow Defends Imposter Grey Owl." *Globe and Mail*, 30 October, 17.

Fulford, Robert. 1992. "Let's Bury the Noble Savage: Indians and Museums Are Working Together to Eradicate Indian Stereotypes." *Rotunda* 25, no. 2: 30–35.

Gaskell, Eric F. 1935. "The Pilgrim (a tribute to Grey Owl)." *Saturday Night*, 16 November, B1.

———. 1936. "Grey Owl: Pathfinder and Artist." *Canadian Bookman* 18, no. 6: 1–5.

George, Chief Dan. 2004. *The Best of Chief Dan George*. Surrey, BC: Hancock House.

Gleeson, Kristin. 2011. "Blazing Her Own Trail: Anahareo's Rejection of Euro-Canadian Stereotypes." *Recollecting: Lives of Aboriginal Women of the Canadian Northwest and Borderlands*, edited by Sarah Carter and Patricia A. McCormack, 287–311. Edmonton: Athabasca University Press.

———. 2012. *Anahareo: A Wilderness Spirit*. Tucson, AZ: Fireship.

Glotfelty, Cheryll. 2004. "'Once a Cowboy': Will James, Waddie Mitchell, and the Predicament of Riders Who Turn Writers." In *Eco-Man: New Perspectives on*

*Masculinity and Nature*, edited by Mark Allister, 127–40. Charlotte: University of Virginia Press.

Godsell, Philip H. 1931. "Spendthrifts of the Fur Supply." *Illustrated Canadian Forest and Outdoors*, July, 340–44.

Goodwill, Jean, and Norma Sluman. 1984. *John Tootoosis*. Winnipeg: Pemmican.

Gordon, Irene Ternier. 2004. *The Curious Life of Archie Belaney*. Canmore, AB: Altitude.

Gray, John Morgan. 1978. *Fun Tomorrow: Learning to Be a Publisher and Much Else*. Toronto: Macmillan.

Green, Rayna. 1988. "The Tribe Called Wannabee: Playing Indian in America and Europe." *Folklore* 99, no. 1: 30–55.

*Grey Owl*. 1972. Directed by Nancy Ryley. Screenplay by Lovat Dickson. CBC.

*Grey Owl*. 1999. Directed by Richard Attenborough. Screenplay by William Nicholson. With Pierce Brosnan, Annie Galipeau, and Nathaniel Arcand. Remstar.

*Grey Owl: A Biographical Note and A Day at Beaver Lodge*. 1937. London: Lovat Dickson.

"Grey Owl Hushed." 1938. *Time*, 3 January, 17.

Grigor, Angela Nairne. 2002. *Arthur Lismer: Visionary Art Educator*. Montreal: McGill-Queen's University Press.

Gutsche, George J. 1986. *Moral Apostasy in Russian Literature*. Dekalb: Northern Illinois University Press.

Halton, M.H. 1938. "Grey Owl Sought Friends in Belaney's Native Town." *Toronto Daily Star*, 19 April, 1, 8.

Hart, E.J. (Ted). 2010. *J.B. Harkin: Father of Canada's National Parks*. Edmonton: University of Alberta Press.

Harvey, Jean-Charles. 1937. "La mort de l'orignal." *Art et combat*, 28–34. Montreal: Éditions de l'A.C.F.

———. 1965. "Hommes et bêtes." In *Des bois…des champs…des bêtes…*, 84–85. Montreal: Éditions de l'Homme.

Hayman, John. 1994. "Grey Owl's Wild Goose Chase." *History Today* 44, no. 1: 42–48.

Hearne, Samuel. [1795] 1958. *A Journey from Prince of Wales's Fort in Hudson's Bay to the Northern Ocean 1769, 1770, 1771, 1772*, edited by Richard Glover. Toronto: Macmillan.

Heidenreich, Rosmarin. 2000. "Inventions of the Self: Canadian Palimpsests." *New Worlds: Discovering and Constructing the Unknown in Anglophone Literature*, edited by Martin Kuester, Gabriele Christ, and Rudolf Beck, 217–38. Munich: Ernst Vögel.

Hollinger, David A. 1995. *Postethnic America: Beyond Multiculturalism*. New York: Basic.

Horwill, Herbert W. 1935. "News and Views of Literary London." *New York Times*, 17 November, BR 8, 23.

Huggan, Graham. 2007. *Australian Literature: Postcolonialism, Racism, Transnationalism*. Oxford: Oxford University Press.

Hulan, Renée. 2006. "Hearing Voices in Armand Garnet Ruffo's *Grey Owl: The Mystery of Archie Belaney*." *Études canadiennes/Canadian Studies* 61: 39–57.

Hutcheon, Linda. 1988. *The Canadian Postmodern: A Study of Contemporary English-Canadian Fiction*. Toronto: Oxford University Press.

Innis, H.A. 1935. Review of *Pilgrims of the Wild*, by Grey Owl. *Canadian Historical Review* 16: 197–200.

Jacquin, Philippe. 1996. *Les Indiens Blancs: Français et Indiens en Amérique du Nord (XVIe-XVIIIe siècle)*. Montreal: Libre Expression.

James, Scott. 2006. *"Pungent Personalities": Arts & Letters Club Drawings by Arthur Lismer, 1922–43*. Toronto: Thomas Fisher Rare Book Library Catalogue.

Jessup, Britt. 1971. Letter to Donald B. Smith, 17 May. Smith Papers. Glenbow Archives. M 8102, Box 5, Folder 55.

_____. 1973. "How Nugget Kept Grey Owl's Secret." [North Bay, ON] *Nugget*, 31 October. Smith Papers. Glenbow Archives. M 8102, Box 5, Folder 55.

Johnson, Brian D. 1999. "Romance Goes Native in *Grey Owl*." Review of *Grey Owl*, by Richard Attenborough. *Maclean's*, 4 October, 54.

Johnson, Brian D., with Susan Oh. 1999. "Rediscovering Grey Owl." *Maclean's*, 4 October: 53–56.

Kallen, Horace M. [1915] 1924. "Democracy *versus* the Melting-Pot." In *Culture and Democracy in the United States: Studies in the Group Psychology of the American Peoples*, 67–125. New York: Boni and Liveright.

Karsh, Yousuf. 1978. "Grey Owl (Archibald Belaney)." *Karsh Canadians*, 68–69. Toronto: University of Toronto Press.

Keeshig-Tobias, Lenore. 2005. "For<e>ward." *Walking a Tightrope: Aboriginal People and Their Representations*, edited by Ute Lischke and David T. McNab, xv–xvi. Waterloo, ON: Wilfrid Laurier University Press.

Kelly, M.T. 1991. "Case History." *Breath Dances between Them*, 125–44. Toronto: Stoddart.

Kettle, John, and Dean Walker. 1968. "Grey Owl Estate Suit 1939: The Secrets of a Celebrity." In *Verdict! Eleven Revealing Canadian Trials*, 171-84. Toronto: McGraw-Hill.

Kirk, Heather. 1991. "Grey Owl as Necessary Myth: A Reading of *Pilgrims of the Wild*." *Canadian Children's Literature/Littérature canadienne pour la jeunesse* 61: 44–56.

Kroetsch, Robert. [1973] 1999. *Gone Indian*. Toronto: Stoddart, 1999.

Lascelles, Tony. 1932. "Master Craftsman of the Wild." *Illustrated Canadian Forest and Outdoors*, February, 49–51.

Lavertu, Yves. 2000. *Jean-Charles Harvey, le combattant*. Montreal: Boréal.

Leacock, Stephen. [1912] 2002. *Sunshine Sketches of a Little Town*, edited by Carl Spadoni. Peterborough, ON: Broadview.

"Literary Rambles." 1935. *Lovat Dickson's Magazine* 4, no. 1: 116–17.

Litteljohn, Bruce, and Jon Pearce, eds. 1973. *Marked by the Wild: An Anthology of Literature Shaped by the Canadian Wilderness*. Toronto: McClelland and Stewart.

"A Little History of Grey Owl." 1936. *Illustrated Canadian Forest and Outdoors*, September, 11–12.

Longfellow, Henry Wadsworth. [1855] 1983. *The Song of Hiawatha*. In *Poems*, edited by Thomas Byrom, 183–258. London: Everyman's Library.

Loo, Tina. 2006. *States of Nature: Conserving Canada's Wildlife in the Twentieth Century*. Vancouver: UBC Press.

Lucas, Alec. 1965. "Nature Writers and the Animal Story." In *Literary History of Canada: Canadian Literature in English*, edited by Carl F. Klinck, 364–88. Toronto: University of Toronto Press.

MacEwan, Grant. [1975] 1995. "Anahareo: The Screams of Suffering Animals." In *Mighty Women: Stories of Western Canadian Pioneers*, 267–75. Vancouver: Greystone.

MacEwen, Gwendolyn. 1985. "An Evening with Grey Owl." In *Noman's Land*, 74–78. Toronto: Coach House Press.

———. 1987. *Afterworlds*. Toronto: McClelland and Stewart.

Mackey, Doug. 2000. "Grey Owl and His Life in Temagami." *Community Voices*, 11 August. www.historycomesalive.ca/canadians/links/greyowllinks.htm. http://www.pastforward.ca/perspectives/august_112000.htm. Accessed 15 October 2012.

Macnab, Geoffrey. 2003. "Eager Beaver: Richard Attenborough." *Sight and Sound*, September. http://www.bfi.org.uk/sightandsound/feature/35. http://old.bfi.org.uk/sightandsound/feature/35. Accessed 5 May 2009.

Massey, Vincent. 1963. *What's Past Is Prologue*. Toronto: Macmillan.

Maurice, H.G. 1936. "Grey Owl." Review of *Tales of an Empty Cabin*, by Grey Owl. *Manchester Guardian*, 4 December, Supplement, xx.

McCall, Sophie. 2013. "Grey Owl's Wife." Review of *Anahareo: A Wilderness Spirit*, by Kristin Gleeson. *Literary Review of Canada* 21, no. 6: 28.

———. 2014. "Reframing Anahareo's *Devil in Deerskins: My Life with Grey Owl*." In *Devil in Deerskins: My Life with Grey Owl*, by Anahareo, edited by Sophie McCall, 189–210. Winnipeg: University of Manitoba Press.

McGuffin, Gary, and Joanie McGuffin. 2002. *In the Footsteps of Grey Owl: Journey into the Ancient Forest*. Toronto: McClelland and Stewart.

McKenzie, Stephanie. 2003. "Chasing Tales." Review of *Tales of an Empty Cabin*, by Grey Owl, and *Grey Owl*, by Armand Garnet Ruffo. *Canadian Literature* 177: 149–51.

McNally, Michael D. 2006. "The Indian Passion Play: Contesting the Real Indian in *Song of Hiawatha* Pageants, 1901–1965." *American Indian Quarterly* 58, no. 1: 105–36.

Mitcham, Allison. 1980. "Grey Owl in the Park." *Northward Journal* 17: 7–11.

———. 1981. *Grey Owl's Favorite Wilderness*. Moonbeam, ON: Penumbra.

———. 1983. *The Northern Imagination: A Study of Northern Canadian Literature*. Moonbeam, ON: Penumbra.

Moffett, Anita. 1935. "Rare Forest Lives." Review of *Pilgrims of the Wild*, by Grey Owl. *New York Times*, 7 April.

Momaday, N. Scott. [1970] 2001. "The Man Made of Words." In *Nothing but the Truth: An Anthology of Native American Literature*, edited by John L. Purdy and James Rupert, 82–83. Upper Saddle River, NJ: Prentice-Hall.

Monkman, Leslie. 1981. *A Native Heritage: Images of the Indian in English-Canadian Literature*. Toronto: University of Toronto Press.

Montgomery, L.M. 2004. *The Selected Journals of L.M. Montgomery*. Volume V: *1935–1942*, edited by Mary Rubio and Elizabeth Waterston. Don Mills, ON: Oxford University Press.

Morris, Peter. [1978] 1992. *Embattled Shadows: A History of Canadian Cinema 1895–1939*. 1978. Montreal: McGill-Queen's University Press.

Munro, Alice. 1968. "Dance of the Happy Shades." In *Dance of the Happy Shades*, 211–24. Toronto: Ryerson.

*New York Times*. 1936. "Indian Lore." Unsigned review of *Tales of an Empty Cabin*, by Grey Owl. 13 December. 12, 33.

Nolan, Maggie, and Carrie Dawson. 2004. "Who's Who? Mapping Hoaxes and Imposture in Australian Literary History." *Australian Literary Studies* 21, no. 4: v–xx.

"Notes on Contributors." 1934. *Lovat Dickson's Magazine* 3, no. 6: 719.

O'Hagan, Howard. [1978] 1993. "Grey Owl." In *Trees Are Lonely Company*, 99–120. Vancouver: Talonbooks.

Oskaboose, Gilbert. 2000. "Grey Owl…Kindred of the Wild." *Village of First Nations*. http://www.firstnations.com/oskaboose/grey-owl.htm. http://toms-randomthoughts.blogspot.ca/2011/01/gilbert-oskaboose-writes-about-grey-owl.html. Accessed 17 April 2009.

Page, James E. 1979. *Seeing Ourselves: Films for Canadian Studies—National Film Board of Canada*. Toronto: National Film Board of Canada.

Panofsky, Ruth. 2012. *The Literary Legacy of the Macmillan Company of Canada: Making Books and Mapping Culture*. Toronto: University of Toronto Press.

Parker, W.A. 1931. "More about 'Game Leaks.'" *Illustrated Canadian Forest and Outdoors*, April, 195–97.

Pessoa, Fernando. 2006. "I'm a Fugitive." In *A Little Larger Than the Entire Universe: Selected Poems*, edited and translated by Richard Zenith, 315. New York: Penguin.

Plumstead, A.W. 1997. "What's the Matter with Grey Owl?" In *Reflections on Northern Culture: Visions and Voices*, edited by A.W. Plumstead, Laurie Kruk, and Anthony Blackbourn, 55–60. North Bay, ON: Nipissing University.

Polk, James. 1972. *Wilderness Writers*. Toronto: Clarke, Irwin.

Potts, Gary G. 2001. Letter to Author, 25 October.

Prose, Francine. 2002. "Going Native." *Creative Nonfiction* 19: 41–48.

Punshon, Lori. 2006. *He Who Flies by Night: The Story of Grey Owl*. Illustrated by Mike Keepness. Regina: Your Nickel's Worth.

Raddall, Thomas H. 1945. "Bald Eagle." In *Tambour and Other Stories*, 25–47. Toronto: McClelland and Stewart. Originally published as "Bald Eagle 'Iggins" in the *Saturday Evening Post*, 6 July 1940, 14–69.

_____. 1947. Letter to Margaret Vollmer, 19 July. Thomas Raddall Fonds, Dalhousie University Archives. Vol. 19. MS-2-202 48.45. http://www.library.dal.ca/archives/trela/letters/800vollmer19jul47.htm. Accessed 27 June 2011.

_____. 1968. "Grey Owl." In *Footsteps on Old Floors: True Tales of Mystery*, 95–156. Garden City, NY: Doubleday.

Rashley, R.E. 1971. "Grey Owl and the Authentic Frontier." *English Quarterly* 4, no. 3: 57–64.

Relke, Diana M.A. 1999. *Greenwor(l)ds: Ecocritical Readings of Canadian Women's Poetry*. Calgary: University of Calgary Press.

Richardson, Bob. 2001. *A Face beside the Fire: Memories of Dawn Grey Owl-Richardson*. Victoria, BC: Trafford.

Richler, Noah. 2006. *This Is My Country, What's Yours? A Literary Atlas of Canada.* Toronto: McClelland and Stewart.

Roberts, Lloyd. 1931. "Beaver Finds Visitor 'All Right' and Demonstrates Logging Art." *Christian Science Monitor,* 5 November, 1, 2.

____. 1937. "Grey Owl—the Man." Lloyd Roberts Collection of Grey Owl Papers. Thomas Fisher Rare Book Library, University of Toronto. Box 1, Folder 11.

____. n.d. "My Friend Grey Owl." Lloyd Roberts Collection of Grey Owl Papers. Thomas Fisher Rare Book Library, University of Toronto. Box 2, Folders 1–13.

Rose, Wendy. 1994. "For the White Poets who Would Be Indian." In *Bone Dance: New and Selected Poems, 1965–1993,* 22. Tucson: University of Arizona Press.

Ross, Colin. 1979. "The Story of Grey Owl." *Compass: A Provincial Review* 5: 79–83.

Rubio, Mary Henley. 2008. *Lucy Maud Montgomery: The Gift of Wings.* Toronto: Doubleday.

Ruffo, Armand Garnet. 1996. *Grey Owl: The Mystery of Archie Belaney.* Regina: Coteau.

____. 2000. "Writing the Water." In *Crisp Blue Edges: Indigenous Creative Non-Fiction,* edited by Rasunah Marsden, 185–93. Penticton: Theytus.

Rutherford, Paul. 1993. "Made in America: The Problem of Mass Culture in Canada." In *The Beaver Bites Back? American Popular Culture in Canada,* edited by David H. Flaherty and Frank W. Manning, 260–80. Montreal: McGill-Queen's University Press.

Sabin, Edwin L. 1935. "Northern Frontier." Review of *The Men of the Last Frontier,* by Grey Owl. *Saturday Review,* 29 June, 5.

Scheffer, Victor B. 1977. Introduction to the New Edition. In *Sajo and the Beaver People* by Grey Owl, xi–xiv. Toronto: Macmillan.

Schubnell, Matthias. 1985. *N. Scott Momaday: The Cultural and Literary Background.* Norman: University of Oklahoma Press.

Seton, Ernest Thomson. [1911] 1981. *The Arctic Prairies: A Canoe-Journey of 2,000 Miles in Search of the Caribou; Being the Account of a Voyage to the Region North of Aylmer Lake.* New York: Harper.

Sheridan, Joe. 2001. "'When first unto this country a stranger I came': Grey Owl, Indigenous Lessons of Place, and Postcolonial Theory." In *Mapping the Sacred: Religion, Geography and Postcolonial Literatures,* edited by Jamie S. Scott and Paul Simpson-Housley, 419–39. Amsterdam: Rodopi.

Shipton, Vicky. [2003] 2008. *Grey Owl.* Harlow, UK: Pearson.

Sianu. 1938. "The Lament of the Beaver People." In *The Green Leaf: A Tribute to Grey Owl,* edited by Lovat Dickson, 8. London: Lovat Dickson.

Simpson-Housley, Paul, and Allison M. Williams. 2002. "Sense of Place: The Case of Canada's Provincial Norths." In *Prairie Perspectives: Geographical Essays,* edited by Bernard D. Thraves, 1–17. Regina: Department of Geography, University of Regina.

Sinnott, Nigel. 2009. "My March to Militant Atheism." 16 November. http://www.sof-in-australia.org/blog.php?blog_id=554. Accessed 6 December 2012.

Smith, Donald B. 1971. "'Grey Owl.'" *Ontario History* 63, no. 3: 161–76.

____. 1990. *From the Land of Shadows: The Making of Grey Owl.* Saskatoon: Western Producer Prairie Books.

Snell, Gordon. 2001. "Grey Owl (1888–1938)." *The Oh, Canadians! Omnibus! Hysterically Historical Rhymes*, 217–19. With caricatures by Aislin. Toronto: McArthur.

Sokal, Alan. [1996] 2000. "Transgressing the Boundaries: Toward a Transformative Hermeneutics of Quantum Gravity." In *The Sokal Hoax: The Sham That Shook the Academy*, edited by the editors of *Lingua Franca*, 11–45. Lincoln: University of Nebraska Press.

Swartile, Katherine. 2014. Foreword. In *Devil in Deerskins: My Life with Grey Owl*, by Anahareo, edited by Sophie McCall, ix–xii. Winnipeg: University of Manitoba Press.

Taylor, Dorell, ed. 1984. *Waskesiu Memories*. Victoria, BC: Classic Memoirs.

Taylor, Drew Hayden. 1996. "Grey Owl Is Dead, but His Spirit Lives On." In *Funny, You Don't Look Like One: Observations from a Blue-Eyed Ojibway*, 96–98. Penticton: Theytus.

_____. 1999. "James Owl or Grey Bond." In *Further Adventures of a Blue-Eyed Ojibway: Funny You Don't Look Like One Two*, 119–21. Penticton: Theytus.

_____. 2014. "Pretending to Be an Impostor." In *Fake Identity? The Impostor Narrative in North American Culture*, edited by Caroline Rosenthal and Stefanie Schäfer, 227-30. Frankfurt: Campus Verlag.

Thorneycroft, Diana. 2009. "The Creative Process: *Group of Seven Awkward Moments*—Interviews with Diana Thorneycroft." In *Diana Thorneycroft: Canada, Myth and History—Group of Seven Awkward Moments Series* by Sharona Adamowicz-Clements, 45–54. Kleinburg: McMichael Canadian Art Collection.

Thorpe, Vanessa. 2004. "Veil Lifts on Jungle Mystery of the Colonel Who Vanished." *Observer*, 21 March. http://www.guardian.co.uk/uk/2004/mar/21/research.brazil. Accessed 8 December 2012.

Tippett, Maria. 2007. *Portrait in Light and Shadow: The Life of Yousuf Karsh*. Toronto: Anansi.

Toufik and Zoran. 1989. "Grey Owl, l'Indien Blanc." *La Presse*, Sunday Edition, 3 September–4 October.

Turner, Frank M. 1993. *Contesting Cultural Authority: Essays in Victorian Intellectual Life*. Cambridge: Cambridge University Press.

Unwin, Peter. 1999. "The Fabulations of Grey Owl." *Beaver*, April/May, 13–19.

Waiser, Bill. 1989. *Saskatchewan's Playground: A History of Prince Albert National Park*. Saskatoon: Fifth House.

Ward, Graham. 2009. "(Dis)honest Indian: Grey Owl, My Mother and Me." 17 April. http://grahamward.blogspot.com/2009/04/blog-post_17.html. Accessed 23 October 2012.

Williams, M.B. *MB: Living and Writing the Early Years of Parks Canada*, edited by Alan MacEachern, Luvneet Rana, and Adam Crymple. http://mbwilliams.academic-news.org. Accessed 23 December 2013.

Wilson, Hap. 2005. *The Cabin: A Search for Personal Sanctuary*. Toronto: Natural Heritage.

_____. 2010. *Grey Owl and Me: Stories from the Trail and Beyond*. Illustrated by Hap Wilson and Ingrid Zschogner. Toronto: Natural Heritage.

Wilson, Stephen G. 2004. *Leaving the Fold: Apostates and Defectors in Antiquity.* Minneapolis: Fortress.

Winter, Gordon. 1988. "Champion of the Wild North." *Country Life,* 15 September, 234–35.

Wood, J.A. 1938. Letter to Lovat Dickson, April. Quoted in "'The Passing of Grey Owl'" by Lovat Dickson. In *The Green Leaf: A Tribute to Grey Owl,* edited by Lovat Dickson, 28–31. London: Lovat Dickson.

# Index

as example of cultural apostasy,
2, 170, 172; extent of his cultural
transformation, 37–40, 139, 148,
149, 171–72; his own confusion
over, 36, 81–82, 168; how book
reviewers assessed his identity,
29–30, 56; how he received name
Grey Owl, 60; how his real identity
is revealed, 112–13, 154; idea that
Aboriginals always knew about,
12–13, 110–11, 147, 149, 171;
information about his background
in his books, 13–14, 17–18, 72–73,
77; L. Dickson's turnabout on, 117–
19; posthumous claims of knowing
about, 125–27; public reaction to
learning his real identity, 1, 37,
90, 112, 123, 125; racism directed
toward in light of, 166–67; theories
on why he became Grey Owl, 5–6,
14; his choice of Anahareo over
Angele, 60, 61, 92–94, 110
PERSONAL LIFE: acrophobia, 105;
Anahareo's claim he told her about
his previous lovers, 105–6, 107;
birth of daughter (Dawn), 52; burial,
139, 155; confessions of early life to
Anahareo, 4–5; conservative nature
of, 105; death, 90, 112; drinking of,
100, 157; influence of Angele on, 16,
92, 139, 148; meets Anahareo, 11–
12, 106; relationship with Anahareo,
58–60, 96–103, 104, 108–9; view of
Anahareo's public image, 108
SCHOLARSHIP AND STUDIES OF:
accused of colonialism, 163–64;
anthologies, 134–35; biography,
38–39, 141–42, 143–44, 146–51;
children's literature, 158; and
Donald B. Smith, 120–21, 134, 143–
44; essays, 122–23, 124, 128–29,
133–34, 137–38, 139–40, 142–43,
147, 150, 151–52, 159–62; fiction,
135–37, 140–41, 144–45; film, 135,
152–55; graphic novels, 155–56;
histories, 145–46, 163–64; and L.
Dickson, 119–20, 121; monographs,
121–22, 132, 138–39; pictures/
paintings, 123, 158–59; poetry, 121,
122, 140, 146–48; satire, 130–32;
travel literature, 156–58, 159
WRITING CAREER: "The Wilderness
Awakes," 114; critical acceptance,
66–67, 90–91, 150, 165; decision
to start, 53–55; early training for,
16–17, 44; effect of on relations
with Anahareo, 57, 62, 63–64, 110;

as effective voice for wildlife, 122,
123, 127, 128–29; and *Forest and
Outdoors,* 18–24; and *The Green
Leaf,* 88–89; his reaction to reviews,
63, 168; importance of hidden
identity to, 60, 61, 74, 78, 169;
influence of Anahareo on, 56–57,
110; L. Dickson serves as publisher
for, 42, 58–59, 64–65, 74–75, 76; L.
Dickson's promotion of, 114–19;
lecturing, 112, 117, 127; as letter
writer, 62, 63, 105, 168; and Lloyd
Roberts, 127–29; meetings with
famous writers, 124–27; negative
feelings about, 55–57, 62, 85, 86;
planned books never written, 63, 64;
relations with editors/publishers,
28–29, 41–43, 62, 74–75; success
of, 1, 167; and "The Tree," 83; use of
fiction in his non-fiction books, 51,
60–61, 78; works for *Country Life,*
17, 18, 20, 24, 28–29, 41–43. *See
also* Belaney, Archie; *The Men of the
Last Frontier* (Grey Owl); *Pilgrims
of the Wild* (Grey Owl); *Sajo and the
Beaver People* (Grey Owl); *Tales of
an Empty Cabin* (Grey Owl)
*Grey Owl* (film), 90, 152–55, 161–62, 172
*Grey Owl* (tv documentary), 135
"Grey Owl" (Brower), 142–43
"Grey Owl" (Raddall), 132
«Grey Owl, l'Indien Blanc» (Toufik and
Zoran), 141–42
*Grey Owl: A Biographical Note and A Day at
Beaver Lodge* (Dickson), 123
*Grey Owl and Anahareo at Beaver Swamp*
(Thorneycroft), 158–59
*Grey Owl and Me: Stories from the Trail and
Beyond* (Wilson), 160–62
*Grey Owl and the Beaver* (Cory), 121–22
"Grey Owl: Mysterious Genius of Nature
Lore" (Cantwell), 133
*Grey Owl: The Many Faces of Archie Belaney*
(Billinghurst), 150–51
*Grey Owl: The Mystery of Archie Belaney*
(Ruffo), 146–50
*Grey Owl's Favorite Wilderness* (Mitcham),
138–39
"Grey Owl-the Man" (Roberts), 128–29
Guerrero, Gonzalo, 169
Guppy, Bill, 7

**H**
*Half-Breed: The Story of Grey Owl* (Dickson),
118, 119
Harkin, J.B., 51
Harvey, Jean-Charles, 133–34